RARE SPIRIT

RARE SPIRIT

A life of William De Morgan
1839–1911

Mark Hamilton

CONSTABLE • LONDON

First published in Great Britain 1997
by Constable and Company Ltd
3 The Lanchesters, 162 Fulham Palace Road
London W6 9ER
Copyright © Mark Hamilton 1997
ISBN 0 09 474670 2
The right of Mark Hamilton to be identified
as the author of this work has been asserted by him in
accordance with the Copyright, Design and Patents Act 1988
Set in Monophoto Poliphilus 12pt
Servis Filmsetting Ltd, Manchester
Printed in Great Britain by
St Edmundsbury Press Ltd
Bury St Edmunds

A CIP catalogue record for this book
is available from the British Library

To my wife, without whose constant support
and encouragement this book would not have been written

Contents

CONTENTS

CHAPTER 12

CHAPTER 13

CHAPTER 14

Illustrations

William Morris and Edward Burne-Jones
Photograph of William and Evelyn (*De Morgan Foundation*)
1 The Vale
William and Evelyn leaving Italy, for the last time (*De Morgan Foundation*)
Evelyn De Morgan (*De Morgan Foundation*)

between pages 178 and 179

Colour

Fireplace in a house designed by Norman Shaw, 1879
The remaing seven plates illustrate vases, dishes and ewers with lustre or Persian
decoration. De Morgan completed these at various times between 1885 and
1900

I am most grateful to Jon Castleugh for allowing me to photograph tiles in his pos-
session and to Geoff Ideson for taking the photographs. Thanks also to Richard
Dennis Publications for the use of transparencies in their possession, and to the De
Morgan foundations for the use of pictures owned by them.

Acknowledgments

For the use of copyright materials, and kind permission to consult and refer to manuscripts and archives my grateful acknowledgments are due to the Archive of the Borough of Fulham and Hammersmith, the Bodleian Library, the City of Birmingham Museum and Art Gallery, the British Library, Cambridge University Library, the Fitzwilliam Museum Library, William Heinemann archive, Leighton House, the London Library, the National Art Library at the V&A, the National Maritime Museum archive, University College Library, the University of London Library, the Beinecke Rare Books and Manuscript Library, Yale University Library, the Getty Center for the History of Art and the Humanities, the Huntingdon Library, California, the Library of Knox College, the Lilly Library, Indiana University, the Sterling Memorial Library, Yale University, the Library of the University of California, Berkeley, and the Library of the University of Virginia.

I owe a debt of gratitude to many people who have helped me in the writing of the book: above all to Prof. John Sutherland who has guided me throughout, to Prof. Dan Jacobson for his interest and encouragement, to Jon Catleugh, Chairman of the De Morgan Foundation who kindly read the typescript and made valuable suggestions, to Alice Hiller for many helpful comments, to Dr Catherine Gordan for her help, to Jason Cooper for typing the book and to the English department of University College London for financial assistance in obtaining a copy of one of the novels in typescript. I must also thank the De Morgan Foundation for making it possible to include colour illustrations in the book. My publisher Ben Glazebrook has given me much friendly support and I am very grateful to his editor Gemma Forster for her meticulous reading of the work.

Introduction

ONE OF THE BEST known portraits of William De Morgan, painted by his wife Evelyn, shows him looking stern, or perhaps tired of sitting still. He is holding one of his lustre pots and on the wall behind his head, to the left, hangs a large lustre plate. To the right one can see three novels on a shelf, his first three, and underneath them is stacked a pile of paper, obviously a new novel in the making. The picture, a striking one, was painted in 1909 when he had abandoned his pottery business, and had already published three best-selling novels. By this time, although conscious of financial failure in his pottery business, he and Evelyn were better off than they had ever been, because of his literary success. Yet, now, in the 1990s, he is remembered as a unique and extraordinarily talented ceramic designer, his wares eagerly sought after by (wealthy) collectors, and his novels are either forgotten or dismissed as being over-long and unreadable. Consigned, in fact, to a sad literary rubbish heap. The only place to find his books is in second-hand bookshops, or, if you are lucky, in libraries.

By chance, I became interested in De Morgan the novelist before I became aware of his achievements as a ceramic designer. I was encouraged by my father to read *Joseph Vance*, his first novel, as being one of the funni-

est books in the English language. I was immediately intrigued by his por-
trayal of old Christopher Vance, and the cockney speech of mid nine-
teenth-century London. Reading his second novel, *Alice-For-Short*,
convinced me that De Morgan was a much neglected writer.

Having found out that he had written nine long novels it was not long
before I discovered his extraordinary plates, pots and tiles, richly decorated,
some of them glowing with lustre. I became curious to know how a ceramic
artist could, at the age of sixty-eight, very late in his life, after many years of
producing and selling his pottery, became an extremely successful novelist.
The authors of excellent books and articles on his ceramics were not very
much help. De Morgan's novels were dismissed out of hand. As far as his
life was concerned, they relied heavily on a biography of William and his
wife Evelyn written by Mrs A.M.W. Stirling, Evelyn's sister. This book,
published in 1922, is essential as a source of information for anybody who
wants to write about the De Morgans, but there are pitfalls. She is very unreliable when it comes to dates, there are no notes of sources and no bibli-
ography. Many letters to and from the De Morgans are quoted, but many of
the originals have disappeared as have diaries and notebooks to which she
tantalizingly refers. Clues, then, have to be looked for in what their friends
wrote about them, in William's novels and in their family backgrounds. De
Morgan was strongly influenced by his parents, particularly his father
Augustus, while Evelyn rebelled against her family and upbringing, which
was rich and aristocratic.

The more I looked at De Morgan's brilliantly imagined and executed
pots and the more I read his novels, the greater was my curiosity about this
rather elusive, very talented man. It was surprising to find that there was no
biography, since the one published in 1922, of this friend of William
Morris, Burne-Jones and their circle.

Reginald Blunt (Chelsea historian and the manager of the De Morgan
works in Fulham) wrote in 1918, a year after William's death:

> Good fiction survives more housemaids than good pottery, and the
> name of William De Morgan will doubtless live as the author of
> *Joseph Vance*, *Alice-For-Short*, *Somehow Good* and the others of that
> wonderful succession of novels – which were all produced in the last
> decade of his life – in the days to come, when his pots and panels are

scarcely to be found, save – one hopes and is promised – in the South Kensington Museum [now the Victoria and Albert].

De Morgan's obituaries remembered him first and foremost as a novelist, mentioning the ceramics as a venture which ended in failure, financially. Now perhaps the wheel has turned full circle.

Chapter 1

William Frend De Morgan b. Gower St, London, 1839 – his
parents Augustus and Sophia – his father's career in University
College, London – Sophia's charitable work – William's
choice of an artistic career – the Academy Schools.

WILLIAM FREND DE MORGAN, born in 1839, ceramic artist and novel,
ist, stands out as a Victorian of exceptional and varied talents. His achieve,
ments as an artist/potter date from the period between 1869 and 1904, and
although never formally part of the Pre,Raphaelite Brotherhood or an
active member of the William Morris firm, he was a close friend of Morris
and his family, and of Edward Burne,Jones and his wife Georgiana. At
various times he collaborated with both men. His novels, written between
1905 and 1917, and published between 1906 and 1921 (two of them pos,
thumously), were not typically Edwardian. Some of them recalled the mid
nineteenth,century London of Dickens, and the almost feudal rural society
of the great country houses and their dependent villages of the 1850s. One
is historical. Others are set about 1900. None belongs to any identifiable
school of fiction.

De Morgan's parents were both highly intelligent and strong,minded
people who, by his own admission, had a lasting influence on his person,
ality. His father, Augustus, descended from a long line of Indian Army
officers,[1] was born in India and when a baby lost most of the sight of his
right eye from a disease known locally as 'sore eye'. This disability ruled out
any career in the army or navy. Young Augustus was brought up by his

mother, his father, a colonel in the Indian Army, having died prematurely, leaving his widow with four young children. His precocious mathematical talent was discovered by a family friend who found the young boy drawing with rulers and compasses. When asked what he was doing, Augustus replied that he was 'drawing mathematics'. The friend showed him what real mathematics was. (The incident bears a close resemblance to the dis-covery by Dr Thorpe of the young Joseph Vance's talents, in William De Morgan's first novel).[2]

Augustus matriculated at Trinity College, Cambridge, and went on to become a popular member of the university, sociable and well known for his ability as a flautist, and for his voracious consumption of fiction. He read mathematics and his mother fondly hoped that he would become an evangelical parson. He had been expected in his final exams to be the senior or second wrangler, but only succeeded in being placed a disappointing fourth in the mathematical tripos lists of 1827, perhaps because of the amount of time he had devoted to the study of music and philosophy. Having taken his degree, it was obvious that the Church was not going to offer him a career unless he subscribed to the Thirty-Nine Articles, which he declined to do. Much of his subsequent antipathy to organized religion – shared by his son – was, according to his wife Sophia,[3] caused by the dreary and incessant churchgoing and endless sermons imposed on him in his early life by his devout mother.

Denied an academic career in Cambridge, as at that time college fellow-ships were open only to ordained clergymen of the Church of England, Augustus came to London to live with his mother, brother and sister, and entered Lincoln's Inn to read for the Bar. It was around this time that he got to know William Frend, his future father-in-law, also a mathematician. Frend had also refused to subscribe to Anglican Church doctrine, and in consequence had been obliged to give up a promising academic career. He had been elected a Fellow and tutor at Jesus College, Cambridge, but after four years his religious beliefs underwent a drastic change and following a controversial sermon given in the University church he was expelled from his college tutorial post. He then, six years later, wrote a pamphlet, provoca-tively published in Cambridge, which enraged the Master and Fellows of Jesus who banned him from the college buildings. A similar sentence of exclusion was passed on him by the University. Banished from the

University for his dissenting views, he became the actuary to the Rock Insurance Office. The twenty-one year old Augustus found a kindred spirit in the older man with his keen interest in mathematics and firm belief in freedom of religion. Frend's daughter, Sophia, later to be Augustus's wife, was educated at home. Her father taught her Hebrew, Latin and Greek, and encouraged her reading in metaphysics and philosophy. Most of her young life was spent at home outside London. As she much later told her daughter Mary, it troubled her at the time, it being an odd and lonely upbringing for a young girl, but she was thankful to have had such an extra-ordinary education.

In 1828 the new University College in Gower Street (later to be part of London University) was looking for someone to fill the post of Professor of Pure Mathematics. The chair had been offered to the distinguished practi-tioners Herschel[4] and Babbage,[5] who both turned it down. Out of twenty candidates who did apply, the College Council chose the youngest, Augustus De Morgan, who at twenty-one was only too willing to give up his legal career. He came with exceptionally strong references from Cambridge and the support, so he said, of two influential patrons, Brougham[6] and Warburton.[7] It may seem odd to us now that a very young scholar should have been appointed a professor, but it was a new university and a comparatively new university subject, and a large number of the teaching staff appointed were similarly youthful.

The new 'godless' place in Gower Street obviously appealed to the young and brilliant professor; it was founded 'to provide a liberal education in classics, mathematics, physical sciences and medicine, without regard to religious distinction either in teacher or pupil'. There is a good description of Augustus at this period by his colleague Thomas Hodgkin:[8]

Towering intellectually above all his fellows as I now look back on him, rises the grand form of the mathematician, Augustus De Morgan, known, I suppose to each succeeding generation of pupils as 'Gussy'. A stout and tall figure, a stiff rather waddling walk, a high white cravat and stick up collars in which the square chin is buried, a full but well chiselled face, very short-sighted eyes peering forth through gold-rimmed spectacles; but above all such a superb dome-like forehead, as could only belong to one of the kings of

thought: that is my remembrance of De Morgan, and I feel in looking
back upon his personality that he is one of the grandest figures I have
known.

There are other eulogies. Professor M.J.M. Hill in an unpublished manuscript,[9] reminiscing about some of the holders of the mathematical chair at
University College, said of him: "amongst the great men who have lectured
within the walls of the College he was probably by reason of his scholarship, by the profundity of his work, and by his personal character, one of
the greatest, if not the greatest of them all." All agree that Augustus had
great sweetness of temper but a formidable mind. His pupils sometimes
found themselves left far behind in his classes. He could be eccentric, and
his dislike of the countryside outside London was notorious. He wrote a
letter to his future father-in-law William Frend in September 1834, declar-
ing:

> I did not exceed but a single day my estimate of the time I could bear
> the viridity of extra-urban scenery. I have been only two days in the
> wilds . . . Conceive me reduced to clip hedges to pass away the time
> till dinner, which I did with great *goût*, seeing that it is reducing the
> sum total of foliage. No letters from you, from which I conclude that
> your thoughts are of trees, only interrupted by the slopping of the
> waves, which are always fiddling at the sand until I long to give them
> a thump, and tell them to be easy. The prettiest thing about the sea is
> the straight horizon and the isochronism of the waves in deep water.
> But near the shore they do not keep time like my pendulum.

Irredeemably cockney in his tastes, Augustus preferred Gower Street and
Camden Town and he was never so happy as when everyone was away
from London in the summer months, allowing him to bury himself in his
library, reading and writing innumerable letters and articles. A professor's
salary at this period was less than generous and it must have been a struggle
in later years to bring up seven children in middle-class decency. When he
was appointed in 1828, a professor was entitled to receive between £4 and
£6 for each enrolled pupil. Later on in 1833, the council recommended a
new arrangement:

Where the fee of the pupils who have entered for the session shall not exceed the sum of £100, the professor shall take the whole fee. Where the fee shall exceed the sum of £100, but not exceed the sum of £300, the professor shall take the first £100, and the surplus shall be equally divided between the university and the professor. Where the fee shall exceed the sum of £300, the professor shall take two-thirds, and the university the remaining third.[10]

In practice, as Sophia De Morgan recalled in her memoir of her husband, his fees never exceeded £500, and in later years seldom amounted to more than £300 annually. For this reward he lectured twice a day and after each lecture went over problems with his pupils. He also took private pupils at home, and his professional advice as an actuary was often sought by leading London insurance companies, recommended by his father-in-law.[11] All this activity was quite apart from his own voluminous writing.

Twice during his career at University College he felt he had to resign – both times on a matter of principle. On the first occasion he had taken issue with the governing body over the hastily formed constitution of the new university. Matters came to a head in 1831 when a colleague, Professor Patterson, was dismissed apparently without reason. De Morgan wrote a letter of resignation which was accepted in a one-line reply from the council. He was persuaded to take up a professorship at the college again in 1836 when there was a vacancy and there had been sufficient reform in the administration to reassure him. In the meantime he had been occupied with the affairs of the Astronomical Society and also the Useful Knowledge Society, a very typical piece of Victorian philanthropy, to bring scientific education to the under-privileged. Neither of these positions carried a stipend and De Morgan seems to have supported himself in the interim by his pen.

The second resignation came much later in his career at the college in 1866 and reflected badly on his employers. A professorship became vacant and the leading candidate was first of all accepted and then passed over in favour of someone less qualified on the grounds that the original choice was a Unitarian. This discrimination on the grounds of religious belief appalled De Morgan. He at once sent a long letter explaining his reasons for resigning after thirty ill-paid years at a professor. The letter was read at the relevant council meeting and all poor De Morgan received was a terse note from the secretary accepting his resignation and not a word of thanks. He lived for only four years after this insulting dismissal.[12]

William's father was obviously a man of lofty principle. He was loved by his family and friends and respected by his colleagues. He had a cheer-ful side to his character and a mischievous sense of humour inherited by William. His correspondence, even letters to distinguished fellow scientists, was characteristically peppered with verse, puns and scientific jokes.

His domestic life had begun happily. Augustus's religious views made it impossible for him to agree to have a marriage ceremony in a church so he and Sophia were married in 1837 in a Registry Office. The newly wed couple settled at 69 Gower Street,[13] very near his work. Sophia[14] says rather sadly of her married life with him: 'The great amount of work which he did at this time as at all times while his strength lasted, filled the day, so that I had little of his society. We both naturally regretted this but it could not be helped.' However, there remained time for recreation in the evening and much of Dickens was read aloud by Augustus to his wife. Besides his daily lectures and classes at the college, Augustus wrote an impressive number of articles and books, as well as editing and translating mathematical works and writing pieces for journals on education and miscellaneous subjects. These ranged over an extraordinary variety of subjects: the possibility of a decimal coinage, calculus, Euclid, algebra, probability, Newton, logic, essays on practical education and on double-entry bookkeeping. As we have seen, holidays away from London proved not to be successful, although occasion-ally he enjoyed France, and it was agreed that when Sophia took the children away in the summer he should be permitted to get on with his research in London. This included taking an active part in the Astronomical Society's proceedings and his name was put forward as a likely candidate for the post of Astronomer Royal. He did not in the event want to be considered and instead persuaded his close friend Sir John Herschel to accept the honour. Augustus obviously had extraordinary energy and accomplished a great deal, but his energy seems to have been concentrated almost wholly on his solitary intellectual work. Nevertheless, he was an affectionate father and William remembered him with great love and respect.

Sophia was, also in her way, an outstanding person. She brought up a family of seven children and managed the De Morgan household which included the standard retinue of servants and a nanny. Like many Victorian families the De Morgans were afflicted with tuberculosis, referred to by Sophia in her reminiscences as 'Phtisis', for which there was then no cure. Their eldest daughter, Alice, lively, naughty and dearly loved by Augustus, died in 1853 at the age of fifteen. In her memoir of Augustus, Sophia inserts a sad little note for the year 1853:

> The end of the year was the beginning of a long period of sorrow and suffering to us. Our eldest dear child, Alice, who had caught cold after a severe attack of measles, died before Christmas. I had feared the termination of the great weakness and delicacy which I had vainly tried to prevent. Her father did not realise the degree of illness till the end was near, and the blow fell heavily upon him. He was not then so used to death and sorrow as we afterwards became, and his want of sight and natural hopefulness of disposition made him unaware of the degree of danger in this and other cases. This hopefulness left him after repeated sorrows. He always dwelt on the belief that whom God loves are early taken, but after we lost Alice his cheerfulness diminished, and I do not think that he ever laughed so heartily, or was heard whistling and singing merry snatches of songs as he used to do when all our children were with us. I cannot write of these events.

Over the years four of her seven children were to die of TB. George, the oldest son, a mathematician who had inherited his father's brains, died aged twenty-six of TB of the throat. William's other brother, Edward, survived to marry and have children, but died at the age of thirty-seven after a fall from a horse in South Africa where he had gone for his health, the spectre of tuberculosis haunting him. He had been an outstanding medical student at University College Hospital and had established a general practice in South Africa. The second daughter Anna Isabella ('Annie') did better; she married Dr Reginald Thompson[15] who worked with William on some of his designs, had four children, and lived to the age of fifty-nine. Of the remaining two sisters, Helena ('Chrissie') died unmarried in 1870, and Mary, also unmarried, died in Egypt in 1907. All but William, Mary and Edward were victims of consumption. It is not surprising that William had a lifelong phobia of TB, and his bad back obviously worried his doctors for the same reason (although TB of the spine was and is rare). His doctors determined that it would be wise, later in his life, for him to winter in Florence to escape the English climate and any predisposition to the disease which had laid waste his siblings.

Sophia herself, born in 1809, did not die until 1892, aged 83, and had an extraordinarily full life quite apart from her family concerns. The Frend family were high-minded and cultured and, as has been said, if anything took their daughter's education rather too seriously. There is a revealing letter from her father, William Frend, to Lady Byron,[16] about Sophia's upbringing:

> My eldest girl, (Sophia) gave alarming symptoms of being a prodigy, but I so effectually counteracted them that her mother began in her turn to be alarmed when she was between six and seven years old lest she should be backward in her learning. She is now between nine and ten and frequently puzzles me with words I am to make out with the ivory letters which have been, and are, a source of amusement to us all. It is by these letters that they have all learned – boys as well as girls – and the youngest now makes a small sentence with them from her book when she has a morning lesson – which is not everyday. No spelling book has been used, and I abominate the system of daily tasks and getting so many words to spell by heart. As to grammar, they shall never learn one, nor be troubled with the false notion it contains.

During her childbearing years, Sophia was fully occupied with her growing family, but after the De Morgans moved from Gower Street to Great Camden Street she had more time for other than domestic matters. She was active in the founding of Bedford College for Women (although Augustus on his part was not apparently wholly convinced of the necessity for women's education) and was a leading member of the anti-slavery movement. A friend of Elizabeth Fry,[17] she worked for prison and work-house reform[18] and was a non-militant lobbyist for political emancipation for women. She also tried without much success to establish playgrounds for poor children of the slums. Later in her life she wrote her reminiscences and a memoir of her husband. She also published a history of the spiritual-ist movement in Great Britain.

Inevitably, with these parents the De Morgan children grew up in an ambience that was kind but high-minded. Augustus, despite the claims of his work, took a proper parental interest in their education. Mrs Stirling, in her biography[19] of William and Evelyn De Morgan, remarks percipiently:

> the mental training of their children, in small matters, as in great, was unconventional as the moral training was rigid . . . The result was a curious mixture of freedom of thought and outlook far in advance of the date at which they lived, combined with notions of conduct which even then were held to be unduly strict and old fashioned.

Despite what could have been rather pressurized upbringing there is no indication that one can discover from William later in life that he had an unhappy childhood in any way. Certain of his personal characteristics can be directly traced to his parents' theories and practice of child-rearing. He seems clearly to have been something of a hypochondriac and this is understandable given the susceptibility of the family to TB. Secondly, he was infused in later life with the feeling he was a failure. Success as an author came at the very end of his life and took him completely by surprise. As we will see, he went against his father's wishes as regards a career and later regretted his obstinacy. (One wonders what his comments would be if he could know what his plates, pots and tiles would fetch at auction in the 1990s, one hundred years on.) Of course, he had complete confidence in the aesthetic value of his designs and ceramic painting. His failure to run a profitable business was attributable not to his workmanship but to his inefficiency as a businessman.

William, writing in 1914,[20] set down some of the main events of his early life:

> I was born in Gower St (No. 69) and resided there – if an infant resides – until my fourth birthday, November 16 1843. I can recollect it! In the spring or summer of 1844, my father moved to 7 Camden St. (Afterwards Mrs Buss's school or college). I went to the University College School at ten years old, I believe in 1848 – probably at the opening of the session. I was there until sixteen, when I went into the College. In that year my father gave up Camden St. for

41 Charlcot Villas, Adelaide Rd (afterwards 91 Adelaide Rd). I
then began art at Cary's in Streatham St. Bloomsbury. I remained at
college until nineteen, and was then admitted to the Academy
Schools in 1859.

The three brothers all went to University College School, William from
1849–55, Edward, 1852–59 and George, academically the brightest one of
the family, from 1856–57.[21] The school had opened in 1832 and was
remarkable for its forward-looking system of teaching and organization.
No corporal punishment, but instead a system of impositions, 'confine-
ments' and monthly reports of progress and conduct sent to parents. No
compulsory subjects, but a wide range taught. Sadly there are no records in
the school archive about the schoolboy William, mainly due to a fire a few
years ago when most of the school records were burnt, and William left no
memories of his school-days. At the early age of sixteen he enrolled as a
student at University College to read classics. He was obviously not an
enthusiastic member of the college and did not get a degree.[22] It must have
been a disappointment to his father that he did not do well at the university,
particularly when compared with his brother George. It is interesting to
read what De Morgan wrote towards the end of his life in *The Old Man's
Youth* which obviously reflects his experiences at this stage of his life:

I think my father's imagination was misled by the word College. He
could not dissociate it from his old University life, with its intox-
icating traditions of ancient learning, its freedom of sacred precincts
where every stone brings back its memories of bygone scholars; its
great silent libraries whose peace alone is stimulus enough to make an
otherwise bookless man read out the day and part reluctantly in the
end with the quarto or folio he never would have looked at elsewhere.
He had never known how much of his own love of the classics was
due to the associations of the spot where they had reached his soul,
and he fancied that his son too might be bitten with the love of
Literature; or, it may be, of the practice of thinking – mathematical
and scientific thinking – by the surroundings of the College. But,
honestly as I believe that there was not in the world, in my time, a
sounder curriculum of learning than the one he offered me, it had one

[14]

defect. There was nothing in the places of study, in their antecedents and surroundings, to catch and hold the imagination of a crude boy, who, behind his many faults – which I do not think my words conceal – had one prominent impulse of the mind, which was ready to grasp good or evil, truth or falsehood, according to the garb it came in. My years of College life – in no sense Collegiate life – placed the banquet of learning before me ungarnished and colourless, and my father wondered why the dishes that had tempted his intellectual palate in the library of the gardens of Peterhouse should be tasteless to his son's in Gower Street. Surely a College is a College, wherever chance has placed it. He attached no weight whatever to University residence, as against home and daily attendance. Of what dis-advantage was it to studious youth to be shut out of his College after hours? Would any amount of gating make study acceptable to an unstudious son? – No – it was manifestly my aversion to letters, devel-oped as soon as application to them became optional; for that was a condition precedent of College manhood, no longer schoolboy-hood.

Before he finished at the college he had already started to attend evening classes at Cary's. This old-established school run by John Stephen Cary, son of the famous translator of Dante, was in a building in Streatham Street, off New Oxford Street. As was usual in those days, the students' main occupation was drawing charcoal copies of antique casts, but this futile practice did not deter William from entering the Royal Academy Schools, for he decided that he wanted to make a career as an 'artist', that is, a painter. His father was not then (or ever) in favour and made his feel-ings plain to his eldest son. But not being the classic heavy-handed Victorian father, once it was clear that William was adamant, he made no attempt to stand in his son's way. His distrust of a career as a painter is set out in a letter he wrote William, who later inserted some comments of his own:

Professor De Morgan to William De Morgan.[23]
7 Camden Street, N.W.,
August 24, 1858.

Dear Willy, –

Now that you have fairly left College, it is time to ask yourself whether you have really made up your mind as to your profession – and if so, whether you have chosen wisely. I have never interfered, because I cared little what you thought at seventeen and eighteen.

Do you really think that you are so likely to adhere to the choice you think you have made as to make it worth while to spend more time upon it? [*In pencil, in William's handwriting*; YES.]

Have you considered your chance of success with any other eyes but your own? Would it not be worthwhile to take the opinion of some persons who have no partiality towards you as to your chances.

Have you considered other things as to how you should like them?

Are you fully aware of the lottery character of the profession of an artist?

Do you know that it is a life subject to very keen mortifications. [*In William's writing*: BLOW THAT!]

Do you know that the preparation for it is very hard labour? That you must work many hours a day for years and years?

[*In William's writing*: THE SAME MAY BE SAID OF ANY PROFES/ SION IN WHICH ONE MAY BECOME AN HONOURABLE AND INDE/ PENDENT INDIVIDUAL.]

Think this over for a fortnight and give me an answer. If, after perfect deliberation, you make up your mind to go on, well and good. But you cannot easily give too much thought to what I have put before you.

Give me no answer for a fortnight at least. But even if you wait till you come here give it me in writing.

Your affectionate Father,

A. DE MORGAN.

[Endorsed in William's writing: '*Received Wednesday, August 25 – '58*'.]

William's answer to the letter has disappeared but he later wrote:[24] 'my father's feeble opposition to my wishes had to disappear, though I do not believe he was ever convinced; he was far too sensible for that! I fancy he consoled himself with the reflection that I was still so young that a year or so spent in demonstrating my incompetence for Art could be well spared.'

William won his argument with his father and was accepted as an art student, but his disillusionment not only with the teaching available in London at this time but with the students and indeed the art world in general was made very plain in various recollections later in life. Obviously one should not take for granted that certain passages in his novels are strictly autobiographical; indeed, in *It Can Never Happen Again* De Morgan in a postscript slightly testily takes to task readers who believe that opinions expressed by characters in his narrative are those of the author. However, May Morris in the *Dictionary Of National Biography* categorically states that *The Old Man's Youth* is 'largely autobiographical', and the author himself conceded that the character of Charles Heath in *Alice-For-Short* is some/thing of a self-portrait. One may look for other transcriptions of his early experience. There is, for instance, a very disillusioned view of the art world and the artist which is worth quoting from *Alice-For-Short*:

> So completely is the image of what constitutes 'an Artist' fixed in the mind of Everyman that as soon as he knows that the stock qualifica/tions of the profession are complied with, he makes little enquiry about what the outcome of it all is. That is the affair of Critics, Purchasers, and Dealers. All that he, Everyman, has to do is to get an affirmative answer to one or more of the following questions, and then he will know that this man is an Artist – to wit: Has this man a Studio? Has he one or more easels? Does he buy large quantities of colours, and get professional discount? Does he employ real life Models? Does he send to the Academy? If he does no one of these things, he evidently isn't an Artist – if he does them all or any fair pro/portion of them, he evidently is. Everyman is satisfied, and no man looks at the results or cares twopence about them. Maybe this was truer in the sixties than it is now, when very few people are not Artists, and speculative builders are running up barracks of Studios in every suburb; when Artists' Colourmen are as numerous as milkshops, and every post brings a new little book of canvas samples; when most of the Times newspaper is taken up with One Man Exhibitions,

[17]

which Everyman is expected to go to, and we never go to unless we have a free pass. In the sixties it was not at all uncommon to hear of a picture sale; in the case of big swells coronetted supplicants were humbly competing with Calicottonopolis for the privilege of possessing their great works as soon as they should deign to finish them. It is all changed now, as far as the buyers go, and Everyman is really weary of Exhibitions. We, ourselves, feel we might pay a shilling of gate-money if only all the Pictures in an Exhibition were hung with their faces to the wall. Not seeing so many pictures all at once would give a sense of rest, and allow us to recruit and become able to rejoice in Treatment and Quality and Due Subordination as of old, and to recognise Values and all that sort of thing instead of thinking it must be getting on for Tea-time.

When young Eustace John in *The Old Man's Youth* shows an apparent talent for drawing, he writes, 'Another landmark, which had painful consequences for me in after life, was my discovery that I had a genius for Fine Arts.' In fact he is discovered to have no great genius but a facility for amusing cartoons, sketches for journals and newspapers, and for book illustration. Like Augustus, Eustace John's father is not keen on the arts as a career for his son. He takes him to an academician who is no help at all, and to a cynical old man in the world of galleries and auctions who maintains that the only standard in painting is the commercial viability of a painter's work: if it sells it is good, and if it does not, it is no good.

The author's view of the art student is less than complimentary in *Alice-For-Short*. Charles, a thoroughly nice but weak young man, very seldom finishes a picture and spends a lot of his time preparing canvases, chatting to his fellow students and buying expensive paints. Later in the novel, having survived a disastrous first marriage, he comes to terms with his obvious lack of talent and after marrying his childhood sweetheart he goes on to write a best-selling novel – much to his surprise. This is a very close parallel with what happened to William in much later life, except that between his early artistic efforts and late literary success he had an immensely interesting and distinguished career as a ceramic designer. Nevertheless, as we shall see, he was not, to put it kindly, a good businessman.

One of William's lifelong friends was William (later Sir William) Blake

Richmond, RA, who went on to become a distinguished portrait painter and was responsible for some of the mosaic decorations at St Paul's. When William arrived, Richmond was already a student at the Academy, and he left a vivid sketch of the new student arriving at the School:[25]

I am not sure if it was in the autumn of 1859 or the spring of 1860, when I was working in the schools of the Royal Academy, that a tall, rather gaunt young man arrived as a *nouveau*, who excited among us of a term's seniority some interest. He was an original, that was evident at starting. His capacious forehead denoted power, his grey eyes tenderness, his delicately formed nose refinement, and his jaw strength. But the commanding characteristic was unmistakably humour. He spoke with a curious accent, his voice, as if it had never quite settled to be soprano or bass, moved with flexibility up and down the scale, and every sentence was finished with a certain drawl. This was a trait caught by many of Rossetti's friends. This youth was William De Morgan, son of the celebrated mathematician and his wife, a distinguished lady, highly cultivated, intimate friend of Carlyle and other leaders of the thought of the times, and much loved by her friends . . .

Well grounded at King's College [sic] he was a fair classical scholar, but it was not in any portion of his character created by education that he was remarkable. Pre-eminently he was original, entirely uncommonplace. He had a quaint invention, he took a quaint view of everything. He was a master of the unexpected, a creator of paradox, a serious humorist. A very delicate constitution forbade ath-letics of all kinds. His body had to beware of excess, his mind could adroitly play with it. Public opinion he cared for not a jot; he was his own critic in as much as he always strove for perfection. The progress of his mind was swift as well as persistent; a bit of wire, a bit of wood provided hours of enjoyment for his creative mind, one moment dwelling on a vast scheme for flying or underwater piracy, another in adding some delicacy to the construction of his bicycle.

There were many talented young men there: Richmond himself, Henry Holiday,[26] who was a designer of stained glass and a painter in the Rossetti tradition, Fred Walker,[27] and the man they all thought had the most talent of all, Simeon Solomon.[28] The teaching from all accounts left a lot to be desired. The Keeper, Charles Landseer, brother of Sir Edwin, came in once a day invariably to remark on a student's incorrectness in anatomical detail, and the great Sir Edwin himself paid an occasional visit to the Life School. Richmond reserved his most critical remarks for Solomon Hart the Professor of Painting: 'How he came to be in the RA no one knew.' Hart gave appallingly dull lectures on anatomy. Other recollections surface in the novels. In *Alice-For-Short* De Morgan describes the Schools and the pathetic old man Verrinder who has been a student there for nearly fifty years, and who hates the cynical and unkind young men who pour scorn on him.

De Morgan was just twenty when he entered the Academy, and wrote much later about his fellow students:[29]

As for those I saw drawing – probates, I suppose, as they had passed through successfully – I was strongly impressed with the persistency with which they gazed on their own work, glancing occasionally at its original for comparison. Now and then, rarely, as a fly occasionally touches the surface of a still pool, the point of a crayon or the bustle of a stump touched the surface of a drawing. The serene contempla- tion of achievement, which filled the gaps between the touches, set thought on the alert to determine when the drawings were actually executed; a task before which thought reeled and staggered speechless. A fair percentage of these matured students seemed morally degener- ate – more reprobates than probates – passing their time in the exchange of repartees, the comparison of the beauty of actresses, or reminiscences of theatrical tit-bits. [*'Morally degenerate' presumably alludes to bawdy talk.*]

De Morgan goes on to say:

My recollection is well supplied with dissolute and vicious units who made up for sheer incapacity, or strong disposition to leave off work at the point at which difficulty begins, by audacious attitudinizing and wholesale quackery. The wonder of it to me has been that such men have been so often taken at their own valuation, and have been worked up by dealerdom, and written up by the press, until any attempt to accelerate the natural gravitation of their 'work' toward Oblivion would only cause a recrudescence of their spurious fame, and defeat its own object.

I was not qualified for a mountebank by nature, and should never have scored a success on those lines. So I never became a Real Artist.

De Morgan's time at the Academy Schools may have been discouraging in some ways but it certainly had two good outcomes. First, he discovered that he was not going to be a good painter, and started work as a designer of stained glass which prepared him for his later inventions in the use of lustre. Joseph Vance, in De Morgan's first novel, says: 'I know of nothing like invention to make life palatable.' De Morgan was extraordinarily versatile, as will be seen, whether experimenting with glazes, pigments or new designs of kilns and this love of experiment would last throughout his life. It is unlikely that if he had stuck to his painting this side of his talent would have been expressed. Personally, he seems to have had no regrets in giving up a career as a painter in favour of glass and ceramic design.

The other result of his time as a student came about through his partic-ular friendships with some of his fellow pupils, Richmond, Henry Holiday, and Simeon Solomon. They would have been much more enthu-siastic about the work of the early Pre-Raphaelites than about the more conventional academicians, and it was through these friends that he was to get to know William Morris and Edward Burne-Jones.

Chapter 2

Stained-glass designing – meeting with William Morris and
Burne-Jones and his work in Fitzroy Square studio –
experiments with glazes and lustre on tiles – death of
Augustus De Morgan.

THE YEARS BETWEEN 1862 and 1872 were formative in De Morgan's artistic career. There was not a great deal to show materially by the time he established himself and his pottery in Chelsea in 1872 but he had realized over the years that he was not going to succeed as a painter of pictures, and most importantly he had discovered what his real métier was going to be.

His family were living at 6 Merton Road, Adelaide Road, north-west London, but it is unclear how much time he actually spent there and how much he was at 40 Fitzroy Square and, prior to that, in London Road and Grafton Street. The Fitzroy Square house,[1] where he had his studio, which he shared with the stained-glass maker James Lyon Tennant, is, in part, the house in *Alice-For-Short* where Charles and his artist friend had their studios. It also had the appalling, dirty and ghost-ridden basement in which poor little Alice and her drunken parents lived. However, the ballroom[2] which plays an important part in *Alice-For-Short* is modelled on the big room in the house in Great Marlborough Street which De Morgan later used as a showroom.[3]

One suspects that the life Dr Morgan led was rather similar (and so he suggests himself) to Charles's in *Alice*. One difference was that he probably worked much harder than Charles, who was adept at organizing his

studio, buying paints and stretching canvases but only too open to suggestion from his friends to go out and have a meal at the local Italian restau-
rant, or stop work altogether to have a friendly talk and smoke cigars.

The most important event for William De Morgan in these years was his
introduction, in 1863, by Henry Holiday (mainly known as a stained-glass
artist) to William Morris in the house in Red Lion Square where the great
man lived and where he had set up his firm Morris, Marshall, Faulkner &
Co. The old Pre-Raphaelite Brotherhood had fallen apart by this time.
Morris and his friends had finished their ill-fated painting in the Oxford
Union[4] and the firm had been established to create and sell useful products
of good design and individual craftsmanship, very much inspired by
Morris's extraordinary talents and driving energy. Around him Morris had
gathered the talents of Edward Burne-Jones[5] who had been at Oxford with
him, Dante Gabriel Rossetti,[6] Ford Madox Brown,[7] Thomas Woolner,[8]
and two who were not artists, Charles Faulkner a mathematician and Peter
Paul Marshall a surveyor and sanitary engineer.

Many years later De Morgan recalled his first visit to Morris:[9]

I first met him at Red Lion Square where I was taken by Henry
Holiday – the very earliest dawn of him to me being the *Athenaeum*
reviews of his earliest poems (Dr Garnett wrote it, I fancy) quoting
Rupunzel. At this visit I chiefly recollect him dressing himself up in
vestments and playing on a regal,[10] to illustrate certain points in
connection with stained glass. As I went home it suddenly crossed my
mind as a strange thing that he should, while doing what was so trivial
and almost grotesque, contrive to leave on my memory so strong an
impression of his power – he certainly did somehow.

De Morgan later wrote, 'Morris was certainly the most wonderful genius I
ever knew. He produced poetry as readily as a bird sings!.' One day on a
visit to the Burne-Jones family De Morgan:

found Morris in the parlour – he was nibbling a pen. And he said,
after a few words of chat – 'now you see, I'm going to write poetry, so
you'll have to cut[11] – I'm sorry, but it can't be helped!' so I cut – and
I have a notion that I know what he wrote that evening, as next

[23]

Saturday when I turned up, as I always did then-a-days, he read us a
lot of the Study of Psyche. So I'm glad I cut! – I recollect his remarking that it was very hard work writing that sort of thing. I took it that
he was speaking of the thrashing Psyche gets at the hands of Venus.
He really felt for her – and was evidently glad it was over.[12]

Nowadays Morris' verse is little read and although one cannot doubt his
extraordinary fluency it is interesting that even some of his closest friends
sometimes found it difficult to keep awake listening to the author's chanting
of his latest poems.

The importance of the meeting between De Morgan and Morris and his
circle can hardly be exaggerated, particularly for the latter. The Morris firm
had started on 1 January 1861. Burne-Jones told a visitor to Red Lion
Square, the painter Price Boyce,[13] 'he and Morris and Rossetti and Webb[14]
were going to set up a sort of shop where they would jointly produce and
sell painted furniture'. As has been said, the firm produced a lot more than
that. In April 1861 a prospectus had been drawn up to send to likely clients.
It is an interesting document; the preamble states: 'The growth of
Decorative Art in this country owing to the effort of English Architects has
now reached a point at which it seems desirable that Artists of reputation
should devote their time to it.' It goes on to say in a very confident, and
perhaps self-important, manner:

These Artists having been for many years deeply attached to study of
the Decorative Arts of all time and countries, have felt more than
most people the want of some one place, where they could either
obtain or get produced work of a genuine and beautiful character.
They have therefore now established themselves as a firm, for the production, by themselves, and under their supervision of:

I   Mural Decoration, either in Pictures or in Pattern Work, or
     merely in the arrangement of colours as applied to dwelling-
     houses, churches or public buildings.
II   Carving generally, as applied to Architecture.
III Stained Glass, especially with reference to its harmony with
     Mural Decoration.
IV   Metal Work in all its branches, including jewellery.

V Furniture, either depending for its beauty on its own design, or
on the application of materials hitherto overlooked, or on its con-
juncture with Figure and Pattern Painting. Under this head is
included Embroidery of all kinds, Stamped Leather, and orna-
mental work in other such materials, besides every article necessary for domestic use.

The prospectus claimed the firm possessed access to a great wealth of talent,
and indeed with the original members they could provide all the necessary
expertise to produce the different goods promised to customers. Stained
glass, on which De Morgan had been working, was a very significant activity in the firm, but it must have struck William as convenient that pottery
was not mentioned and none of the original members of the firm specialized in the making or decoration of ceramics.[15] It proved lucky for him later
on in his career that he was able to market some of his products, both pots
and tiles, through the Morris firm's shop at 449 (originally 264) Oxford
Street. This shop, unusually for buildings of the time in the centre of
London, can still be identified.

It must have been enormously stimulating and exciting for William to
have been accepted by this group of extremely talented young men who
were putting into practice revolutionary ideas on arts and crafts, and selling
the products, challenging set Victorian ideas on furniture, decoration and
painting.

Two years earlier, in 1859, Morris had commissioned Philip Webb, the
architect, to build him Red House at Bexley. The same year he had married
Jane Burden. In this house Morris, his wife, his family and friends, and particularly Burne-Jones, were able to apply their theories and ideals in design,
whether for painted furniture, tapestries or curtains. They practised the
crafts which they were going to use to good effect in Morris's business.
Morris's firm included a wealth of talent and he and his friends between
them had started to create and make a great variety of objects: tiles, furniture, embroideries and tapestries woven by Jane and her sister using the
designs of Morris and Burne-Jones, and of course painted textiles and wallpapers. Stained glass was also produced. At Fitzroy Square De Morgan
experimented with both stained glass and designs for tiles.

As it happened, stained glass was much in demand at this time.

Convulsions in the Church of England earlier in the century, when the Oxford Movement and the Tractarians had shaken the Church out of its eighteenth-century somnolence, led to a great deal of church restoration and new church-building, much of it Gothic revival, inspired by A.W.N. Pugin's work and often designed by G.F. Bodley.[16] De Morgan was encouraged in his efforts in stained-glass work by Morris, and as far as one can tell the glass he designed was for Morris's firm to market. It is important, and De Morgan thought so too, to stress that although in his early days he worked through Morris's firm as far as the marketing of his products was concerned, he was never an established member, but always independent. 'A common error', he wrote later in his life, 'is to suppose that I was partner in Morris's firm. I was never connected with his business beyond the fact that, on his own initiative, he exhibited and sold my work and that subsequently he employed my tiles in his schemes for decoration.' De Morgan's firm, which confined itself to the designing and making of tiles and pottery, was always independent from the start in Chelsea in 1872 to the final closure in Fulham.

Some examples of his stained-glass work survive in five different churches, such as the David window in Layer Marney, Essex, and the east window and St Michael window in Rocester, Staffordshire.[17] There were some roundels and figure panels in Old Battersea House where Mrs Stirling (the biographer of William and Evelyn De Morgan), lived for many years. In his typical self-disparaging way he described himself as 'a feeble and discursive dabble in picture making. I transferred myself to stained glass window making and dabbled in that too until 1872.'[18] However, some people thought rather better of his efforts. His friend Sir William Blake Richmond wrote: 'I've seen some very interesting work from his hand, in that difficult branch of art into which incompetence too often strays and where genius is so rarely visible.'[19] May Morris, William Morris's daughter, said many years later that she had seen specimens of his glass hanging up in his house and they had struck her as 'being singularly rich in colour and simple and dignified in design'.[20]

It was also in Fitzroy Square that De Morgan started designing and experimenting with tiles, initially to sell through Morris's firm. Later, when he started producing them in quantity, Morris routinely ordered any he wanted from William's firm.

De Morgan's decision to work with ceramics came at a key moment in the history of the English tile. The great period of English tile-making had been in medieval times (principally encaustic tiles for flooring in cathedrals, churches and monasteries),[21] but production ceased with the Reformation. A.W.N. Pugin used encaustic tiles in his churches made by the manufac-turer Herbert Minton and also used colour-printed tiles, still to be seen, for instance, in the smoking-room in the 'new' House of Commons. At the beginning of the nineteenth century the tile was 'simply a roofing tile', as an anonymous author wrote. By the late 1860s they were used extensively in ordinary middle-class homes and by 1867 they had reached a peak of popularity. The Paris exhibition that year had a big area devoted to English and French tiles. George Gilbert Scott introduced richly coloured tiles in to the Foreign Secretary's room in the Foreign Office and, most extraordi-nary achievement of all, Messrs Copeland of Stoke-on-Trent agreed to dec-orate with tiles the nine domes of what is now the reading-room of the Bibliothèque Nationale in Paris. When the project was planned many firms were approached in France, Germany and Holland but none of them would undertake to put 36,000 tiles on the underside of the domes. Royalty and architects of major new buildings also ordered tiles from firms such as Minton, Maw & Co. and Copeland.

Elizabeth Aslin in her authoritative essay[22] on tiles in the nineteenth century sets out very clearly what distinguished De Morgan's work from that of others in the same field:

From the outset able and even distinguished artists and designers were employed by tile manufacturers, a practice which continued through-out the century, and tiles can be found to illustrate every style of design current in Queen Victoria's long reign, from Gothic revival to Art Nouveau. The list of artists and architects who included tiles in their work ranges from A.W.N. Pugin and G.E. Street at the beginning of the period to C.F.A. Voysey, Walter Crane and Lewis F. Day at the turn of the century. Curiously, in the light of the many theories propounded about the suitability of design for material, it would appear that with the exception of William De Morgan in England and Theodore Deck in France, none of these artists, even those working for the Morris firm, were concerned with ceramic technique.

The tile was regarded as one of the many forms of pattern design comparable with wallpaper or printed textiles. Strictly speaking, De Morgan was alone in this field, for even Deck couldn't be described as a designer of tiles in the normally accepted sense of a single unit repeated over a large area. During the 1860s, the period in which his technical researches into colours and glazes interested and impressed De Morgan and others in France and England, Deck was making large earthenware slabs on which figure, subjects or landscapes were painted by his friends.

De Morgan's experiments in Fitzroy Square in glazes for tiles (and the firing of them) and his work on stained glass led to his 'rediscovery' of lustreware. Lustre was nothing new, it had been made in the Near East, Iznik in Turkey, Egypt, Spain and Italy. It had always had a unique and peculiar fascination, particularly gold and silver lustre, and there was a certain amount of mystery attached to its production, which was and still is very difficult with a high rate of failure in the firing. In the Great Exhibition of 1851 there is no mention of lustre pottery, and certainly there had been very little made in Europe for two hundred years. De Morgan himself wrote about the 'discovery' in a paper he delivered to the Society of Arts on 31 May 1892, and which was published in their journal on 24 June 1892:[23]

In fact, re-discovery appears to have dogged the footsteps of the lustres from the beginning. I rediscovered them myself in 1874, or there-abouts, and in the course of time some of my *employés* left me, and re-discovered them again somewhere else. I do not think any rediscoveries of this sort contributed in any way to the very general diffusion of the process in the potteries at this moment. Very likely some of them have an earlier record than mine, but the only one I chanced upon when I was in Staffordshire was that of the late Mr Clement Wedgwood, who showed me a number of experiments which would have been successes if the glaze had been suitable, and a small sample shown me by the late Mr Colin Campbell. As far as the technical difficulties of simply evolving a copper or silver lustre go, I see no reason why (as in the case of the Arabs and Italians) every discovery should not be totally unconnected with every other. But

[28]

there was one thing the Italians found out, when they reproduced the Moorish firings, namely, how to make a strong, and beautiful, and original use of their materials. It may be that the less we say about the modern parallels of their case the better.

Perhaps we may now make a new departure, and consider the process is as well known as any other process in the arts; at any rate, I will contribute what I can to make it so, by telling all I know of it myself. I got nothing from Piccolpasso,[24] as I did not see the work until long after, nor from any printed information, except the chem/ ical manuals I had read in youth. The clue was furnished by the yellow stain of silver on glass. When overfired this shows iridescence, which is often visible on the opaque yellow visible from the outside on stained glass windows. I tried the stain on Dutch tiles, and found them unsusceptible in the glass kiln but, in the small gas muffle I found that both copper and silver gave a lustre when the gas was damped down so as to penetrate the muffle. I pursued my investiga/ tion, and, after an interruption, occasioned by setting the house on fire and burning the roof off, I developed the process in Chelsea. This was 1873–4, since which time it has not varied materially, although I have tried many experiments, with the view to improving it.

One has a lot of sympathy for the landlord of 40 Fitzroy Square, who, De Morgan said, 'was not at all amiable'[25] when he found his tenant had set fire to the roof, having connected the chimney from a small kiln he had built into the ordinary fireplace in his room. Also, one has sympathy with a Miss Laura Hertford, tenant of the floor above, who warned De Morgan when she saw his kiln: 'you will burn the house down.' She became a dis/ tinguished painter, the first woman to exhibit in the Royal Academy.

Morris certainly encouraged De Morgan in his designs and experiments with tiles, and so did a friend and fellow tenant, Horatio Lucas: [26] When he saw the first tile William had produced – a rather dull pink one – Lucas said to his wife, 'keep that, for one day De Morgan will be a great man'. He also encouraged De Morgan to try his hand at making stained glass. Everything had to be learned from first/principles. May Morris wrote:[27] 'It was the dilemma of the period that artists were unskilled in an exacting craft . . . the technicians of the commercial factory were not artists.' She complained of 'the necessity of spending valuable time experimenting in the ABC'. This elementary research was what really fascinated De Morgan. As he said later in his Society of Arts paper, when he started his experiments with glazes and kilns he had to rely on schoolboy chemistry books. The architect Halsey Ricardo,[28] who later became a partner in his business, said:

> He was so keenly interested in the physics of this craft, and its con-
> tributory constituents that were it not for the wealth of inimitable
> objects that came from this kiln one might have classed him as a sci-
> entific enthusiast, absorbed in his investigation of pottery-making,
> glazing and firing – independent of any decorative treatment.

Even though there was very little to show from his work before 1872 and the move to Chelsea, it is safe to assume he must have experimented a great deal, not only with stained glass and tiles but also with pottery decoration. Morris, as we have seen, was content later on to use De Morgan's tiles and he was never particularly involved in the making or designing of pots – so there was a gap to be filled, particularly by someone with the quite extraor-dinary talent of De Morgan.

These years are significant in William's life in quite another way. They were the years in which he cemented lifelong friendships with Morris and Burne-Jones and also the last years when the De Morgan family was still a complete unit with the exception of the eldest girl, Alice, who had died of TB. A warm friendship grew up between them and William's artistic friends. Adelaide Road was a centre of music-making and games-playing. Victorian families, especially fairly large ones, in the peaceful days before the telephone, radio or television, tended to look to their own resources for entertainment, whether singing, playing music or staging dramatic entertainment. The De Morgans were no exception. Henry Holiday writing in 1864 says:[29]

> We became intimate the Spring, and I was often at Adelaide Rd.
> where his family lived. His father, Professor De Morgan, well known
> for his writings on spiritualism, the three sons, William, George and
> Edward and the daughters Annie, Chrissie and Mary, formed an

attractive and interesting household, not the less so to me that they were most of them musical. Professor De Morgan played Pleyel's sonatas for the piano and flute with his daughter Annie. Edward played the violin and was in great request with amateur orchestras; and most of them sang.

No mention is ever made of William playing an instrument or singing, but it is obvious that he loved listening to music and had a considerable knowl-edge of many well-known works. Of Beethoven's 'Waldstein' Sonata for piano, he said: 'It is the best argument for immortality that I know!'[30] It was also a great solace to poor Joseph Vance – in the first novel – after the death of his wife. The 'Kreutzer' Sonata for violin and piano plays a prominent part in *Somehow Good*, where a talented Mr Bradshaw with his Strad eclipses the talents of other members of a quartet, and later gives a super-lative concert performance of Beethoven's 'Kreutzer' Sonata.

The De Morgans and their friends also amused themselves with games using comic verse, a game called 'Cartoons'. Such scribbling is not usually interesting to an outsider, but as William was going to become a best-selling novelist and Holiday, Burne-Jones and William were all going to succeed as artists, they do have a certain fascination. The only copies of the verses and drawings are those reproduced in Mrs Stirling's biography and seem to date from the 1860s.* One of their circle of friends, Amherst Tyssen, wrote:

The entries in my diary show that in 1863 William De Morgan was strong, active and enterprising. He was also well informed, clever and humorous. This came out particularly when we played the games he and his family were fond of, such as drawing pictures and writing stories on those drawn by the others, also making a list of words and finding rhymes to these, thus fashioning sets of verses. It was not always easy to find a rhyming connection with a given word; but William solved the difficulty by introducing a negative. He discov-ered that it was always possible to find a rhyming word about some-thing which the given subject did *not* do or was *not*! One evening we

* See Appendix A.

had a competition in finding as many rhymes as possible to the word 'piano' and William won by inventing a number of ridiculous combinations of words which supplied the necessary rhymes. At this date, too, he and Henry Holiday on wet days were jointly painting a picture which represented the body of the Lady of Shalott floating down the river to Camelot and exciting the wonder of spectators on the bank. Each did a small portion of the picture, as the spirit moved him, and then left it to his collaborator to continue as the latter saw fit. The result was curious and rather beautiful.[31]

Characters and cartoons were often included in letters written by De Morgan and Burne-Jones, and many of the extraordinary and weird animals used on William's plates and pots are very similar to those in his letters. Fortunately, he concentrated on prose at the end of his career as a potter as there is not much evidence of any great talent as a poet in the quoted fragments.

In 1864 the Holidays, Henry and his parents, went to Beddgelert in North Wales for the summer. In the next village, Betwys-y-Coed, the De Morgans were staying, the whole family except for Augustus, who could rarely be persuaded to leave London for the country, which he detested as we have seen. Henry Holiday, De Morgan, Amherst Tyssen, and the athletic rector of Beddgelert made a number of expeditions, up Snowdon, along the coast at night, and some foolhardy experiments on the scree slopes where they all got slightly hurt. Obviously William was not at all delicate, or suffering from a bad back, until much later on in his life. The athletic rector bears some resemblance to the Rev. Athelstan Taylor in *It Can Never Happen Again*: an unorthodox and attractive example of muscular Christianity and down-to-earth common sense.

In reading about the Pre-Raphaelites with their eccentricities, particularly William Holman-Hunt, the marital problems of Morris and Rossetti, Rossetti's long drug and drink problem late in his life and not forgetting poor Ned Burne-Jones's predilection for affairs with his models, one cannot but get a rather false and jaundiced view of an agonized and deeply unhappy group of people. Added to that, many of their paintings, whether one admires them or not, do have an extraordinary atmosphere, otherworldly and full of a despairing quality. As young men, though, they seem to have had a rather jolly middle-class life, full of ideals and the talents to realize them. It was not always serious discussion in the evening and we are told that in Rossetti's lodgings they often played whist in the evenings. Morris's firm had got off to a good start backed by family money, Burne-Jones had plenty of work with his designs for stained glass and furniture decoration, and Rossetti, already a successful painter, was a magnetic personality and inspired revolt against the Establishment. Morris had inherited money which helped him entertain his close friends at Red House in a lavish style and the gatherings were often, according to his biographers, hilarious affairs with plenty of practical jokes to be played on Topsy, as Morris was called. There was very little 'artistic bohemianism.' Perhaps because this was London and not Paris, they were not starving artists in cold garrets nor did they drink absinthe and take drugs in their younger days. It is in fact a far cry from the world of Paragot in the *Beloved Vagabond* or indeed the somewhat idealized world of the student in *La Bohème*.

One curious habit of some of the Pre-Raphaelites was to write and speak a pseudo-cockney. William De Morgan took to this particularly in correspondence with Ned Burne-Jones. Typical is a letter from Burne-Jones:[32]

> My de$^{\lambda}$r de Morgan,
> do you re$^{mem}_{\lambda}$ber a frame i likt at your house it wus a frame from florrence it wus a nice one and i likt it may Mr. Va^{s}ani make me one lik it may he call at your house and i may add your good ladies' house on Monday nex about 12 or so I will try to come round on Sunday afternoon to adentify the frame i hope u are quite well this seseonable winter i am 1/2 ded so is most people i hope to get good news from you and all your famly with wishes for a happy new year when it comes i am
> Your affectionate
> NED

De Morgan, of course, later in his life was very successful in writing dialogue in many of his novels, whether middle-class, aristocratic, or more particularly working-class. One thinks of Joseph Vance's father, or a slightly ghoulish but comic scene in *Alice For Short* when a bricklayer is asked to dig a floor which he has just laid as it is suspected that it might cover the skeleton of a dead girl.

It is a small mystery how Augustus, taking into account his meagre salary and resignation in 1866, managed to support a large family. It is possible that Sophia may have had money of her own from her father, William Frend, and Augustus, a tireless worker, must have had some commissions to write articles and edit books (not very well paid work at the best of times). We know he also did actuarial work. He certainly wrote articles on the subject, and there is one rather fleeting reference to a connection he had with a big insurance firm. As far as one can tell, none of the surviving children were earning any money, until William set up his firm in Chelsea in 1872.

The few years before 1872 make melancholy reading as far as the De Morgan family was concerned. Alice's death had occurred earlier but George, founder and secretary of the Mathematical Society, was to die of TB of the throat, Edward went off on an eighteen-month voyage because of his health, and Chrissie, one of the wittiest and most sparkling of the family, died in 1870. Poor Augustus never really recovered from his resignation and the deaths of his children. A letter he wrote at the time to his friend Sir John Herschel is typical of the man:[33] 'A strong and practical conviction of a better and higher existence reduces the whole thing to emigration to a country from which there is no way back and no mail packets, with a certainty of following at a time to be arranged in a better way than I can do it.' Also typical of this resolute man is a sentence in his will: 'I commend my future with hope and confidence to Almighty God; to God, the Father of our Lord Jesus Christ Whom I believe in my heart to be the Son of God but whom I have not confessed with my lips, because in my time such confession has always been a way up in the world.' Augustus De Morgan died in March 1871.

William had to move in 1872 from Fitzroy Square following the fire he had caused. He obviously had to have somewhere more practicable to build a kiln, and he also had to provide for his mother and his sister Mary who were the only members of the family still dependent on him. Annie seems not to have moved to Chelsea and as we have seen was married two years later to

Dr Reginald Thompson, a physician at the Brompton Hospital and a close friend of William's. In 1906 William wrote to one of his admirers in America: 'A friend offered capital and I removed from the ruins of my Carthage. I started afresh as a potter but I lost my stained glass which was bringing me more than I've ever earned since.'[34] This was of course written before his novels started earning. We do not know who the friend was, possibly Reginald Thompson, or perhaps Horatio Lucas who was enthusiastic about his 'first' tile.

Chapter 3

WILLIAM, his mother Sophia and sister Mary moved to 30 Cheyne Row
in Chelsea where a kiln was built at the bottom of the garden. Frank Iles
joined him and remained his kiln master for all the 35 years the pottery lasted.
Chelsea in 1872 still retained its village atmosphere. May Morris wrote:

> Cheyne Row was an unpretentious old-world corner at the upper end
> of which stood the beautiful little house built for G.P. Boyce by Philip
> Webb, the tree tops of its pleasant garden waving above the high brick
> wall; from here, looking down the Row, one caught glimpses of the
> light on the river and the red-sailed barges, and for us one of the
> charms of the place was the sense of adventure that a quiet corner
> gleans from that sight of the way into the open world.[1]

In fact, Chelsea was an excellent place for a potter's family to move to.
There was a history of pottery-making; Wedgwood amongst others had a
large workshop near by, not too far from Cheyne Row, and in it Wedgwood
made among other products the famous dinner service for the Russian royal
family. Some of De Morgan's close friends lived within easy visiting distance – Burne-Jones had moved to The Grange, Fulham, and William

Morris was to buy a large house in Hammersmith Mall which he christened Kelmscott House as a companion to Kelmscott Manor in Oxfordshire. Also, not too far away in Hammersmith, in Beavor Lodge, lived William Blake Richmond, his old friend and fellow student at the Academy Schools.[2] In Cheyne Row itself there lived the formidable Thomas Carlyle, whose thick Scottish accent made him difficult for even close friends to understand. Sophia had known him for many years.

The kiln De Morgan had had built with difficulty at the bottom of the garden proved too small for his needs. While his family remained in no. 30, he rented a large old house called Orange House on Cheyne Row; a Roman Catholic church stands there today. The new site gave plenty of room for his workmen and women and by its side there was a coach house where he built his bigger kiln. Rather rashly, considering the experience he had had in Fitzroy Square, the flue was channelled into one of the chimneys of the new house. No fire resulted, but he was very impatient with his first firing and blew the top off the kiln. He had received an order for a thousand tiles of a fan-shaped flower pattern which he called the 'BBB' after the manufacturers Barnard, Bishop & Barnard. With typical good humour, when the entire kilnful was ruined he said the BBB order 'was temporarily re-named the DDD.'[2]

Reginald Blunt in his *The Wonderful Village*[3] was able to get some particulars of Orange House from Fred Passenger,[4] who in 1879 joined the De Morgan firm where his elder brother Charles already worked – both of them highly skilled ceramic decorators. There was no room for the firm to make its own pots, vases, plates and tiles (the kiln at Orange House was used only for glazed-work firing), so these had to be bought in, although towards the end of the Chelsea period De Morgan started to make his own tiles. The kiln was in the coach house, the showroom and a storeroom at the back filled the whole of the ground floor. The decorators worked on the first floor: namely, the two Passenger brothers, a young artist called Mr Bubb, Mrs Beaty and Dr Reginald Thompson,[5] who as we have seen in 1874 married Annie, De Morgan's sister. Several girls employed on tile-painting had a room in one of the Upper Cheyne Row houses. Blunt recounts the enjoyment the De Morgan painters got from being next to the showroom where they might see the would-be purchasers come in to examine the objects which they, the painters, had had a hand in making.

[37]

The prospective purchasers were known as the carriage folk, because on the whole De Morgan's customers were very superior people. De Morgan himself[6] was very much in evidence, not merely making the designs, packing the kilns, and personally attending to customers, but also coping with the larger-than-life William Morris who would often pay a visit at the end of the day's work. May Morris writes:[7]

> Many a time, when our Hammersmith quartette paid a visit to the Chelsea trio, we would go round to Orange House after tea and spend part of the long summer evening wandering through house and garden eager over the latest experiment. There were times when a kiln spoilt cast a slight cloud on the gathering, in spite of the gentle cour-tesy of our friend, who would not even mention the mishap; times when a pot that had roused no special expectation came out a triumph of shining colour amongs the ruin of a whole firing; there were 'spoilt' pieces that one could not help loving for some special quality in them – in short a whole chapter of the story which passing under the eyes of those familiar with the building-up of a craft, was alive with inci-dents hailed and followed with keenest interest.

Reginald Blunt,[8] later to be De Morgan's manager, writes from first-hand experience of working with De Morgan of the strains and tensions involved in the firing of a large kiln filled with decorated ware. These had probably taken weeks if not months to produce and might very well have been ruined by some very slight and unforeseen variation in temperature. 'More than once', he writes,

> I have been by William De Morgan's side at these supremely critical moments and admired the coolness and resource – the high pitched voice never quitting its resonant drawl – which marked the excitement of a big issue in the balance. But the end, whatever it was, was sure to reveal the rare good traits, the grit, perseverance, and invincible good humour, at the worst an object lesson or a clue won, and registered, with a smile, from failure.

De Morgan was not a potter in the sense that he 'threw' pots. He employed throwers, but Blunt says that he was never known to have thrown one himself. He always, however, designed the decoration which went on to his vases, plates, dishes and tiles. His painters followed his instructions faithfully, and he of all the work-force was the only chemist, so the colours were entirely his; and above all the distinctive De Morgan lustre was his personal creation. It must be admitted that many of the pots which he brought in from other firms are of undistinguished shape. In fact many of them are clumsy, even lumpy, but their decoration, designs and colours are truly unique and stand out from other people's work in the same period for their extraordinary quality. If one goes to a large exhibition of nine-teenth and twentieth-century pottery a De Morgan pot is instantly recognizable.

One of the best accounts of what it was like to work in the De Morgan firm was written by one of the painters, a Mr Bale.[9] His testimony is worth quoting in its entirety for the technical insights it gives in to the workings of the firm in the 1870s:

It is about fifty years ago I was sent to Mr. De Morgan, on the recommendation of Mr. William Morris, as painter. This was the first time I ever saw anything of the tile and pottery work; everything was so strange and fascinating that it acted like a spell upon me, and I could not resist studying it night and day.

Well the first thing I had to do was to outline on a piece of glass the design in brown colour, the same as is used in glass painting – I sub-sequently found out. This piece of glass with the design was fired, then given to me with sheets of tissue paper cut about eight inches square, then a solution was made, tinted green. I had to dip the tissue paper in the solution, lay it on some blotting paper to take up the superfluous water, then I had to paint on the glass (with the design on it) a solution of gum and glycerine round the pattern, pick up the damp paper and lay it even over the design, then paint on the paper the design in different colours when thoroughly dry, then gently pull the paper off the glass and lay it aside to be eventually stuck down with a solution of soluble glass upon Dutch enamel tiles. This was given to the kiln man who covered it with a powdered soft glass, then put it in the kiln to fire.

Mr. De Morgan at this stage often used Dutch enamel tiles, it was a long time before he made his own tiles. When he got his own (which were always made of fire clay) he had to get a white ground, this white ground, or paste, was made of silica, and was the medium for sticking the paper paintings onto the tile. This paste was extremely good; but unfortunately there was always likely to be trouble – and one which was hardly ever got over, as it used to split up into little holes, consequently they had to be touched up and refired. I maintained that this was the cause of a great deal of loss, and if it hadn't been for the vases and plaques in the lustre and Persian designs, he could never have kept on with the expensive business.

Also he never painted straight on to the tiles, like the vases, he did them on tissue paper ... Every Persian vase, or nearly so, had a starting by his own hand; of course often he would supply drawings to be carried out by his painters, – but while he superintended the work he never allowed any of us to put our own designs on.

I remember one occasion when I took it upon myself to break through this rule and finish a pot I had been all day at work on. Mr. De Morgan would begin a design, say with a flower or a bit of ornament, and then tell us to put just so many around; and we had to wait sometimes hours at a time before he came back, and meanwhile we did not dare to put another little bit here or there. Well, on this particular pot there was just a little space left to finish the design, and I had been waiting such a very long time that at last I didn't think it would make any difference if I finished it the same as the rest. No sooner had I done it, however, than he comes to finish it, and directly he says – 'why did you put that in?' – I answered (quite simply), I thought it shouldn't matter and would save time! 'I thought', he repeated – 'please understand I don't pay you to think! If you think again, you must think elsewhere!'

Ever after that I took care not to think, but calmly waited. It taught me a lesson for the future though, he was cross about it. I must say he was a very kind hearted man to all who worked for him, and always thinking of the welfare of his men.

Ever inventive, De Morgan decided to use a new technique for some engravings which he executed for illustrations in a children's book called *On A*

Pincushion, by his sister Mary.[10] It was a clever technique but never, as far as one can tell, one which he repeated. Mr Bale continues:

> He would get a sheet of window glass; upon that he spread a very thin coating of his paste, or white ground, which he used for his tiles, just simply let it dry without heating it, and he then used a fine needle and scratched or engraved the subject just as anyone would do an engrav-ing on steel! And where he wanted greater depth in the block he piled his paste high up. When all was then dried by the fire he pours over it, to the depth of a metal block, say three quarters of an inch of molten sulphur or brimstone. This used to come clean away, and he would send this block of sulphur to the printers and they could print direct from it, but on account of the pressure they used to make a metal cast instead.

Mr Bale also gives an account of a technique De Morgan developed for making mosaics. He was helped by his expert knowledge of chemistry. But although he and William Morris subsequently experimented with quite a lot of mosaic work he did not continue with this line of work.

May Morris[11] describes how De Morgan's work changed over the years and divides his pottery working life into three periods which, roughly, coin-cide with his three different places of work, Chelsea, Merton Abbey and Sands End. As she records: 'simple and occasionally naive work in the early Chelsea time, to the bold-minded period with big strong masses enriched with smaller ornament [Merton Abbey] and then to the later work, elaborate and full of curious invention [Sands End]'. As well as looking at his plates, vases and tiles in major collections such as the Victoria & Albert Museum or Cardiff Castle, it is something of a revelation for the modern student or collector to look at the designs[12] in the print room at the Victoria & Albert Museum which were given to the museum by Evelyn De Morgan in 1919. Seeing many of these designs on a flat surface rather than on a rounder pot or plate make it clear what an extraordinary gift De Morgan had for filling a comparatively small space with a complicated picture and at the same time giving the figures or decoration a sense of move-ment and life. This went together with his mischievous humour, which breaks through in the most unexpected places. Unlike many of his contemporaries, he was almost never sentimental and there is a clarity and vividness in these designs which makes someone like Walter Crane,[13] for all his originality and talent as painter and illustrator, look pale and unsure. Perhaps the best description of his work was written by May Morris in the *Burlington Magazine* in two articles in August and September 1917, the year De Morgan died. Another long quotation is in order here:

> The time when he was studying the finest of the potter's art at its source produced some splendid echoes of Asia Minor and Persian types, and later his passion for the sea expressed itself in patterns that have to my mind a curious relation with Mycenaean work. No one would call it an attempt at reproduction; it is rather as if the same forms suggested the same type of ornament to inventors so far sun/ dered in time and space, as though the same impulse toward sea things, the same passion for the twilight gardens of the deep, had moved the nineteenth century craftsmen and those dwellers around the Middle Sea.
>
> Some of the decorations on the pots and vases of the late middle style, which one may call the Merton Abbey and early Fulham Period are wonderfully subtle in both form and colour, two designs are spe/ cially in my mind; one (a pot) has a ground of dead/white on which is a lustre fish under a network of green/white; another (a vase) has a pale pinkish lustre ground and lustre figures under a scale/pattern in white. The atmospheric impression obtained by this plane upon plane is remarkable, and a simplified concentration of the symbol/ drawing stimulates imagination and produces a feeling of reality – the vivid dream/realism which is more especially the possession of an artist and poet. The deeps of the sea – fishes seen behind clustering seaweed in a pale green light – are suggested in several of these 'plane upon plane' patterns . . . The finest periods of art give us, in textiles, in ceramics and in other crafts, countless examples of one pattern laid upon another, but I cannot at the moment recall any example of note in which the slighter, mechanical pattern, reversing the usual prac/ tice, is used as a veil for the principal design. I hope it is not straining a point to dwell upon this feature in some of De Morgan's patterns; the suggestion of an *essential* seen through shimmering water or other

[42]

screen of detail; it occurs to me as a quite unconscious expression –
perhaps notable only to anyone on the look out for such expressions –
of the reaching through a tangle to things that count: peering through
the ordered pattern of trivial matters to the real life behind . . . The
special bent of De Morgan's invention was in winding beast-forms
and great sweeping lines round difficult shapes; the more difficult the
space to be filled then the more fantastic the beast pattern, the more
enjoyment is evident. The symbolism story told is vivid and apt . . .
many an episode of the drama of nature has been concentrated into
the symbol drawing, the first word, it may be the latest, in all human
decoration of life on this earth. One design for a plate he has named
'Stranded fish', a monstrous creature taking up one half of the circle,
while the other is occupied by tiny men in tiny boats hurrying to
secure the spoils. Another he labels 'Sea birds island', another 'the
Snake eater', another shows a lizard standing gaily on his tail and
smiling. These and many others are racy jokes – and so De
Morganesque in their daring and enjoyment! Among the designs for
tiles may be noticed a splendid wild boar, an amazing chameleon, a
serpent charming a rabbit, a frankly bored leopard – a handsome
beast, and a hippo shedding absurd giant tears. There is a spoon bill
too, trying to get its bill into a De Morgan pot (with a background of
Chelsea church and the factory chimneys of the Surrey side of the
Thames, if my memory serves me) . . .

The freedom of his studies for designs puts them (if I may once
more note the comparison) on a level with the spirited drawing of
Mediterranean ancient art. Some bird drawings in two sweeps of the
brush have a Chinese swiftness and crispness . . . in the midst of all
this rich and decorative invention one comes across pots and vases
which are severely simple – just a fine spacing of dark and light, and
a sightly disposition of some plain line-and-spot bordering. They are
masterly in their effect of noble emphasis.

The colouring of this ware with its Eastern force and depth, needs
no description, though one may note the principal colours used; the
polychromatic pieces have a magnificent dark blue, (darker than the
Egyptian night sky, but full of that luminosity), a very brilliant
turquoise blue and real malachite green; of course a manganese

[43]

purple of the uneven 'atmospheric' quality that is familiar in Eastern art; an Indian red is used, also orange, but more rarely, and a pure lemon yellow; black, of course, of different depths. These are the usual colours; but to name them is to give no idea of their quality and arrangement – to tell how the jewel-like birds fly across a blue black sky, the pallid fish shine through green water; how the turquoise and purple flowers star the wooded lawns, how the python glitters in his forest lair; such is our potter's handling of incomparable material.

The production of tiles[14] was of course a major part of his business in Orange House. We have seen that in the early 1870s he bought in tiles from various firms and also dishes and plates for lustre, but later on he began to make and fire his own tiles from clay supplied by the Morgan Crucible Company, Battersea. He found the wet clay used in the production of tiles, once it had been slowly dried, stood up to wear (particularly out of doors) better than tiles industrially produced made by compression from dried clay. He himself wrote:

At some date in the early seventies, I was struck by the fact that the employment of tiles in European buildings never approached in extent the use that I have always understood had been made of them in other countries, especially in Persia. This seemed particularly noticeable in external work. In my frequent conversations with archi-tects, I noticed the reason invariably alleged for this last was that the tiles would not bear the frost or hold tight on cement or mortar. Observation confirmed this. I also remarked the tiles pointed at as having these defects were always the pressed dust tiles, or Minton tiles (so called, because the invention of the press was either Herbert Minton's, or because he had bought the patent). In time I came to the conclusion that the artificially compacted clay differed in molecular structure from that of natural shrinkage from the wet. It is more absorbent, or rather absorbs with greater capillary attraction (for I doubt the same bulk of pressed tile absorbing as much water as one of ours; but I don't know). Of course I did not then *know* that the tiles I made myself from wet clay *would* stand frost and wet. I only believed it.[15]

One has only to look at the surviving brilliant tiles in the entrance of Debenham House in Addison Road, Kensington, to see how well they have survived the acid polluted air of London. De Morgan's ingenuity and inventive powers were put to good use in his tile-making. Over the next few years he designed his own machines for the grinding and sieving of clay and the drying of the tile squares. Halsey Ricardo[16] was particularly admiring of the method he devised for the painting of his tiles, for preserving continu-ity where the same design had to be reproduced, and also for preserving the 'register' where the total pattern exceeded the area of a single tile:

> The 'pattern' (its leading lines only) was drawn in strong black line on tracing paper and this was pasted onto a sheet of glass. On the other side of the glass was fixed (temporarily) a square of the paper and the glass easel-fashion was set up in front of a window. The lines of the pattern were easily visible on to the paper and the painter pro-ceeded to follow them with his pigments, filling up the rest of the pattern according to his discretion as to the intensity and so forth of his colouring, a colour tile or drawing at this side dictating to him the effect required.

The process was repeated as often as it was required and the painted paper was placed on to the surface of the tile square, prepared for the purpose by coating a white slip. The bright white of the slip was an important factor in the making of the brilliancy of colour, combined with a thick glaze. The paper was laid on the slip, paste was brushed over with silicone soda and powdered glaze was sprinkled on to the adhesive surface. The tile was now fired in the glaze kiln, the glaze melted and incorporated with the pigments while the paper was reduced to an ash which disintegrated and floated away in the draught of the kiln. 'Nothing could be simpler,' says Ricardo, 'and yet who would have had the imagination to hit on the answer to this problem?'

During the years 1872–82 De Morgan was to produce more than three hundred different distinct designs for tiles. The designs in the Victoria & Albert Museum give one a very good picture of the variety and imagina-tive quality of these tiles. Jon Catleugh[17] in his book has pointed out how difficult it is to establish an accurate chronology, although the impressed mark on the back of the tile is sometimes a guide. The influence of Morris is more evident in some of the early Chelsea designs but De Morgan himself pointed out that he used very few Morris patterns. William Gaunt and M.D.E. Clayton-Stamm[18] have given a very good summary of the variety and development in De Morgan's tile designs in this period:

> At the beginning of the series, animal and floral designs, excluding birds, are found in almost equal numbers. Up to 1875 bird motifs shared popularity with animals. After 1875 he concentrated on flowers and plant forms, ships and a small number of miscellaneous subjects accounting for the rest.

Dr Reginald Thompson was undoubtedly involved in some of the designs but it is impossible now to tell to what extent. Mrs Stirling writes: 'He and De Morgan would vie with each other in inventing grotesque beasts and monsters, and laugh like happy school boys when either succeeded in evolving some more than usually fantastic creatures.' This was of course hearsay, as Mrs Stirling knew neither of them at this time, but it sounds like William, who never lost his childlike sense of humour. His bird designs changed during this period. Early on they had been fairly simple ones, storks, herons, seagulls, swans and pelicans all appear, but later on in the 1870s they were more ambitious and he tended to concentrate more on plumage – typical of one of the best among his later style is the peacock with the flowering tree on a dish in the Victoria & Albert Museum.

His plants and floral motifs have been divided into two groups – those treated naturalistically, and those obviously influenced by 'Persian design'.[19] The naturalistic group of designs is more akin to those produced by Morris and Burne-Jones, while the so-called 'Persian' items show the influence of Islamic (particularly Turkish Iznik) pottery. The marvellous collection of Near-Eastern ceramics in the Victoria & Albert Museum obviously had a considerable influence on De Morgan and his friends. William Morris declared to the architect Philip Webb: 'You and I are two of the half dozen people for whom the South Kensington was made.' We don't know if De Morgan was included in this select group, but the shape of many of his pots, his treatment of birds and foliage and his colours, both lustre and non-lustre, show knowledge of what the Victoria & Albert

Museum had in its collection. Besides the considerable interest of the Near East, if one is looking for sources for the remarkable plants, trees, animals and mythical creatures which appear on De Morgan's pots, tiles and dishes, his own unusual imagination and droll fantasy supplied a great deal. The doodles which he and Burne-Jones delighted in were obvious precursors, and many of William's drawings were grotesque beasts and monsters which subsequently appear in his pottery.

During the decade he had two very unusual if not very profitable commissions. The first was from the artist Frederic Leighton for the house he had built in Holland Park Road and lived in since 1866. Earlier in life Leighton had travelled extensively in the Middle East and had, with his friend Sir Caspar Purdon Clark (later appointed a Director of the South Kensington Museum) and Sir Richard Burton[20] made a large collection of tiles acquired mainly in Damascus, Rhodes and Cairo. Leighton planned an exotic and (for Holland Park) eccentric Arab hall in his house. His architect was George Aitchison; Walter Crane designed the mosaic frieze and Sir Edgar Boehm carved the rare birds and the capitals of the columns. There were not enough tiles to complete the hall – partly because of break-ages and partly because some of the Middle Eastern tiles were imperfect. We are told that Leighton over one of his famous and punctual 8 a.m. breakfasts asked De Morgan to supply the missing items. The work was begun in 1877 and not finally completed until 1881. It was an extraordi-nary challenge to match the peacock-blue tiles and it is just about imposs-ible even to the trained eye to detect which are the work of De Morgan and which the originals. A number of tiles which he had laboriously made had to be thrown away as they were not as perfect as he required, and at the end of the job De Morgan reckoned he was some £500 out of pocket. Being the least greedy of men he never disclosed this to Leighton, despite the fact that the painter, President of the Royal Academy, knighted and made a baron just before he died, was by now one of the grandees of the English art world and very wealthy. The panels of tiles are thinly rimmed with gold and the total effect of the Arab hall is overwhelming. It is good to know, in view of the De Morgan connection with Leighton House, that there is now a collection of his ceramics on display there (including a number from the Bushey Heath pottery designed by Fred Passenger in the style of De Morgan's work).

The second unusual commission for tiles in the 1860s was for the Tsar of Russia's yacht *Livadia*, named after one of the imperial estates on the Black Sea. Sadly, the potentate's vessel was probably broken up in 1926. One could have got some idea of De Morgan's work for this commission from two panels in Old Battersea House in a warehouse destroyed by fire some years ago: one was of a knight (comprising forty-five tiles) the other of a Russian chancellor of the exchequer holding a symbolic money-bag, accounts and a rolled scroll. These rather sombre works, although technically skilful, were not examples of De Morgan at his best or most likeable. The *Livadia* panels had one excellent result, however, attracting the attention of the directors of the P&O shipping company, which later on resulted in some very large-scale work.

With these ambitious commissions, and demand for his work increasing (both for individual pots and tiles for houses), by the turn of the decade production was going well and William had every reason for feeling optimistic. By the end of his time in Orange House he had seen the success of his experimentation with his lustres, kiln-building and glazes. His works during the decade 1860 to 1870 show a growing freedom of design. He had also proved himself to be an employer capable of gaining the complete loyalty of his work-force. Three of his employees lasted until the end of the pottery, even, with De Morgan's approval, carrying on when the Fulham factory was closed down. The painters, as Reginald Blunt[21] recorded, enjoyed the atmosphere in Chelsea at Orange House. It was a pleasant place to work and the business was expanding. The surviving members of the De Morgan family were settled in 30 Cheyne Row; Sophia was occupied writing a memoir of her husband, and Mary completed her children's story, *On A Pincushion*, with illustrations by her brother. She followed it up with more writing for children and a novel which she published under a pseudonym.

Unfortunately, as has been suggested, it became apparent early on in his career that William De Morgan had no head for business. He had no extensive capital to call on and running such a firm with a sizeable number of employees and constant outgoings (not only for salaries but for clay, ready-made pots and rent) was a risky matter. He said himself of the factory: 'It is not well organised, it is very ill De Morganised in fact!' Mrs Stirling has immortalized some stories of his quaint business methods. A very wealthy prospective customer went to Orange House eager to buy an expensive pot and De Morgan pointed out some of his most successful products. 'What do you want it for?' he asked. The customer replied, 'I want it for a wedding present.' 'Is it for so-and-so's wedding?' asked De Morgan. 'Yes,' was the reply. 'My dear chap,' De Morgan said, 'don't give the bride any more of my pots – she's inundated with them! You take my advice and just go round to Mappin & Webb's and choose her an unusual piece of silver. She'll like it ever so much better!' His selfless advice was duly taken. Another time, a prospective purchaser who wanted tiles for a nursery was told to go to Minton as De Morgan tiles chipped very easily and were excessively expen-sive. A princess of the royal family, on another occasion, having inspected the showroom, bought a tile for £1 and then asked for the loan of a panel worth £50, the design of which she wanted to copy. De Morgan's reply to this rather impertinent suggestion was: 'I would suggest that you first copy the tile you have bought, and by that time I shall know whether I can spare the panel.' Off went the princess. One has considerable sympathy for De Morgan, although it was perhaps not an obvious way to encourage a dis-tinguished potential client.[22]

The above examples are perhaps apocryphal, but it does seem from what Reginald Blunt found when he took over the management of the factory that the accounts side of the business was chronically neglected, and although De Morgan is reputed to have invented a novel method of book-keeping, it was not a subject which took up much of his time or attention.

The relationship between the De Morgans at 30 Cheyne Row and the Morris family became much closer in the 1870s. They frequently visited each other and of course the Burne-Jones family at The Grange. William was a very welcome visitor, remembered with much affection by May Morris, at Kelmscott Manor in Oxfordshire. He contributed greatly to the high-spirited and at times quite childish practical jokes and party games. Morris's socialism was not a side of his activities which received much support from De Morgan, and it is noticeable that the fascination with an idealized medieval age which Morris and his other artist friends affected never influenced De Morgan, whether in his designs for pottery or in his novels. This made little difference to his relationship with Morris which lasted until the latter's death in 1896.

[49]

By the late 1870s, before the move of the workshop from Chelsea, De Morgan[23] tells us that he had established his technique for making lustre-ware and that he hardly changed this for his remaining 25 years as a potter. Of course, the designs changed and by the time that he was working in Sands End, Fulham, the products were considerably more ambitious. It is instructive to compare the lustre from the Chelsea days with some of the magnificent plates and pots he was making not long before the winding up of his firm in 1905. The Sunset and Moonlight suite are obvious and really extraordinary examples of his finest achievements. The actual decoration was carried out by Charles Passenger. This is not to decry the achievements of the Chelsea period; there are some very successful tiles from the Orange House workshop, for instance a dado panel of three tiles with one of De Morgan's typical snakes curling round a tree with flowers and a big half-sun behind.[24] There was a real demand for De Morgan tiles, if only for the surrounds of domestic grates, and there are still some impressive examples of this work in private houses.

In 1873 Morris had rented Kelmscott Manor[25] and seven years later he had also found a London house in Hammersmith Mall, called The Retreat, which he renamed Kelmscott House. There was only a narrow road between it and the Thames, and as J.W. Mackail writes in his Morris biography:[26]

> One hundred and thirty miles of stream between the two houses were a real, as well as imaginative link between them. He liked to think that the water which ran under his windows at Hammersmith had passed the meadows and grey gables of Kelmscott and more than once a party of summer voyagers went from one house to the other by water, embarking at their own door in London and disembarking in their own meadows at Kelmscott.

Happily there is still a log extant which describes the journey undertaken by Morris and his wife Janie, their two daughters, 'Crom'[27] Price, the Hon. Richard C. Grosvenor and William himself. May Morris well remembered the voyage: 'with De Morgan in the foreground, always genial and content,

Portrait of William De Morgan by Evelyn, 1909. His
hands holding a vase, now in the V and A and
showing the titles of his first three books on a shelf.

Interior of Old Battersea House in Mrs Stirling's time.
Portrait of William – artist unknown – and some De
Morgan tiles.

Interior of Old Battersea House with dishes by De Morgan and paintings by Evelyn.

Detail of the tile-panelled walls of the public bar of the
Tabard Inn, Bedford Park, West London, opened in
1880.

Four fruit and flower tiles.

Ship tile, and three ship tiles in a panel (above). A ship
panel over a fireplace in a house designed by Halsey
Ricardo 1886-7 (below).

Tiles of deer and rabbits.

Tile panel of a heron and one of peacocks.

whether called upon to scull our uncouth boat with its ragamuffin crew through the crowd of genteel regatta, or to celebrate the voyage in verse and picture'.[28] But a finer description perhaps, is in a letter which William wrote to little Margaret Burne-Jones, Ned's daughter (suitably illustrated of course):

Kelmscott
August 16–'80.
No! August 17–'80

MY DEAR LITTLE MARGOT, –

As to writing an account of our most eventful voyage – how can I? It would take all the columns of a copy of the *Daily Telegraph*. Besides I can't remember one thing from another –

Very generally speaking, I did not exert myself at all to do any-thing, but I exerted everybody else very much indeed. I lay in the boat engaged in the manufacture of puns and bad jokes, and every one else rowed and steered and pushed and slapped and pinched the boats to make them go.

Our boat had one sail (which we didn't use) and the helmsman never looked particularly pale, at least till the end of the voyage, when several characters, strange to say, were unwell, this was because they towed the boats and got squeezed – I can tell you when a chap tries to tow, he gets exactly like curried fowls in tins, inside, owing to the compression.

We set sail from Hammersmith as 'twer on Tuesday and arrived here so to speak on Monday. We slept at Sunbury on Tuesday, and were waken by a cock-a-doodle, but wouldn't say *doo*!

There were once seven towns built by the inhabitants of Sunbury – it was the first thing built – Monbury and Tuesbury are extinct – Wednesbury still exists – Thursbury not – Freibury is in Switzerland where natives call it Fribourg-en-Swisse, but that is because they are foreigners and cannot help it – Saturbury was never finished owing to the half-holiday.

Our next Station was Windsor, where the Castle is too large to move, but large enough to take the Queen for all that, and any number of Bishops and Knights in the bargain.

I looked for Newton, but I couldn't see him —

Eton is a pretty place, it is called so after the fish which are eaten there —

Then we came to Great Marlowe, which reminded us of little Margot.

We stayed at the Complete Angler. It is called so after an Angle of 360° in the immediate neighbourhood. We saw the Obtuse Angler staying there.

Then came to Sonning — a very pretty crib — it is so called from the French *sonner*, to ring a bell, because we rang the bell so often for things.

The next place was Wallingford, *scilicet* Wallingfold because the bill was very high and we lamented — and a very silly set we were not to ask beforehand what inn to go to —

The next was Oxford, when in spite of Mr. Morris's dreadful revolutionary sentiments we slept in the King's Arms. There are many derivations of Oxford, and it probably comes from all of them, though every one has his favourite.

Auksford from the Auks — they are not there but in the Orkneys — that doesn't matter — if they like to give their name — let them — that's their look out.

Arxford — from the inquiring spirit of the Dons.

Arksford — because a narrer mind only wants a narrer 'at [an Ararat]. They are ashamed of this and always wear broad ones. Also Boxford and Coxford because they cannot easily take in more than one idea at a time — [erasures] that's enough!

Then we came on here yesterday. We were towed by Mr. Bossom (who continually unbossomed himself from the bank into Mr. Morris's sympathetic ear until the latter murmured against him) as far as Bablockhithe, or Badbloke⁄hithe, so called from Wm. Morris and your Uncle Crommy Price. We got through lots of weirs, and unhappily I passed without noticing it (so as to mention it) Weir 7, on which Wordsworth wrote that pretty poem. We nearly got drowned getting through Radcote Bridge — some strong language was used, but I name no names. It is very difficult going uphill thorough Bridges.

However, we are all safe and sound after many perils past. We

didn't finish the ham and we have still got 12 pounds of the cheese –
four bottles of the champagne arrived safe – the remainder was gone,
and we cannot account for it.

With all their loves accept mine from your loving UNCLE.[29]

William's friendship with Morris was a close one, and up to a point, they
shared the same opinions: he agreed with Morris's support of the Liberal
protest against Turkish atrocities in Bulgaria, but was disconcerted when
he found out that some people equated this with a sympathy with Marx. He
was also drawn into the meetings which resulted in the foundation of the
Society for the Protection of Ancient Buildings – the so-called 'Anti-
Scrape Society'. Asked by Morris to recruit his near neighbour, Thomas
Carlyle, he did so. But Morris had to read a letter from Carlyle at the first
public meeting in which he extolled Wren, and De Morgan was much
amused as Wren was one of Morris's particular *bêtes noirs*. De Morgan and
Burne-Jones did join Morris in the campaigns for the general election of
1880, taking the side of the National Liberals: the result of the election was
triumph for the Gladstone government. De Morgan was not led further by
Morris into his socialist campaign. Later in his life he wrote: 'Top [Morris]
chose to call his religion "Socialism". First tell me what is a socialist and
then I can tell you if I am one.'

Orange House was proving too small and impracticable for his expanding business and De Morgan and Morris discussed the possibility of com-
bining their efforts to find a site to set up their two factories near each other.
May Morris again:

The country easily accessible from London was explored a long time
in vain: then one summer holiday a disused silk-mill with most of the
necessary qualifications was discovered in a remote village, one of
those jewel-like clusters of grey buildings which nestle among the
slopes of the Cotswolds. All the points in favour of this site (so far
removed from 'the Great Wen') were seriously and eagerly considered
those against it being set aside for future consideration. However, this
dream of reviving the crafts from the part of the country where they
formerly flourished had to be regretfully abandoned by the two friends
and the laughing waters of that wide free country to be exchanged for

sleepy Wandle and the melancholy of the once-country struggling against conversion into town.[30]

The choice of Merton as this site was not made until after much discussion and several journeys. De Morgan himself relates:

My own settlement at Merton came about in this wise. Morris and I were always talking over an imaginary factory which I was to occupy jointly with him. It wasn't so much that we believed in it – indeed, we always called it the FICTIONARY – as that it gave us an endless excuse for going over premises. We raised the hopes of many a proprietor of unsaleable property, always going carefully into the minutest details and arranging the rooms, which was to have which, and so forth, till the miserable owner really believed a deal was assured to eventuate. We brought away bottles of water for analysis to make sure that it was fit to dye with. I recollect Morris's delight when a certificate was sent from an eminent analyst to the effect that a sample taken from pipes supplying all Lambeth was totally unfit for consumption – and could only result in prompt zymotic disease! 'There's your science for you, De M!', said Morris. I explained that, if the analyst had known that 250,000 people drank the water daily, he would have analysed it different. This was in Battersea, and never came to anything.[31]

The Cotswold factory was the only other feasible site but distance from London proved too much of a problem. Merton Abbey may have been too near the metropolis for their taste, but it had compensations. Mackail has left what is perhaps an idealized picture:

As one turns out of the dusty high road and passes through the manager's little house, the world seems left in a moment behind. The old-fashioned garden is gay with irises and daffodils in spring, with hollyhocks and sunflowers in autumn, and full summer by summer, of the fragrant flowering shrubs that make a London suburb into a brief June Paradise. It rambles away toward the mill pond with its fringe of tall poplars; the cottons lie bleaching on grass thickly set with buttercups; the low long buildings with the clear rushing little stream

running between them, and the wooden outside staircases leading to
their upper story, have nothing about them to suggest the modern
factory; even upon the great sunk dye-vats the sun flickers through
leaves, and trout leap outside the windows of the long cheerful room
where the carpet-looms are built. 'To Merton Abbey', runs an entry
in a visitor's diary on a day at the end of April, 1882, when the new
works had settled fairly down to their routine: 'white hawthorn was
out in the garden: we had tea with Mr Morris in his room in the house,
and left laden with marsh-marigolds, wallflowers, lilac, and
hawthorn'.[32]

The premises at Merton were on the site of an abbey, the stones of which
had been pillaged by Henry VIII to build Nonesuch Palace. It was later to
become the site of a silk-weaving factory started by Huguenot refugees, and
still later a print works. The River Wandle supplied clear water for Morris's
dyeing and next door to his factory, but separate from it, De Morgan set up
his works in 1882. Moving a pottery business was evidently a harrowing
business but De Morgan had his own way of coping. According to his
employee Mr Bale:

> when Mr. De Morgan was clearing out to go to Merton, it was a
> strange sight. He was always slapdash in those days, and he couldn't
> stand the thought of packing. He just sat on a chair and put a hammer
> through dishes worth £2.10s and £3.00, at the same time saying, 'Go
> on boys help yourselves!' which you may be quite sure we did.[33]

When he pulled the kiln down to go to Merton Mr Bale comments: 'bothered if he didn't give all his bricks (especially his fire brick) to the borough
of Chelsea and actually paid the cartage! When he must have known that
he would want them badly at Merton.' He would have had fine material for
breaking up to mix with his fireclay in making his tiles and vases. Not the
way, perhaps, to run a business economically!

Chapter 4

The move to Merton Abbey next door to William Morris's
works – marriage to Evelyn Pickering and move from house
in Cheyne Row to The Vale, Chelsea.

DE MORGAN had every reason to feel optimistic in 1882 when he set up his
factory in semi-rural Merton Abbey next door to the Morris works. The
business was expanding and his reputation was growing steadily with his
increased mastery of the various complicated and difficult techniques
involved in the production of tiles, pots and dishes. Morris and his close
friends (De Morgan was one of the closest) were nothing if not Romantics,
and the idea of producing beautiful objects in the English countryside was
an attractive one and a powerful critique of mass production in the big
potteries. But there were drawbacks to working in Merton and living in
Chelsea – namely, the distance, and the time it took to travel each morning
and evening. Seven miles does not sound very far until one recalls that in
1882 there were only the Metropolitan Railway (the electric railway did not
open until 1890), horse-drawn buses, and the main steam railway. Philip
Henderson[1] in his *Life Of William Morris* records that: 'to get [to Merton]
from Hammersmith (unless he walked or drove, as he sometimes did)
meant going by the Metropolitan Railway to Farringdon St., crossing the
city to Ludgate Hill, and then taking another train to Merton, a journey of
about two hours.' This kind of journey was to prove a major drawback to
De Morgan, who was less robust than his comrade, and it meant that his

stay at Merton Abbey was limited, in fact, to six years, several years less than at other work-places.

During this time he broadened the scope of his pottery. As we have seen, during the Chelsea period the main output had been tiles, and these con-tinued to be manufactured up to the time the pottery was finally closed in 1905. Stocklists of 1885 and 1887[2] and a price-list of tiles of about 1897 are still extant, and show that many of the tile designs of the Chelsea period were being produced as late as twenty years after their first appearance. De Morgan kept a showroom in Orange House even after the pottery had moved to Merton. The Chelsea showroom was only given up in 1886 when he rented the ground floor at 45 Great Marlborough Street, which con-tained Mrs Siddon's ballroom. This was the ballroom, haunted by ghosts, which would later appear in *Alice-For-Short* as part of the Soho house where Alice lived and Charles pretended to be a painter.

As before, many of the pots which De Morgan decorated were supplied as blanks, others were thrown under his supervision.[3] Davis of Hanley, whose name can be found on the bases of many of the pieces of this period, supplied bowls which were manufactured for export to the East as rice dishes. By the year 1885 the workshop was using a large variety of shapes – vases with two handles, bottles, long-necked jugs and so on. Quite a number of the products have the impressed factory mark, the painter's ini-tials or sometimes a stock mark. For those which were unmarked when they left the factory it is very difficult to establish dates of manufacture and a chronology. Often it is impossible to work out whether a piece is of the Chelsea or the Merton Abbey period. It has been pointed out,[4] for example, that some wares have the Merton mark, but since the factory had later been transferred to Fulham they may actually have been manufactured in either place.

What is clear when one studies the enormous variety of designs in De Morgan's work is, first of all, the many sources from which he gained inspiration. Secondly, the amazing way in which he absorbed styles from other periods and artists and yet retained his originality. As has been said earlier, it is fairly easy to trace these influences from the designs themselves and from what De Morgan later wrote. He was very much aware of the lustreware produced in sixteenth century Deruta and Gubbio, in Italy, using techniques derived originally from Spain and further back from the

Middle East. The Italians used designs and ornamentation which they in their turn derived from the Renaissance painters who themselves sought inspiration from Roman decoration on monuments. Decoration obviously inspired by Persian potters is sometimes mixed with designs more familiar in Pre-Raphaelite painting. Animals, mythical beasts and flowers and foliage appear and give De Morgan scope for his humour and extraordinary talent for using a limited space in the best possible way, keeping the picture alive and moving. There were not, apparently, many vases produced during this period. De Morgan has been criticized for the poor quality of the shapes of some of his pots, by Bernard Leach[5] amongst others, but this criticism is, I would suggest, misdirected. He was not a studio potter or artist's crafts-man of the sort we know today and his primary purpose was always graphic. Clay pots were merely a surface for his decorative art.

He only spent six years at Merton Abbey before events in his life made him start to doubt the wisdom of setting up his factory there. His back pains made the journey to and from Chelsea very tiring, and understand-ably, in view of the past family history, there was always the threat of TB looming over him. This fear must have been increased by the death from TB of his sister Annie. Mrs Stirling quotes a letter from William Morris, from Kelmscott House on 19 January 1884. Morris writes:[6]

My dear Bill,
Of course from what you said to me I've been expecting your sad news any day. What is there to say about it save that it is a sad tale? However life is good as long as we can really live, and even sorrow if so taken has something good in it as a part of life, as I myself have found at times – yet have nonetheless bemoaned myself all the same.

So in spite of yourself I wish you a long life, my dear fellow, to play your due part in.

Give my love and sympathy to your Mother and Mary – I shall hope to see you soon.
Yours, affectionately,
WILLIAM MORRIS.

According to Mrs Stirling, he had toyed with the idea of living in Merton to be near his factory, but in addition to everything else he was finding the factory too small for some of the more ambitious projects he had in mind, among which was a very large pot he was designing for Lord Ashburnham, which would not go into the biggest kiln in Merton. Most important was his engagement to Evelyn Pickering in 1885. Typical of the man was the way he announced the happy event to Burne-Jones:[7]

Dear Ned,

I meant to come in yesterday evg: but I was engaged to be married and couldn't!

I wanted to convey the news to you of *two* engagements that have just come to pass. One is my own – I am engaged to a lady. The other is Evelyn Pickering's – she is engaged to a cove, or bloke.

Having supplied you with the data . . . she and I are both strongly disposed to come around some time and see if you can guess whom we are respectively engaged to. Don't give it up!

We send you all our united kind love in which my mother and sister commingle.

Yours affectly,

DM

Burne-Jones wrote back:[8]

My dear DM,

I'm so glad, but you might have knocked me down with a crow-bar, I was so surprised – regular took aback I were.

Now that's pretty comfortable I call it – we are just where we were and no unpleasantness between parties.

We are all glad about it.

Find a day next week for a feast and come both of you and we will have larks.

Yes it is admirable – in former merrier years I would have called it capital, but the word terrifies me now and when I see it I slink away.

My dear fellow, I feel as if I had suggested it!

Always your afft,

NED.

The engagement caused a certain amount of good-humoured amusement in the factory. Mr Bale wrote:[9]

> Mr De Morgan was, as I have said, a very generous master. If any man was in trouble, his hand went to his pocket at once. One day a lad in his employ came to him with the news that he was going to get married. Mr De Morgan at once said, 'then you'll want more money if you're going to keep a wife, so I'll raise your wages.' After that all the lads were for getting married and he had to treat them all the same. At last he could stand it no longer, when a fresh one came to him with the same news, he said 'now look here, boys, I can have no more of this. The next man in this factory who gets married will get the sack.' But the laugh turned against him, for the next man to get married was Mr De Morgan himself.

De Morgan met his future wife at a party given by Mrs Walter Bagehot, and whether or not the story given by Mrs Stirling is strictly accurate, it certainly rings true.

> Evelyn in rose colour (it was a fancy dress party) wrote herself down as 'a tube of rose madder'; De Morgan, asked to name his costume, described it as 'madder still'. The new acquaintance was clinched in typical fashion. Perturbed at the perversity of a glove which refused to be buttoned he at length turned despairingly to his partner, 'if you will button my glove for me', he pleaded, 'I will give you one of my pots.' The bargain was struck, the glove was buttoned, the pot accepted, and the comradeship cemented for all time.'

Evelyn Pickering came from a very different background from William's. Her father was a QC and Recorder of Pontefract, and her mother Anna Maria Spencer Stanhope, daughter of John and Lady Elizabeth Spencer Stanhope of Canon Hall, Yorkshire. Her family was rich and eminently well connected. The young Evelyn was brought up strictly, to take her place in society, make a good marriage and bring up nicely behaved children. However, from quite an early age she was determined to be an artist and despite her family's opposition she secretly painted in her bedroom at 6

Upper Grosvenor Street, and afterwards at 48 Bryanston Square. Eventually she was allowed to enrol at the Slade School where women had only recently been admitted. This was an achievement but she found out that she was not allowed to go there unescorted. A carriage and pair were provided, to her horror, and when she objected she had to agree to a chaperone.

Evelyn's talent was soon recognized and between 1873 and 1875 she was a prizewinner and gained the Slade Scholarship. She felt, however, that she would not profit from staying long at the London School. She refused point-blank to be presented at court, threatening if she was made to she would kick the queen, and she set off to study in Rome. This, of course, horrified her family but out she went none the less, living frugally and working hard. Life cannot have been easy for her; apart from anything else she caught what was then called Roman fever – presumably malaria – which would recur throughout her life. Eighteen months after she had returned to England her father died and Evelyn left home for good, renting rooms near a studio. In May 1877 the Grosvenor Gallery[10] opened, and Evelyn, now aged twenty-one, was invited to contribute to the first exhibition – a painting of Ariadne in Naxos. In all her early struggles to become a painter against the wishes of her family, she was supported by her uncle, Roddam Spencer Stanhope, an artist and member of the Pre-Raphaelite Brotherhood.[11] Evelyn and her uncle were considered by her family to have put themselves beyond the pale, and by taking up painting as a career to have adopted an unacceptably Bohemian way of life, although by our present-day standards of behaviour they were very respectable indeed.

She was professionally successful and exhibited in many galleries in England, America and the Continent. She was highly regarded, May Morris records,[12] 'as an artist of distinction'. Her paintings, although out of favour today, have a power in detail of drapery and the depiction of detailed backgrounds of Renaissance gardens. The faces of her female figures are sad in a languishing Pre-Raphaelite way. Her pictures often feature nude women, but they are quite extraordinarily unsensuous. Many of the paintings are based on Greek myths and are obviously influenced and inspired by Italian Renaissance painters, but early on in her career she found her own style which is quite distinct from her uncle's paintings or from those of close friends such as Burne-Jones. She had great energy and dedication, and hated wasting time away from her work. She was a serious person, but this did not exclude a quirky sense of humour which was remarked on by many of her friends and was something which she shared with William. This humour was almost never unkind, and De Morgan himself is remembered as someone who hated quarrels or over-heated discussion and was character-istically the peacemaker when things threatened to get out of hand.

Evelyn's family greeted the news of her engagement with some incredul-ity. One of her brothers[13] remarked unkindly: 'Evelyn would never look at any man unless it was a picturesque Italian organ grinder.' William's intro-duction to the Pickering family over Sunday lunch at their grand house in Bryanston Square went well, although the fact that he manufactured pottery must have caused a certain amount of dismay, and moreover his income by Pickering standards was negligible. Evelyn's uncle, Roddam Spencer Stanhope, was again helpful. He knew De Morgan and 'had heard nothing but good of him'. 'We are only engaged,' Evelyn wrote to her uncle, 'we should not dream of getting married for at least fifteen years.' 'All the better,' he teasingly replied, 'there will be less time to quarrel in.' De Morgan himself remarked on the length of their engagement: 'I don't see where the hurry is – why, I waited over eighteen years for Evelyn to be born.'[14] Evelyn was nearly thirty-eight in 1887, when the couple were married, and William forty-eight. (William's arithmetic seems a trifle odd).

The wedding was a quiet one shrouded in a yellow London fog. They made no plans for their honeymoon but drove to the nearest station to take the next train available. This was to the Isle of Wight! De Morgan wrote to Burne-Jones from there:[15]

> *Black Gang Chine,*
> *Isle of Wight,*
> *March 6, '87*

Dear Old Ned, —

I must just send you a line to spare you the shock of seeing the Noose in the Noosepaper [in the Newspaper]. I have busted and bloomed and blossomed into a married man, after having been single, man and boy, for more than forty years. I hope it will turn out well. When I have misgivings, I console myself with the rare old adage, *Vixere nupti ante Agamamnona*. If my recollection serves me right

[62]

though, Agamemnon didn't come off so well as *I* deserve to – as for him, no doubt it was all right, for he was no better than the heathen. Now *I'm* a rate payer!
Me and Mrs.

Demorgannéepickering (it wants a whole line) are going to reside in a Wale, where indeed Mrs. Mould told Mrs. Gamp we all reside – but this is an *Imperium in Imperio* – a subwale – just oppersite Paulton Square, where they murdered an 'ousekeeper and shoved her in a box and buried her in the back garden – this is considered in the rent. By the way, we don't pay any, having bought the lease, and perhaps if they'd done this in the case of the Wale of the Temple there wd have been no rent – anyhow the Wale is there.

We don't know our number. The postman he says one number, Mrs. Whistler's French bonne opposite she says another – the rate-collector he says another. *Quot homines, tot sententiae! –* However, I will speak no more French – Besides a new studio calls the paper-boy's attention to the Mansion. He cannot pass by, neither, because he can't as you'll see when you come. If he depends on passing by, he'll have to come on the Parish – I'm sorry.

Now to the point. Robbed of all linguistic decoration, all flowers of language, and figures of speech (my wife is agitating me by remarks) it is that I am and always shall be
Your affectionate friends
WM. DE MORGAN.
EVELYN DE MORGAN.

She began it with a P.!
and the reply from Ned – undated was full of an invalid's self pity:

My Dear D.M., –
We all live in a WALE.
Me as well as you does.
I have been ill. I have been uncommon ill, and can't go out, I can't; so I can't come to you, not brobly for days to come I can't . . .
Did you expect an answer to your letter, dear fellow? Have you known me these forty years and still expect answers to letters?

I should like to see that house – yes, I should. But I have been ill. I have had a bad illness – I was in danger of swearing very often – it was a cold – nothing is worse than a cold except 2 colds, I have had 2 colds – I am much weakened. I have not been happy. I hate being unwell. I hate the least discomfort. I like things to go happily, prosper- ously and smoothly – that's what I mean by Ethics, and I mean the same thing by political economy, and my aspirations in socialism are all founded on my being well and prosperous and happy.
I am your affect. friends,
E. BURNE-JONES.

Despite the surprise and disbelief the engagement caused their family and friends, the marriage, as far as one can tell, was remarkably happy. They were both deeply involved in their separate artistic lives and shared not only a sense of humour, but an extraordinary, delightful and trusting unworld- liness. This, though, quite often led to embarrassments. For example, when they took on the care of a handsome kitten just as they were about to go to Italy, they were puzzled by reports from England that it had an enormous appetite and was growing very large. They returned to be greeted by a young puma, which was hurriedly removed to the zoo. Another mishap occurred when they brought over from Italy their cook and his girlfriend. The couple proceeded to milk the De Morgans. After they had gone back to Italy it was found that not only had they purchased all sorts of luxury goods from Harrods to take back with them, but had also made off with Evelyn's jewellery.

William had a tendency to depression which was already established and Evelyn was good for him. She hated to waste time and, as we will see, refused to let her husband feel sorry for himself when the pottery business wound up. A cousin of De Morgan's, who was at the Academy Schools with William, wrote:[16]

There is one point on which I, having known William much longer than you have, may venture to offer criticism. You picture him as constitutionally cheerful and hopeful. My memory recalls him as subject to states of serious depression – but only before his marriage. Evelyn cured all that. She would never allow him to mope. She gave him new vigour, and brought into his life just what he wanted – her own splendid courage.

There were no children of the marriage. Perhaps this is not surprising, given their ages, and in any case it is possible that they would have been dis⁄couraged from starting a family given the history of TB in William's. It is pointless to speculate on the intimate details of a marriage which took place over a hundred years ago. All one knows from comments from friends is that they appeared to have been unusually well⁄suited and happy together, with a healthy respect for each other's careers.

Marriage entailed a move from 30 Cheyne Row, and the couple found a house off the King's Road, Chelsea. No. 1 The Vale is well described by Eustace John in *The Old Man's Youth*, the last novel.[17] Eustace John has just lost his mother and his father had decided to give up the big house in Mecklenburgh Square and find a smaller one. Young Eustace John goes on several house⁄hunting expeditions with his friend 'Cooky' and they:

> found themselves walking back along the King's Road, Chelsea, on a glorious summer evening. In those days you could walk from Putney to Chelsea through fields all the way, by keeping off the road a little . . . Just beyond the kink of the road that must have been caused by some antediluvian pond, Cooky was brought up short by a 'to let' notice over a gateway on the left. It announced the existence of an eli⁄gible bijou residence with a quarter of an acre of garden and a coach house . . .
>
> The lane was lined with trees on either side, elm and chestnut, and was entered through a swing gate as a private carriage way, shared by two or three residences at the end. The gravel pathway made a circle between them around some larger older elms to make turning room for things on wheels. At the end on the left, unseen at first, was a garden open to the roadway except for chains on posts, that hardly counted, and its owner certainly deserved the rich crop of peas that were helping the universal scent of hay in the kitchen garden behind, if only for having planted the standard roses on the smooth bit of lawn

in front. However it was not our business any more than the house on
the right or its large garden in the rear, or the meadow beyond the fence
at the end, or the two fallow deer, – actually fallow deer! – that were
browsing in it . . . The house – such at least was my impression – laid
claim to the name *bijou* chiefly because of certain verandas on the
ground floor in which wood trellis, curvilinear fretwork, and a graceful dip in the lead roof combined towards an ornate character.

The two boys persuade the old man to show them over the house and when
Eustace John's father comes to see it he immediately wants to live in it. The
De Morgans were equally enthusiastic.

There survives an excellent photograph of The Vale with Evelyn and
William sitting in deck-chairs each side of the garden door. The house is
just as Eustace John describes it; obviously a rather untidy garden, with
William's study on the left and Evelyn's studio on the right of the door, and
a lawn which looks pleasantly unkempt. This was to be their home until
1909 when the leases of their house and the two others up the private drive
(rented at one time by Whistler[18] and Austin Dobson[19]) fell in and the three
houses were pulled down by the owner. The Vale was obviously an oasis of
quiet in the middle of an already busy and noisy Chelsea and the house
must have been delightful with its Morris wallpapers, William's lustrous
pots and Evelyn's rich paintings. There is no trace of the 'oasis' now. The
Vale – quite a pleasant road, most of it rebuilt since the De Morgans' time
– has lost its peace, and the deer park described in the novel has of course
disappeared.

By this time, 1887, William was finding it more and more difficult to run
the Merton Abbey factory and he finally resolved to build a bigger one in
Fulham, the Sands End Pottery, Town Mead Road. Nothing of course is
left of the buildings at Merton Abbey but it is pleasant to record that the
Fulham Pottery is commemorated by 'De Morgan Road'.

Chapter 5

A new factory, Sands End Pottery, built in Fulham –
partnership with Halsey Ricardo – increasing money worries
– involvement with Arts and Crafts Exhibition Society –
lecture to Society of Arts – Report for the Egyptian
Government.

THE MOVE TO FULHAM in 1889 proved a good one. Sands End was not
far from The Vale – an easy bicycle ride, in fact – and the short journey must
have relieved De Morgan of much of the stress he had suffered travelling
daily to Merton. He also decided (and it was on the face of it a wise decision) to enter into partnership with Halsey Ricardo. There were two main
reasons for the arrangement: the first was that Ricardo put £4,000 into the
business, matched by Evelyn with another £4,000; secondly, William
obviously hoped that Ricardo would help in the running of the firm. As
we have seen, administration and financial management were not his strong
points – nor indeed, as would become evident, were they Ricardo's.

Halsey Ricardo was an architect by profession, but as his son has
written:[1] 'he was more interested in the aesthetic rather than the construc-
tional side of architecture – an artist by instinct and inclination'. A happy
and cultured man, a keen musician and a talented designer, he became a
close friend of the De Morgans and of the Burne-Joneses. When he left
Rugby School in 1872, he went to Italy ostensibly to study medieval architecture but in fact he led a pleasurable vagabond life there. On his return
after three years he met De Morgan and according to his son it was not long
before the two men had started to make plans for a factory in Fulham.

Ricardo designed the building and De Morgan the machinery – a gas engine driving a grinding mill,[2] a pudding mill[3] and a potter's wheel mechanically driven by a very ingenious variable-speed gear designed by De Morgan himself. In addition there were of course new kilns to be constructed under William's direction. It was not until 1888 that the new factory was launched, but finally stock and staff moved from Merton Abbey[4] early in 1889. The Ricardo–De Morgan partnership was to last for ten years. The best description of De Morgan and his work at Fulham was written by Halsey Ricardo after De Morgan's death:[5]

My first meeting with him in 1876, at Orange House, where I had been sent by Mr. Basil Champneys (the architect) to see about some tiles required for Mr. H. Holiday's house at Hampstead.

I was instantly captivated by the originality and charm of his manner, as well as by the beauty of the ware he was producing. I was consequently delighted when, during the alterations that were being carried out at Herd's Hill, I had occasion to visit his showroom and confer with him about the arrangement and so forth of the tiles to be used in that house. From this grew up a friendship which lasted till his death.

Soon after the removal from Chelsea to Merton – two adverse conditions revealed themselves – the first, and the most important, was that it was too far from his home in Chelsea, and the daily journey too much for his health, and secondly the site chosen (and I understood the only available) was too small for the purposes he had in mind. I agreed to join him in the search for more adequate premises nearer home, and eventually we decided to purchase a piece of land near Wandsworth Bridge (Fulham) and build a factory commensurate with his schemes for the future. Although these expectations were never realized to the full – and the expense of so large (relatively) a factory became too great a burden for the venture to bear – I am still of opinion that the step was, as far as human foresight could have gone, a wise one.

The factory was equipped with machinery (for power) and the ovens, kilns, mills and the appliances generally were devised and built under his superintendence, and from his designs.

[68]

His power of invention was boundless: almost every article and tool in the place was the outcome of his observation and invention.

Every oven and kiln that was fired was made to reveal some poss- ible modification or improvement: every failure in the ware — from the 'biscuit' to the finished article, was seized upon by him, and made to serve as the stepping stone to some higher result. It is hardly too much to say, that it was the failures that gave him the most interest in his work, and gave his imagination the most material to work upon. Apart from their power to resist exposure to climatic influences — what gave his tiles, and the pottery, their pre-eminence, is their charm of colour — splashes of colour comparable to jewels — the pools of colour into which one can dive and scarce plumb the full depth: due to the rich thickness of the glaze and the brilliancy of the porcelain 'slip' underneath.

To achieve this result was the search of endless experiments: one difficulty was to adjust the conflicting tensions of the glaze and the slip, leading to 'crazing' small fissures in the glaze: another the composition of the glaze so as to bring out the full value of the stain.

In the firing of lustre ware — the right moment had to be seized: if the piece was withdrawn from the kiln too soon, the lustre failed to materialize — if kept in too long the lustre became a dry metallic overlay — or else melted, a pale turquoise blue, into the glazed surface. The firing of a lustre kiln was necessarily a most anxious affair — a threading of One's way between Scylla and Charybdis — and during this critical passage, help could only be got by withdrawing from time to time the small test pieces put with the ware in the kiln, and deduc- ing the state of development from their appearance.

The 'throwing' of the vases, pots and bowls, was done under De Morgan's eye, and the ware was left to dry just as it came from the potter's hand off the wheel. There was nothing that did not engage his invention — the grinding and sifting of the clay — the drying of the wet 'wedged' clay tile squares between glass plates — the 'harp' for cutting these squares the required thicknesses — the composition of the 'frit' (glaze) — the selection and compounding of the colours — all were specially contrived and peculiar to his methods of production.

The result of Mr. De Morgan's genius — as a potter, chemist and engineer, is a ware technically unsurpassible, nor is such ware ever likely to be reproduced again.

But there is, moreover, another side to Mr. De Morgan as a crafts⁄ man: his inexhaustible powers of design – design specially bent to comply with the nature of the material to be decorated, the tools by which the decoration was to be applied, and the capability of the painter's hand which held the brush.

Although not devoid of incident – there is no desire to force his ware by painting, to masquerade as pictures, as so much of the 16th century majolica ware attempted.

His power of design came to him early in life – not without the usual artist's training – his imagination, of course was inherent.

But from the outset, his scheme of decorating his ware, was based on the material, its limitations and its capabilities. Within these bounds, his fancy roamed, exuberant, whimsical and humorous. It shewed itself in everything he did, wrote or spoke. A few lines on a postcard betrayed the writer – his conversation was like no other man's.

This humour, so kindly, so sympathetic, laughs out in his designs: the way he treats his birds, beasts and fishes, to obey his spacing and place themselves in almost impossible situations, without protest and with the suspicion of a grin – is only rivalled by the Japanese in their illustrations to their fairy stories. The Egyptians were masterly in the way they drew their fabulous monsters and divinities – their sympathy with the wild and tame life about them was every whit as great – but it was serious: in all that collection in the British Museum of the graphic art of old Egypt – there is no laughter: the only smile is on the face of the spectator at the strangeness of these far⁄ off times. One is shy in the presence of these formidable personages, with such uncustomary possibilities of admonition and oppression. Protective they might be – but familiarity was scarcely to be thought of.

Whereas who would not be delighted to go a⁄sailing in one of Mr. De Morgan's dream⁄ships or venture into the garden where such pea⁄ cocks are proudly flaunting their plumage. One's heart goes out to the poor Raven who tries to look dignified, and to ignore the vulgar ges⁄

tures of the rude little asp in the corner of the tile: or to the exasperated fish who is trying to keep its tail out of its mouth.

The frog that is regretting its too generous lunch – the parrot that
is not as wise (so says the adjacent snake) as he looks – the strange
flowers that might so easily have existed – all this incessant play of
fancy without the least taint of conscious superiority and upholding
the dignity of High Art. In all that amazing collection of his designs
(given by Mrs. De Morgan) in the Victoria and Albert Museum –
there is not one that shews any flagging, and derogation from the standard of joyous animal spirits, that was raised at the outset of his work.

The vigour and certainty of line – even when traced through a
feebler hand, is an outstanding feature of his rapid creations: it was as
if his brush were more than willing to further his conceptions – and
in the matter of colour, his decisions were faultless.

One may be sorry to reflect that no tradition of his manufacture survives – but in truth its nature was individualistic. Whilst De Morgan
was able to keep the factory going and his health allowed him to
manage and superintend the various activities under that roof – it was
a living and developing art – and when he had to relinquish it, there
was no one who, under the unfavourable financial postulates of its
working, was able to carry it on, providing the necessary sap and
impetus to keep it living and progressing.

During this decade there developed an extraordinary contrast between the
achievements of the pottery *qua* pottery and the increasing financial crisis
which beset the business and eventually led to its closure. One must remember that to move a pottery is a very costly business, involving a near total
rebuilding of workshops and kilns. The accounts from the builder who
undertook the work at Sands End show that the building continued from
1888, through 1889 and into 1890 and the cost from this one builder,
Charles, was £3,110.3s.8d. There was further expense in 1895 to cover the
cost of new WCs. Yet some of what has been judged the most successful
and richly inventive De Morgan pottery was produced at Sands End.
Sensibly, the two partners divided the products between the money-earning
plain-coloured tiles, and the lustreware richly coloured pots and the hand-
painted tiles for which De Morgan was already famous. In this Fulham

period, for the most part, De Morgan manufactured his own tiles. The pots were thrown to his own design and the clay, was mixed with the 'grog'[6] which he, too, prepared.

Gaunt and Clayton-Stamm[7] warn that products bearing the Sands End mark are not necessarily of the Fulham period. Designs which were in demand were reproduced and stamped with the Sands End[8] mark even though they might date back to Merton Abbey or even Chelsea. Work showing the influence of Morris reappeared during these years, as did the 'Persian' flowers. The variety of designs created in Fulham is most impressive; De Morgan's fully developed imagination was shown in his strange birds and trees – peacocks, flowers, squirrels and fish are set against fruit trees and shimmering water. May Morris's is the best description of his artistic achievements[9] which include the famous sunset Moonlight suite.[10] The problems of firing such pottery could only have been overcome by someone with long experience and much experimentation behind him as well as with endless patience.

His growing reputation and his friendship with William Morris led to an early involvement with the Arts and Crafts Exhibition Society. From the catalogue of the society's exhibitions, from the first one in 1888 to the last one, in 1906, in which De Morgan exhibited work, one can easily see how much he was involved. In 1886 with Walter Crane as president, Morris, Burne-Jones and De Morgan were on the committee. For a short time Evelyn was also included. In the first exhibition[11] De Morgan showed a decorative panel in tiles, a chimney-piece, a vase thrown by Hodkin, a panel of tiles with a ship design painted by Fred Passenger and many other objects. Evelyn showed a head, a Medusa in bronze, and Roddam Spencer Stanhope a relief in plaster of Andromeda.

The firm of De Morgan & Co. continued to contribute a number of exhibits in the years 1889, 1890, 1893, 1896 and 1899. In 1903, with Walter Crane president for the second time, there were two works by De Morgan, but shown by the Morris company. In 1906, De Morgan was no longer a member of the society. The firm of De Morgan & Co. had virtually ceased trading. The very last exhibit is a lustre vase priced at £13.5s.

What is very noticeable in the catalogues is the care William took to record the names of his painters. For example, in 1889 one of the composite exhibits was:

A pyramid of tiles and pottery designed by William De Morgan,
Large panels painted by Charles Passenger, an owl panel painted by
Joe Juster, some Luca Della Robbias painted by Fred Passenger and
H. Robinson and pottery painted by Charles and Fred Passenger and
H. Robinson and pottery painted by Charles and Fred Passenger, H.
Robinson, E. Porter, J. Hersey, Joe Juster and J. Birch.

The Arts and Crafts Movement owed much to the teaching and influence
of Ruskin and William Morris. It was started partly as a revolt against the
dead hand of the Royal Academy which was only, as some wit remarked,
interested in 'oil paintings in gilt frames'. More important, it was a craft
revival against industrial production. The Exhibition Society was separate
from the Art Workers Guild and De Morgan's membership brought him
into contact with many such as Walter Crane, Lewis Day, the expert on
ornament, and W.A.S. Benson, who specialized in metalware (in which
capacity he was closely involved with William Morris's company).

In 1892 De Morgan was asked by the Society of Arts to read the paper
on his particular speciality, lustreware, and was awarded the Society's silver
medal for it. The paper was published in the Society's journal on 24 June
1892. It gives a valuable insight into the curiously erudite, but remarkably
lucid quality of De Morgan's mind.*

He starts with a lengthy history of the origins of lustre, why none was
made in China or Japan and where it probably originated – with the
Arabs. He also deals with the earliest decorative pottery made in Egypt and
Syria. Much good-humoured scorn is vented in his examination of the
various theories about the spread of the use of lustre in Renaissance Europe.
About one such theory he writes: 'One of these had its origin from the existence of *bacini*, *bacili*,[12] with which the walls of certain churches at Pisa and
elsewhere are decorated. Marryat, the historian of pottery, ascribed a
Saracenic character to these, and framed a theory to account for them which
is so picturesque that I wish it were true.'

De Morgan shows a healthy scepticism in discussing other theories about
the spread of lustre techniques around the Mediterranean countries and
guesses at more plausible dates for the earliest production of lustre pots. He

* See Appendix B for complete paper

himself is quite definite about some dating: lustre was produced in Italy for about sixty years and then from 1550 until 1850 disappeared. 'Modern' lustre production started again in Italy – in Gubbio and near Florence as noted earlier – but he adds: 'In the catalogue of the Great Exhibition of 1851, which is a sort of death register of the arts of antiquity, not a hint of pottery appears.'

The remainder of the paper is devoted to the technique of producing lustre pottery. How many potters with a knowledge of chemistry were in the learned audience is not known, but what De Morgan has to say is crystal clear for the layman and he presents his practical conclusions of many years of experimentation. It is significant in this regard that his first lustre formula, put to the test in 1873–74, did not vary materially, although he tried many experiments throughout the rest of his career as a potter. He emphasized not only in his lecture but in private letters that the firing process is crucial. If something goes wrong in the firing an entire kiln-full can be ruined and weeks of work rendered worthless. He adds:

> I have, of course, tried endless modifications of the ordinary process, such as using special woods for smoking, sawdust, shavings, paraffin, and other combustibles. Any of these answer the purpose, the application being slightly varied. But nothing material has come of any of these experiments, and the process remains substantially the same as at first. I believe that if there had been any new opening for the application of chemistry, although I might not have followed the clue succesfully, I could hardly have missed it altogether.

There is a notable and magisterial concluding paragraph to the paper which can be quoted at length:

> In conclusion, I may say that I believe we have learnt all there is to know of the chemical and mechanical side of the art, as it was known to the ancients. What remains to be discovered in order to produce original work, equal to that of the Renaissance, is not a technical mystery, but the secret of the spirit which animated the fifteenth century not only in Italy, but all through Europe. We have got the materials and many more, but the same causes that forbid the attainment of new

[74]

beauty with the new ones, have stood between us and the revival of old beauty with the old. In saying this, I do not suppose myself to be going outside a universally accepted truth, or at any rate, one that is very rarely questioned. Some day there may be a new imagery and a new art. In the meanwhile I can only say that if anyone sees his way to using the materials to good purpose, my experience, which I regard as an entirely chemical and mechanical one, is quite at his disposal.

One thing that emerges from a reading of De Morgan's lecture is his excep-tional clarity in discussing the complicated history of a specialized type of pottery and in setting out the scientific basis for lustre production. He has no problems when it comes to dismissing rather fanciful writing by arm-chair experts on the subject. None of what he says appears egotistical, and the criticisms of other people's theories are never spiteful, but often gently humorous. Nevertheless the confidence in the writing and the firmness with which he states his opinions is impressive. One wishes he had gone on to write a whole manual on the subject.

This paper and the report he prepared for the Egyptian government, on the possibility of establishing a pottery in Egypt, in 1894, are the only pub-lished writings we have before *Joseph Vance* appeared on the William Heinemann list in 1906.[13]

De Morgan was recommended to the Egyptian government by the head of the South Kensington Museum, Thomas Armstrong, as the ideal person to investigate the possibility of establishing a glazed-pottery indus-try in Egypt. The report is not long but very detailed and thorough. His researches in Egypt – and he was there some weeks – covered costs, clays, glazes and kilns. Many samples of clays were sent home for analysis, and his brother-in-law Spencer Pickering appears to have been helpful, also his staff at the Sands End pottery. His conclusions, which he sent to His Excellency. Yacoub Artin Pasha (the Under Secretary of State for Public Instruction), were clear and not very encouraging:

1. White earthenware and porcelain were out of the question.
2. No difficulties existed with respect to other pastes and glazes.
3. He had grave doubts as to whether problems over fire-material for kilns and their accessories might be overcome.
4. The main stumbling block was the cost of fuel.

Apparently this last point was very serious. Coal would have been too expensive to import and the only alternatives were 'durrah' stalks or cotton-wood – the first a kind of corn, Indian millet, and the second the name of various species of poplar. He explains that an enormous quantity of these two possible fuels would have to be used in lieu of coal, and wood in Egypt was scarce. To add to these difficulties, the Arab method of throwing pots was different from the English and he complains to His Excellency, after he has returned to Italy, as at this stage of his life he was spending the winter months there, that he could have done better if he had been given more notice of the visit.

His main contact with the Eygptian Government was Douglas Dunlop, the Inspector of the Ministry of Public Instruction. They met in Florence before De Morgan went to Egypt, and agreed what he should be paid – £1 per day for general expenses, and a fee of £5 each week – together with first-class return fare from Florence to Cairo. We do not know whether, as a result of the report, a pottery was started but research went on until 1896. While he was still in Cairo, he wrote home to Ricardo: 'You can have no notion of the slowness of things here, and all has to be done in 8 weeks! Of course nothing will be done. But I shall have had a trip to Egypt and a trip to Egypt is well worth having if only to see the Arabs laugh and ride the donkeys . . .'[14]

Chapter 6

William's mother Sophia dies — the De Morgans decide, on
advice from William's doctors, to spend every winter in
Florence — P&O commission — more financial crises and the
De Morgan-Ricardo partnership dissolved in 1898 — Morris
dies in 1896, Burne-Jones in 1898 — De Morgan's work as a
designer finished in 1904 but firm survives until 1907.

IN 1892 two events occurred which made a considerable difference to the
lives of William and Evelyn. William's old mother Sophia died, which
meant that there were now no members of his immediate family whom he
had to care for. In addition his back was again giving him trouble and, conscious of his family's predisposition to TB, his doctors advised him that he
ought to be out of England during the cold and wet winter months. The
place the De Morgans chose was Florence — an obvious choice if only
because Evelyn's uncle Roddam Spencer Stanhope and his wife lived there.
They, particularly Evelyn, had been to visit them in their palatial villa on
the hills above the city in Bellosguardo, but from the point of view of
William's health it was a slightly odd decision as Florence during the winter
can be very cold and damp.

Spencer Stanhope suffered from severe asthma[1] and found that the only
place which gave him relief from asthmatic attacks was the area outside
Florence, where he had purchased the Villa Nuti and the surrounding
land. The villa was a large, old building set in the middle of terraces over-
looking the city and the hills of Vallombrosa. From Mrs Stirling's account
it seems to have been an idyllic place to live. Stanhope was a rich man and
no expense was spared in the furnishing and decoration of the house and in

the upkeep of the estate which went with it. Florence in the 1890s still retained its rich Anglo-Italian community, and their grand villas were a curious mixture of Italian splendour and English country-house amenity. Snobbery among the English was comparable, as Mrs Stirling[2] points out, to that in an English provincial town in the mid nineteenth century, and the Anglo-Italian community was presided over by the Misses Murray and their brother, General Murray, who lived in the via Dei Bardi. The Spencer Stanhopes, however, refused to be bound by the archaic social conventions they found there. Of course he had rebelled against his family when he became a painter and a member of the Pre-Raphaelite Brotherhood, and as we have seen, was a great help to Evelyn in her efforts to overcome her family's prejudice against painting as a career for women.

May Morris recorded: 'Thus, began their dual existence, tantalizing and somewhat mournful to a man of warm affections and keen interest in his own country[3] but yet not without its compensation.' He did miss his friends, as this letter to Burne-Jones shows:[4]

> *15 Lungo il Mugnone*
> *Florence*
> *Nov 27 '93*

Dear Ned,

I said as how I was going to write an persuade you to come out and winter here, and here's half the winter gone, and it's a hawful pity. And there you are choking in the fogs, and not painting all the poss-ible pictures by Burne-Jones and you're the only cove that can do them that I know – Well I'm just a writing now because my conscience struck me when I saw stuck up App:Studio, only I haven't been out much owing to stopping in the house of a cold, so I hadn't opportu-nities for to see App:Studios before. Well I went and saw it and found it was nice and big an only Seshento Shinwarnter per annum, that is 605 L. only in Italy 650 L. means about 26 pounds English. And I thought to myself what a pity Mr. Burne-Jones couldn't be a painting in this here studio instead of. I stopped short there because I don't wish to say anything against my native village. However I know it seems cruel to twit you with your circumstances, so I will say not a word about what the colour of the sky was when I came out from that studio, nor will I so much as hint at what it was over the Carrera mountains, and I will draw a veil over those mountains that you may remain in ignorance of a particular complection they got off of the sunset. These are things that it is only Christian to conceal from this Northern sufferer. I could not wish you (for your own sake) to realise that its along of the snow on the mountains that they got that colour, and that it doesn't come down here, and the flowers (fiori di terra) are a blowing and a growing still, and you can buy any quantity you like for trentashingking at the stone bench along by the Strozzi – No! My only doubt is if I oughtn't to write and assure you that the whole place is changed into Bayswater, which it isn't and can't be, though they've done a good lot that way, and that its a cold cold place and a reeking nest of typhoid, and a few more similar bloody lies to console you for your winter quarters.

We've never seen you friend M. Duprée – that was him wasn't it. But then we've done a good deal of stopping in the house, because some American left the window open on the rail in the Appenines and I catched cold, and all the while they thought we wanted it open, and they didn't! *Why* did Columbus discover America, one may well ask.

Give my love to your wife and children, and children's children.
Yours aff
DM
No! Destrée

Indeed, Florence proved to be a very pleasant city for the expatriate De Morgans. Even today, with all the motors which De Morgan so disliked, the Via Milton where he and Evelyn had their flat is a quiet tree-lined road with a little canal in the middle with grassy banks. There is only a trickle in the summer, but in the winters months, when they were there, there must always have been fresh running water. Pleasant houses, and the road has not been spoiled by ugly modern development. The hills above Florence, where the Spencer Stanhopes lived, were and still are a delightful change from the busy centre of the city. During the week the De Morgans lived and worked at Via Milton in the centre of the city and their weekends were spent at the Villa Nuti, which was only half an hour's walk or a short drive from the middle of the city. William established a workshop in Florence and took on untrained workmen, who were taught his methods: he found the Italians very quick to learn.[5]

During the winter months, with Ricardo in England – very much part-time – and De Morgan in Florence, there were considerable difficulties in keeping the business going. These got worse over the next decade. May Morris writes:[6]

> The invention which enabled the pottery to continue under these changed domestic conditions was applied to the tiles, which formed a large part of the business, which were now all painted in Italy. The design was not painted direct on the tile but on a whitey-brown paper (they could not get it bad enough in Italy, the home of beautiful carta-mano) stuck with a little soap on a slightly slanted piece of glass, the semi transparency giving the draughtsman greater power over the colour. When a quantity of the paintings were ready they were sent in rolls to the London factory: here the painted paper was fixed on the tile and the whole was covered with the glaze and fired, when the paper burnt right away, leaving the paint on the clay unimpaired. Specimens of a new design, or of a change in colouring were sent over to Florence to be looked at and corrected if need be.

There was necessarily considerable correspondence between Fulham and the Via Milton, by post and by telegraph. While rolls of painting were despatched to Fulham, very thin tiles were specially prepared and baked in London and then sent by post to Italy for approval. De Morgan also relied heavily on the telegraph for urgent instructions. Pots were painted in England, except for a few later on during this period which were baked in the kilns of the Cantagalli[7] factory.

This rather cumbersome way of working was used to cope with the very large and valuable commission from the P&O Line in 1894. Someone in the company had obviously known of the tiles made for the Tsar of Russia's yacht *Livadia*. When they were building six new passenger boats (*Arabia, China, Malta, Palawan, Persia* and *Sumatra*) the shipping firm approached De Morgan & Co. for pictures in painted tiles for staterooms and companionways. The P&O had been using tiles on a number of their passenger liners before the De Morgan & Co. commission but these had been manufactured and designed by large potteries and not hand-painted.

There were difficulties in executing such an ambitious project. De Morgan turned down the idea of large tile pictures of large figures and rejected a time-limit of seven or eight months for finishing the work. He concentrated instead on an imaginative voyage round the world depicted in tile, starting with the Thames and continuing with mountains and rivers, sirens, sea serpents and other products drawn from his extraordinary imagination. Mrs Stirling states that De Morgan only made tiles for six ships but Jon Catleugh is informative on the subject and gives details of twelve ships for which he supplied tiles, the work lasting from 1882 to 1900. It is very difficult now to know precisely what De Morgan made for P&O. Contemporary records give descriptions of the luxury provided for the pas-sengers and the graceful lines of the ships but very little detail about the decorations. Sir Colin Anderson, chairman of P&O, writing in 1967 remembered (and I quote from Jon Catleugh):

> tales of a dining room ceiling of heavy decorative tiles (from De Morgan, I have always hoped) which started, in rough weather, drop-ping one by one like ripe pears, so that for the rest of the voyage meals had to be eaten crouched beneath the dubious protection of a stretched velarium of netting into which from time to time another tile would bounce.

There survives very little to show us what De Morgan interiors looked like on the ships. The *Arabia*, with a full complement of passengers was torpe-doed on 6 November 1916 and sank in the Mediterranean. The *China* was torpedoed in 1915. The *Malta* survived the First World War but was sold to Italian scrappers in 1928. The *Palawan* and *Sumatra* were sold in Bombay in 1914 and the *China* was sold to the Japanese to be broken up in 1928. There are still some photographs in the P&O archives, but these do not give a precise idea of what the tiles looked like. De Morgan wrote in a letter to Ricardo:[8]

> My pictures, represent a voyage on a ship around the world and all the strange dangers she meets with. First, she runs on the rocks – then an

earthquake shakes her off – then I propose to do her dangers from the Sirens and the Sea Serpent, only the Sea Serpent will also be attracted by the Sirens and eat them – the ship will get off scott-free. If the Directors think this improbable we must rationalise the topic down to correctitude. As far as it goes, now, there is no physical impossibil-ity in the incidents – except to the very narrer-minded blokes.

The big pictures the China India, the Overland Route, Japan and you and me and Colcutt (of the P&O) tiger-hunting when we were in the army, in the Deccan and the Punjaub. The 'ansum one is me. The two Islands with panthers and sich-like are, for instance, Surinam and Krakatoa – anyhow nasty places for mariners to be driven on shore in – but capital sport for a rod and gun. These are done in a hurry and the geography will have to be sorter sifted out and arranged before we proceed. The blue in the friezes is enough to freeze the soul of any ship's crew – Macte, virtutibus – you and Fred all.

The 'difficulty', he wrote in a later letter,

has been to know what to do and how to do it, especially the quasi-naturalisms foreign to the nature of my designs – because their nature is to have no nature. The last panel contains: 1. The ruin of a Corinthian temple; 2. Pentonville Prison; 3. Fiesole, and in the middle distance, Eel-pie Island – it's very local.

May Morris obviously saw some of the P&O work and writes about it:[9]

It is saddening that nearly all, if not all, of these great ships are now at the bottom of the sea . . . The work had to be done to time, time being the first thing that matters to the man of commerce, and the last thing that matters to an artist, so everyone concerned was worried: but the tiles and drawings I have seen are bold and splendid, a fitting decoration for the purpose. Among the designs prepared for this work is a sheet of drawings of cities and famous places that the boats pass on their voyages; One, that first glimpse of the cliffs and the green of England; another, the city of London, the ancient city with its Abbey and its Cathedral so beautiful. Then there is the storm with lightning and tiles falling; another scene showing volcanoes smoking, with a background at white heat, very cleverly rendered with the potter's 'realism' and intensity of colour, purple mountains against sullen dark blue. Then the island scenes such as a fruit-laden island with three tigers and four palms; then China, charmingly rendered, with wooded hills and a yellow chess board sailing junks. Japan is a picture of storks and fisher boats drawn with Japanese grace, and an elegant landscape with Fujiyama in the background. India gives us a tiger hunt in which the grey elephants and the golden tiger form destined patterns.

The correspondence which survives from this period between De Morgan and Ricardo is a chronicle of increasing financial difficulties and worries about the running of the factory. Much of the latter might well have been avoided if De Morgan had been there twelve months of the year but Evelyn was adamant that her husband's health must come first and he must not risk the consequences of a winter in England. The tone of a letter to Ricardo from the Villa Nuti was reasonably cheerful although concerned about detail. This is at the beginning of his winter stays in Florence and was written on 17 October 1892:[10]

My Dear Ricardo

Thinks go slowly here – but I'm hoping to have everything ready for start in a week or two – I've got the drawings and tracings of tiles ready – and I believe there will be no difficulty about painters – I'm sending some suggestions for a thrower in case by any run of luck you feel equal to putting Hodkin on again.

It will probably be better to stick to the mixture clay for all the pots throughout as it is equally good for Persian grounds and enamels. Those scoopy in and out pots will make very good lustres as they only want borders and scales and such like painted on them. The larger flat-handled pots might have raised patterns done on the handles like embossed tiles. The little drawing of blue bottles is to fire you with the idea of a vast multitude of quite small pots to be sold at no exorbitant price but to keep Hodkin occupied all his time. – I think a good way would be to limit him to six of each sort of large pots or thereabouts but to go straight on with endless little bottles in the interims. Be very careful (if all this comes to pass) that no pottery gets in to the big oven – it spoils it – it should all be cooked at a long, low heat in the old lustre kiln. This is intensely, excruciatingly true about dishes and bowls which are wanted considerably. I am taking for granted that Fred [Passenger] has plenty of drawings to adjust on departure to the present as I shall not send him anything new until we have left the Villa and settled in the old crib – I have secured a capital workshop for 4£ for the six months! Send me word how finances are going as I must arrange accordingly –.

Late in the same year he and Ricardo discussed ways of raising capital much needed in the business. There is a slightly muddly letter from De Morgan to Ricardo which is worth quoting:

I believe a new syndicate might perhaps be got to take the factory at £350 per annum for rent and concomitants which would nicely cover the interest of our sunk capital – we could then dispose of the stock and call it income as it came in. We should only have to pay wages to painters and prezzo fissato for materials and firing – Ooray! Sim'lar likewise we should charge a %age on all the sales we made for the factory and be the principal agents.

Firing the kilns, always tricky, presented many more problems when De Morgan was absent. One cannot blame poor Halsey Ricardo, who did his best, but he could only spare half a day each week day at the factory and was not there to supervise the whole time. His architectual practice claimed much of his time and energy, and like De Morgan he lacked business acumen. Added to that, the morale of the workforce suffered without De Morgan's presence. He realized this, and wrote in a letter to Ricardo: 'I'm as certain as I can be of anything human, that Iles, Passenger, Ewbank, Dring[11] – all of them will work well in proportion as they feel in direct communication with me.' In another letter[12] he notes:

The difficulty of the position forced upon me by these alterations of England and Italy is almost insuperable. I was during the last few weeks before leaving England completely bewildered by the demands of business, the desire to see what I could of my friends, and the inability to achieve satisfaction in either point owing to physical exhaustion always supervening at unfavourable moments, just when I wanted to rush here or gallop there to see after this, that or the other. We started with everything undone and incomplete . . . A new spine and new eyes will be welcome. Forgive my apparent extinction for long periods! I always seem to be somewhere else. This constant occupation swallows me up.

There survives rather a sad letter to De Morgan in Italy from Frank Iles, his faithful kiln master from the Chelsea days, reporting friction between himself and Bill Dring (the tile and pottery glazer).[13] All De Morgan could do in reply was feebly to advise Iles to try to avoid disagreements.[14] And in another letter to the long-suffering Frank Iles:

Dear Frank,

I am glad to hear things are going on so well.

As to Bob, if you and Mr. Ricardo are agreed that there is no cure for his irregularity, he must be sacked. But I think before doing this it would be as well to put him on piece-work. The only question is about what price should be given. Tell him that unless he comes regularly and gives no more trouble he will have to go on to piecework at the rate of a shilling a hundred six inch tiles, doing all his own wedging, and I think he will probably change his ways. I hope he might well think it over, and not be a fool.

As for the others if they give trouble, you must find someone to come on in their places.

What worried William as much as the never-ending financial crises was his fear that without his presence there might be a deterioration of standards. Apparently 1895 and 1896 were not good years. Letters between London and Florence went astray, illness was rife among the staff at Sands End and an unusually cold February in 1895 deprived the factory of water. Friction is also apparent between Ricardo and De Morgan. The latter wrote:[15]

Sad news about the big kiln, why did you or Iles expect a different result? Of all the warnings we have had about what to avoid the most conspicuous and unmistakable have been those against packing wares for baking in the same kiln with glazes. But I won't nag from afar at those on the field of battle. It is too bad of me not to be there myself.

Ricardo, normally as good natured and gentle as De Morgan wrote impatiently on 7 March 1895 over a misunderstanding about some of the tiles for one of the P&O vessels:

Like Brer Rabbit,[16] I am getting anxious whether I am not getting 'fibble in my min' for I don't seem to be able – to judge by your letters – to make myself intelligible. By the curve of the tiles in the companion way I don't mean any curvature on plan, I mean those lines that in a terrestrial building are horizontal, but in a ship follow the lines of the ship's curvature.

He sent diagrams with his letter to make it plainer.

It is clear from the extensive correspondence[17] between De Morgan and Ricardo that while there were real difficulties with kilns and firings in De Morgan's absence in Italy, it was the lack of money which was the chief worry. An arrangement with an Italian firm, Doccia, was suggested; that came to nothing. Then there was the problem of what to do about the money which Ricardo had put into the firm if he decided to leave – De Morgan suggested raising a mortgage. In 1897, when De Morgan had been sent the latest accounts, there was talk of liquidation.

Despite all these difficulties the ships' tiles turned out successfully, and towards the end of 1895 De Morgan wrote and told Ricardo of his satisfaction. Nonetheless, finances were a real and pressing problem:

I've	Now how about	Missus
got	MONEY	has got
none		none

and Poncini wants his rent and I shall have no money for wages next week. I know the pressure but it's simply a question of stop or go on here. I was hoping to get a tip about the state of the till but you are ret-

icent. I suppose as soon as the ship tiles are well out to sea we can ask
for sommat on account . . .

One wonders whether Ricardo, in chilly winter London trying to cope
with the endless problems of the factory, was not sometimes envious of De
Morgan in Florence and it is also possible De Morgan was vexed by the little
amount of time Ricardo seemed able to devote to the pottery.

The De Morgan–Ricardo partnership was finally dissolved in 1898. Its
termination could hardly have been a surprise to either of the partners. Not
only did Ricardo have his architectural practice, which was fairly busy, to
look after, but in November 1896 he accepted a post as instructor in architectural design at the new LCC Central School of Arts and Crafts. The
principal was William Richard Lethaby and among the other talented staff
were May Morris, who taught embroidery, and, later Eric Gill,[18] who
taught lettering. Before Ricardo left the factory it was decided to appoint
Reginald Blunt both as general manager and as someone who could bring
some order into the firm's finances. Blunt and Ricardo overlapped so that
Ricardo could pass his expertise on to his successor.

Blunt was an interesting and talented man. Son of the rector of St
Luke's, Chelsea, he was an engineer by trade, had been an inspector of railways (working for Ricardo's father-in-law Sir A.M. Rendel), a businessman, a writer and an historian of Chelsea. He soon started to work hard
'at the chemistry of fluxes, grounds and glazes' and reorganized the records
and accounts of the firm. In his relations with staff, he did his best to get rid
of some of the bad feeling which had caused friction in the factory and sent
a bulletin each week to Florence to keep De Morgan in touch with all the
good or bad news. Blunt wrote about the time he spent as general
manager:[19]

William De Morgan, fine artist that he was, was first and foremost an
inventor. There is hardly anything that he was not prepared to
improve upon, from a fire grate to cycle gear to an aeroplane or submarine. His ingenuity was amazing and he was sometimes a little
exasperating to his factory manager who, when awaiting some fresh
and lovely designs from Florence, might receive instead an elaborate
treatise on a new method of accounting which was to show at one

glance the whole position of the company's finances, output, profits and prospects, – things of which his 'chancellor of the exchequer' really now knew much more than he did. All the same, those three years were a great and lively experience. De Morgan's generous trust in his manager was really touching, and although there was some-times nothing left in the Treasury to pay that manager's reputed salary he was free and was constantly urged to take it out in pots and panels. So the occasional enrichment of Glebe House [where Blunt lived] and the provision of some lovely wedding presents. In spite of the ever present shadow of approaching failure, Bill's inventive schemes and genial humour were alike unquenchable: and it was with keen delight that a few years later I welcomed their richer and more prosperous developments in novel form.

Blunt's appointment as general manager was very much a stop-gap in that he had never worked as a potter himself, and although he rationalized the organization and the finances of De Morgan & Co. he was not full time and nothing much could be done to arrest the decline of the firm, particu-larly with De Morgan still away half the year. When the partnership with Ricardo was finally dissolved in 1898 a new more extensive partnership was established with the two Passengers, Fred and Charles, and Iles, which lasted for the next few years. It was to the credit of both Halsey Ricardo and William De Morgan that there appears to have been no unpleasantness or rancour between them – unlike the stormy break-up of the original William Morris firm.

Despite what must have been a pleasant life for the De Morgans in Italy – half the year – it was, inevitably, a sad time. William managed the affairs of his firm as best he could and Evelyn had her painting. But as William remarked at the time, the writing was on the wall for the firm and they must, both of them, have been very saddened by the deaths of their old friends William Morris in 1896 and Burne-Jones in 1898. William recorded in a letter written in 1899 to J.W. Mackail that Mackail's biography of William Morris really cheered him up, and he evidently had a great admiration for it.

Some economy was achieved by closing the showroom in Great Marlborough Street, and a new showroom was established in its place at

the Sands End factory. It greatly saddened William to have to discharge
some of the workers; a depression in trade, partly due to the Boer War, was
not helpful. He wrote in a letter:[20] 'It is melancholy, to think that my men
should be driving omnibuses. What I am curious to see is if, when any of
them come back (if they do), they will be happy, and won't find it dull by
comparison.'

The William Morris firm helpfully suggested that he should remain in
England and give them 'the monopoly of his output'.[21] This was not
acceptable to him as he would not spend the winters in England, neither
was he prepared to give up his commercial independence. He was
simultaneously facing problems with the operation in Italy as he lacked sufficient funds to pay his workmen. There is a sad letter to Blunt in October
1899:[22]

> I've had to resort to a desperate measure to raise £5 for the chaps here,
> lest they should go dinnerless. I have written a cheque on my bank
> knowingly an overdraw ... I should think some cash must have come
> though if it has, there will be very little left for the rest of the quarter.
> Our very existence hangs on the completion of the Bedford panels[23]
> now, and this will scarcely tide us over Xmas. Who would be an Art
> potter?

Mrs Stirling quotes from a number of letters written[24] by De Morgan to his
general manager which are informative if melancholy reading, but with the
occasional flashes of his familiar humour. They also, of course, inevitably
show increasing anxiety and frustration at not being able to keep the firm
going:

November 14 1897[25]

From what Iles says about the big kiln, I imagine that if the floor
holds out long enough he will get it into complete working order,
and run up a stock of plain tiles to cheapening point, which I look
to as a Millennium – clay in barges of eighty tons from Stourbridge –
a mill turning out five tons per diem of body – all the room was
full of workers and 18/- a yard for turquoise tiles – that's my idea of
things ...

Are you making use of the revolving grate at the factory? I mean has it been put in so as to revolve properly and illustrate its smoke consuming properties with only Wallsend coal? If not, please make Fred Iles put it on a pivot so to spin freely, see that the chimney is clear and give it a trial . . .

Re the lustre – of this I am certain, that every glaze that is susceptible at all can give a good lustre. Because on a six inch tile every now and again one always gets a gradation passing from mere red to copper metal, such as you might rightly object to.

Re price of pots [this was in answer to a query from Blunt who wanted a basis for fixing prices] I know that there is some way of doing this. Multiply the height in inches by the largest diameter in centimetres and divide by the number of hours employed. Multiply this result by logarithm of the number of shillings per week, and it will give you the price of the pot in halfpence – but who shall discover it?

The only thing is to make trials and see.

Suppose we try the *contents* of the pot as a gauge – say a shilling an ounce for decorated pots? None of our pots contain less than 5 or 6 ounces of water, and none is priced under five or six shillings. I can't remember how many ounces go to a pint, so I can carry the enquiry no further. But see Ewbank [he was the company's manager] and get him to make a record of how much a selection of pots contains per head and what the present marked price is. Perhaps it would be fair to consider the bulk of the pot as a factor. This could be done by weighing it dry and calculating the bulk of an equal bulk of water from the relative sp. Grs. and adding it to the contents. Perhaps it would be wise to let it alone!

It is hard to believe that this rather facetious reply was very much help to poor Blunt.

I'm so horribly stupid in taking for granted that others know things because I do! – I say to myself 'why *I* know that surely *he* must?' In the case of the tin and aluminiums I was taking it for granted that at the Polytechnic the commercial preparation of Calcine, or combined oxides of lead and tin, would be in the mouths of babes and suck-lings. It is the only known method (recent discoveries perhaps apart) of causing the suspension of the white tin oxide in glass undissolved. It is like mechanical suspension in water, I take it. And the white enamels and Majolicas lack the hardness of crystaline glaze accord-ingly. Calcine is prepared by raking the scum off melted lead and tin. This scum is the calcine oxides which are true compounds or not according to the proportion of the metals.

January 15, 1898

The vicious appearance of so much modern earthenware is due to the dry lathing much more than the tint of the body – and none can vary tints ad lib by a solution of colouring salts . . . I shall be sending this week the Daisy and Anemone patterns for the great Rothschild. I understand he wants turquoise blue to be turquoise blue and not green, like Ally Sloper's boy who wanted tea for tea and declined whisky.

If the devil don't take the Fulham vestry he don't deserve to be devil no longer as a Lincolnshire farmer said.

March 17, 1898

I hope the weak lustres have gone or will go well. All that's necessary for their success is a continued low temperature and much longer firing.

Bismuth makes very good and very soft glazes but they are dear. I never investigated them properly.

I don't like the red on pottery tiles nor any hand glaze. It's too violent and butcherous. But a glaze containing some soda say the materials of the hand glaze we use on the tiles mixed with tin calcine might do very well.

Mrs Stirling quotes from a large number of letters. Many of them are full of precise and practical advice to Blunt who must none the less have longed for De Morgan to be present himself overseeing matters. Some of the letters are despondent:

March 1898

I am glad you take such a sanguine view of the work, my view is san-
guinary! I observe that our tiles now cost us more to make them than
our calculated expense in Chelsea twenty years ago. Ewbank's report
looked very poor as to finances. Don't soften anything. Show it to me
at its worst. I fear you are having a dreary time, but 'just now' is always
dreary!

To Blunt again: 'As I shall have nothing coming in from the home factory,
and I am nearly cleaned out, I am endeavouring to run the concern here [in
Florence] at a small profit with a view to making something for myself.' To
Halsey Ricardo he wrote: 'I'm sure you will be surprised and pleased to
learn that I owe you a sum of money, even as I am surprised and disgusted.
But then *your* delight will be qualified by hearing that I cannot pay!'

Occasionally a letter strikes a more cheerful note. William always, and
Evelyn sometimes, travelled to and from Italy by sea as he felt that train journeys were too great a strain on his back. In any case he loved the sea voyage,
away from worries, and it was very peaceful. One jovial letter which he
wrote to Blunt when he was on the point of sailing back to England at the
end of April read:

Our boat says it sails from Genoa at noon on Wednesday. We are here
[at Levanto Riviera Ligure] because we thought three or four days
holiday by the way would do us good. We've hit on a place of most
amazing loveliness and a very good hotel. I am simply eating and
sleeping and taking long walks – so I shall (I hope) be in a state of
diabolical activity and aptitude when I arrive in London on the 10th
or 11th. I shall need to be, for the task I propose to myself is no less
than that of *forcing* the concern into a paying form. I am satisfied that
we can do it, from the fact that it had done no worse than it has in
these last shopless months. We shall see! If we have a financial collapse outright, I hope it will bring itself home to us immediately – the
sooner it happens the more time I shall have in England to get straight
again.

Meanwhile I hope to have credited the Bay of Biscay with the small-
est possible investments on my part. A Riverderci!

With activity at Sands End more or less at a standstill, De Morgan got the Cantagalli factory in Florence to do some work for him. Evelyn was at pains in 1917 to make the position clear about the relationship between William and Cantagalli. She wrote:[26]

> With regard to the Italian position of the factory, I want to emphasise that there was no sort of connection whatever with the De Morgan work in Italy and the Fabrica Cantagalli. Some time after Signor Cantagalli's death, my husband got them to paint a vase from his designs, also about four or five dishes, the materials employed being their own. These designs, executed by them for him, were not in any way connected with the output of their own firm, merely an order given to them by him. With regard to the experiments on a paraffin ground, the one successful plate was painted by him himself and he employed his own men on other attempts of the kind, but merely sent the dishes to be fired in the Cantagalli kiln – Cantagalli's people having no more part in the experiment than the Doultons have when a sculptor sends his terra-cotta work to them to be fired.

These works are not perhaps his best work, nor is the rather strange head of the god Pan. This is to be seen in Cardiff Castle Museum and is unusual in being three-dimensional. Inevitably reminiscent of Della Robbia, it was said by Mrs Stirling to have been modelled by Evelyn, painted by William and fired by Cantagalli. Another piece a two handled vase, is more success-ful. It is in Cragside, the amazing Norman Shaw house in North-umberland. Cherubs make music, but more sinister are the snakes curled about their legs, the serpent lower down the vase, and the serpentine handles. Gaunt and Clayton-Stamm suggest this design might symbolize the gradual strangling of the pottery factory. This may be a little fanciful, but the rather sombre decoration of some of these pots and dishes fired by Cantagalli might very well mirror De Morgan's understandable depres-sion. Christmas 1899 bought a sombre letter to Blunt:[27]

> I am staying here [Villa Nuti] for Xmas – I have a card from you, but I suppose there is really nothing to tell and that the business is torpid ... There is nothing here to make Xmas any better than in London

– indeed I should imagine that for us English it is worse. We are kept in constant fever by false alarms, cooked up by a press, which always has a glee in reporting news in a sense disadvantageous to us. Then the anxious, expectant faces of my men thrown out here, to whom I unfortunately owe money still which I can't pay, make an unpleasant incident. I am trying to get through some work in decoration but it is only in the summer that much of this sort of work is going about . . . I am hoping to have from you a general statement of how we stand. Anyhow I wish you an Xmas not further clouded than we are at this moment of writing, even perhaps with a silver lining creeping round the cloud's corner

In early 1900 he wrote to Blunt:

As I understand matters now, we have just enough owing to us to carry through to Lady-Day on the reduced scale. If I diminish this by 50 now either I shall have to find another 50 by March or we shall have to close the factory. Well – what must be must! Anyhow, if I cannot have 50 to clear we are stopped. Just look at the Italian account – it's awful.

Nevertheless the strategy is all to hold on, although the field tactics all point to surrender . . . but for the moment I am owing money to the men here still (about £20) and have nothing to live on so that 50 is a *sine qua non*, through it isn't a *cum qua multum*.

February 8 1900
If the pottery is finally strangled by the Boers, I shall have to take to something else permanently but this will be compulsion not choice.

Both Ricardo and Evelyn still had capital tied up in the old partner-ship. William's concern in letters to Ricardo was to try to save the busi-ness: 'The reason I am so very anxious . . . is that I find finances here are slipping into the old way of my borrowing of my wife to pay Torquato and Co., greatly to her perturbation . . . It would I think be a much more sat-isfactory way to post me a cheque every week for £4.' Later, in May 1901 he said:

I am much less influenced than you think by attachment to the factory and the work – I conceive it to be my duty to do all I can for my wife's sake and for yours, and also because I have brought up a number of men from boyhood to earn their living at this particular work and I am by no means sure that some of them would not be landed in the work house if they lost it.

On his part, Ricardo thought that De Morgan was 'prolonging the situation beyond its natural term',[28] but was obviously very understanding about his position, and Evelyn was determined to support the firm financially to the last gasp. A short note from De Morgan to London said: 'The cheque has arrived – and I am delighted. For I had exactly 10 cents in the world, and two more halfpenny papers would have reduced me to beggary.'

By January 1903 De Morgan had to close the pottery temporarily and stop paying wages. A little later, a final misfortune came his way. 'The last shell was pitched into the works, when neuritis gripped my business thumb and stopped my drawing. I threw Art aside after forty odd years.' He recalled with rueful humour in 1905, 'my old joke with Morris about the Fictionary which became a Factory is now reversed. sic transit'.[28] 'My former works', he writes in another letter 'are now the source of that far more useful stiff, blue-bell polish!' The Bluebell Polish company had taken over the Sands Ends works.

A number of factors contributed to the closure of De Morgan & Co. The lack of competent financial management is an obvious one, and De Morgan's absence in Italy for more than half the year made for very real difficulties. What nobody could control was a change in fashion – tiles of the sort that De Morgan & Co. produced were not, by the turn of the century, so much in demand and, in addition, the price of the tiles, in comparison with what some of the big manufacturers charged, was very high indeed. As Jon Catleugh has pointed out, 'It must have been difficult to persuade a client that a plain green De Morgan tile at 1s 3d was really superior to a plain green commercial tile at 4d.' There are some price lists still in existence,[29] one from 1887, and the other undated, which show that De Morgan's prices are about three times more expensive than those produced by Maw & Co. and four times more than the printed designs of Walter Crane. De Morgan, though, was determined not to lower his standards.

There was also, as was mentioned earlier, a recession at the time of the Boer War, and there was not much money about to spend on luxuries, however beautiful and superbly produced.

De Morgan's work as a designer effectively ceased in 1904, but the firm staggered on until its final closure in 1907. By that time his novel, *Joseph Vance*, had been published (in 1906), and quite unexpectedly had been a great success. Reginald Blunt wrote:[30]

> Good fiction survives more housemaids than good pottery, and the name of William De Morgan will doubtless live as the author of *Joseph Vance, Alice-For-Short, Somehow Good*[31] and the others of that wonderful succession of novels – which were all produced in the last decade of his life – in the days to come, when his pots and panels are scarcely to be found save – one hopes and is promised – in the South Kensington Museum . . . Pity it is – as one must always feel with what-soever things are lovely and of good report – that the making of William De Morgan's beautiful Chelsea ware has to be numbered amongst the vanished things from among us . . . The lustre bowls, the glowing pots, the turquoise tiles, beautiful as they were, remained always – though not by his wish – the prize of the few . . . and his pottery, at its rare best achieved a richly imaginative but yet a very limited and precarious heritage.

It is ironic that Blunt's forecasts have for the most part been proved quite wrong. The books have been out of print and unobtainable, except in libraries and second-hand book shops, since the 1930s (with the exception of *Joseph Vance*). De Morgan has very few readers now in the 1990s and the books written on his ceramics have tended to dismiss the novels in passing as both over-long and unreadable. The bowls, plates, pots and tiles are, however, accessible in collections and are eagerly sought after by collectors, but only by collectors with a great deal of money as in the last twenty years sales prices have rocketed.[32] Luckily there survive some notable monuments to De Morgan's years as a potter accessible to the general public. The Victoria & Albert Museum has a good collection,[33] much of it given by Evelyn, and since her death increased by bequests and purchases. It also has (and this is equally impressive) Evelyn's gift to the museum of 1,248 sheets or original drawings of designs for tiles, tile pictures, plates and vases and some meticulously drawn plans for machinery and various kinds of kilns. Surveying these sheets of drawing gives one a marvellous and comprehensive view of De Morgan's imaginative and inventive powers.

Perhaps the most extraordinary monument to William's years as a designer of tiles is at 8 Addison Road, Kensington, London.[34] Ernest Debenham (later Sir Ernest Debenham) of the large stores Debenham & Freebody, asked Halsey Ricardo to design him a London house. Ricardo and De Morgan had for a long time shared an enthusiasm for the idea of tiling houses on the outside as well as the inside in brilliant colours which would be manufactured and glazed in such a way that they would be impervious to the smoky and destructive air of big cities. Ricardo's efforts in publicizing this project found in Debenham somebody with the imagination to agree to something quite new: to decorate the outside of the house with plain tiles, and the inside and the covered way up to the front door with decorated tiles. Ricardo must also have had it in mind that by using most of the remaining stock of tiles in the Sands End pottery there would be some return on the capital sunk in the business. There was a complication, however, as De Morgan felt a dual responsibility to the old firm of De Morgan & Co. and also to De Morgan, Iles & Passenger, but they seem to have sorted matters out quite reasonably.

Much of the Peacock House (as it is sometimes called), particularly on the outside, is nothing to do with De Morgan. In the Arts and Crafts tradition, Ricardo recruited a number of artist craftsmen. The mosaic in the dome above the large square hall, Byzantine in spirit, was carried out by an Italian, Gaetano Meo, who had been an assistant to De Morgan's old friend Sir William Richmond in his work on mosaics for St Paul's Cathedral. The plaster ceilings were designed by Edward Gimson, a cabinetmaker, and the gates and doors by the Birmingham Guild of Handicraft. The brilliant Addison Road facade has grey Staffordshire bricks on the bottom storey, framed by cream Doulton glazed terracotta Cararra Ware. The deepgreen and brightblue panels above were manufactured by the Leeds Fire Clay Co., better known in the decorative ceramic world as Burmantofts, and the brightgreen roof tiles were made from tiles bought in Spain. A colourful and unexpected if rather garish sight in sedate Kensington.

But much more impressive is the De Morgan contribution. Many of his best tiles are to be seen in the covered way to the main entrance to the side of the house. Trial runs for the P&O ships are there and in the loggia and breakfast room, a peacock design in the vestibule. They have an extraordinary effect in the hall, on the staircase and in the passages. The magnificent bathrooms and lavatories are also richly covered with decorated red lustre and peacock-blue tiles and, as May Morris wrote, the tiles in the surrounds to a number of fireplaces were 'arranged by Halsey Ricardo with genius.'

The house was finished in 1907, the same year as the final closure of the Sands End pottery. Not unexpectedly, it attracted a lot of attention. Ricardo sent an article on the house in an architectural journal to De Morgan in Florence, and had a rather lacklustre reply in a letter dated 21 March 1907:[35]

It's really a pleasure to write to you with no damn business in it! This time only thanks for the shiney-paged journal, with the really wonderful pictures of THE HOUSE in it. It is a beautiful palace – there's no doubt of it.

But Millionaires aren't half millionaires not say at once 'let's build a city that-wise forthwith' Not a mere house but a town of houses and plant all the gardens forthwith straight away, to be ready when the houses are finishing fifty years hence.

I don't much care for the figure a-top of the dome – seems to me to wan *impersonality* – is that intelligible, or otherwise?

I hope you overstated the non-existence of orders for new houses – of course over-statement is cut off at a limit in this case. Well! I hope what you said was short of the limit.

Them's my idea about the house.

We do not know whether he ever saw the house.

When Sands End closed, the Passenger brothers and Frank Iles opened a business at 162 Brompton Road with the manager from Sands End, F.L. Ewbank, in charge of sales. They did not make tiles, but De Morgan was happy for them to use his designs on pots and dishes as long as the marks did not mislead customers and made it plain that the painting was the work of CP or FP – Charles or Fred Passenger – not the work of William De Morgan. Later Fred Passenger worked until 1931 for the Bushey Heath Pottery started in 1923 by the wealthy Mrs Ida Perrin. It is sad to look at most of the products made after 1907 because although they were made by William's craftsmen, they clearly lack his inspiration and are – this is particularly true of the Bushey Heath ware – rather dull and lifeless and without the amazing colour of the best of De Morgan's work.

Typical of the man was what he wrote in 1901. It was not the production of beautiful objects which he missed so much as the scientific side of his work: 'Investigation and experiment seem now to belong to a remote and happy past.'[36] And he obviously missed the never-ending excitement of opening kilns and seeing what they contained after the firing. His care for his workers never stopped. He wrote in 1907 from Florence to his sister-in-law Ada (Edward's widow):[37] 'Here's the factory at an end for good, and I know it will mean reproachful faces of men out of work at all points of the compass for me when I come back.'

Chapter 7

The De Morgan family involvement with writing Augustus,
Sophia and Mary – their keen interest in the spiritualist
movement – William starts his first novel in Florence – *Joseph
Vance* sold to William Heinemann.

IT IS NOT UNCOMMON for people when they retire to try to write a book,
usually with lamentable results. Sometimes such a book achieves publication, but very rarely does someone in their late sixties embark on an extraordinarily successful career as a novelist and produce nine full-length works, a
flow of fiction only interrupted by death.[1] De Morgan wrote very little
during his pottery years and tells[2] us he only had leisure for very occasional
reading. In order to appreciate his late-life career as an author it is instructive
to review what his family earlier achieved in the literary field, and indeed
what subjects had particular interest for the De Morgans. This will have an
obvious bearing on William's novels, when one examines them in detail.

Many Victorians of all classes in the second half of the nineteenth and
early twentieth century were fascinated by and much involved in spiritualism:[3] the De Morgans were no exception. In particular, Sophia took the
whole business very seriously[4] and she and Augustus were two of the earliest supporters of investigation and experiment in this field. It was a great
boost to other spiritualists to find a professor of mathematics, known for his
writings on logic and his cool scientific judgement, writing a preface to his
wife's book *From Matter to Spirit: The Results of Ten Years Experience in Spirit
Manifestations'*.[5]

The spiritualist movement had its origins in the United States of

America. Starting with some extraordinary happenings at the home of the Fox family in New York state in 1848, interest in extra-sensory phenomena grew rapidly. Spiritualist societies proliferated and mediums appeared in states across the country: in Brooklyn alone there were fifty spiritualist circles by 1851. Although many people and organizations, including the Churches, opposed the movement, quite prominent figures in public life, among them judges and clergymen, were 'converted'. As in England when spiritualism took hold, the majority of spiritualists were sincere and moderate people, but there were also many cranks and much fraud, particularly in seances.

The movement reached England in 1852 when a Mr Stone, an authority on 'animal magnetism,'[6] brought a well-known medium, Mrs Haydn, across to London, where she gave many demonstrations of her powers. There was scepticism, mainly in the press and among scientists, but some eminently respectable men in public life were convinced that Mrs Haydn was genuine, even that well known rationalist and socialist Robert Owen. Augustus De Morgan showed an early interest and carried out several investigations of Mrs Haydn's seances in his own home. The anonymous book *From Matter To Spirit: The Results Of Ten Years Experience in Spirit Manifestations* was published in 1863 by 'CD' with a preface by 'AB'; it was partly a result of these investigations (CD being Sophia, and AB, Augustus). Augustus was aware, as he says in his preface, of dangers arising out of his advocacy: 'My state of mind, which refers the whole either to some unseen intelligence or something which man has never had any conception of, proves me to be out of the pale of the Royal Society.' One can sympathize with his anxiety when one realizes that most scientific opinion was unconvinced, particularly the country's leading authority, Michael Faraday, who attacked the spiritualist interpretation of psychic events in a letter to *The Times* dated 30 June 1853.

Augustus's preface is balanced and lucid and bears comparison with what Dr Thorpe had to say in *Joseph Vance* on the subject of the supernatural and the possibility of life after death. This is what Augustus writes about the pros and cons of spiritualism as set out in Sophia's book:

I am satisfied, by the evidence of my own senses, of *some* of the facts narrated: of some others I have evidence as good as testimony can give.

I am perfectly convinced that I have both seen, and heard in a manner which should make unbelief impossible, things *called* spiritual which cannot be taken by a rational being to be capable of explanation by imposture, coincidence, or mistakes. So far I feel the ground firm under me. But when it comes to what is the cause of these phenom-ena, I find I cannot adopt any explanation which has yet been sug-gested. If I were bound to choose among things which I can conceive, I should say that there is some sort of action or some combination of will, intellect and physical power, which is not that of any of the human beings present.[7]

He ends his preface by assuring the reader that neither he nor the 'author' had read the other's work until both were complete: 'Between us we have, in a certain way, cleared the dish: like that celebrated couple of whom one could eat no fat and the other no lean.' Like his son after him, Augustus was never at a loss for a whimsical or irreverent comment.

Sophia's book is written by someone who is in effect a 'convert' to spiritualism.[8] This is not to say that she had disavowed Christianity. Many spiritualists found no difficulty in reconciling their basic Christian beliefs, with spiritualism, and even with recent scientific discoveries. What disturb a late twentieth-century reader are some of the statements in *From Matter to Spirit* if, as we are to understand, these are written by an educated and highly intelligent woman of the time. For instance, Sophia's blind acceptance of the value of phrenology,[9] or statements such as: 'When our pulmonary breathing and spiritual breathing are brought into harmony of action, or polarised together, we should all be receptive as a natural condition of everyday life, of the streams of influx from higher beings.'[10] Delusions and illusions experienced by the dying are explained as spiritual experiences, when one suspects they resulted from heavy doses of laudanum (a good example is the death of the second, wicked, wife in *The Old Man's Youth*).[11]

Sophia's book is exactly as it is subtitled, *A Guide to Enquirers*, and covers all the important aspects of spirit manifestations: table-turning and rapping, automatic writing, mediumship, etc. Considerable space is devoted to what she called 'Correspondence and Development' and her beliefs on these topics clearly derive from Swedenborg's teachings. She writes: 'The very clear explanation of Correspondence given by

Swedenborg has not received the attention it deserves, partly because from the *positiveness* and *great copiousness* of his style, and partly from the difficulty found in apprehending the reality of the doctrine by those who have had no conscious experience of spirit life.'[12]

One has considerable sympathy with anyone trying to come to grips with the turgid mass of Swedenborg's writing without 'the conscious experience of spirit life'. It is better to turn to Chapter 1, The Society of Swedenborg, in Conan Doyle's *History of Spiritualism* (published by Cassell in 1926) where he gives a clear and concise account of the extraordinary Swedish mystic.

How far did William De Morgan believe in the movement and in the book his mother wrote on the subject? It is impossible to tell from the few remarks that have survived, and although there are prominent supernatural elements in his novels this does not prove that he either supported or disbelieved in spiritualism. It is fair to assume that William, from what one knows of his character, and taking into account the great respect he had for his father's opinions, would have remained ambivalent. Nevertheless, he and Evelyn did over a long period (probably around the turn of the century) investigate automatic writing, and produced a book which was published in 1909 called *The Results Of An Experiment*.[13]

To us, nearly ninety years later, this work seems very curious. The 'editor' explains that the two people involved have found that other experiments in the supernatural and seances which they had witnessed have been unsatisfactory and the 'bulk of results were due to imposture'. So M and N, as they are archly referred to throughout the book, decide to see if they can get better results from automatic writing. The experiments are conducted over many years, for a short time each evening. For the uninitiated the method is explained:

One person holds a pencil as though writing, and the second places his or her hand on the wrist of the writing hand of the first. The point of the pencil of course rests on a blank sheet of paper. Under these circumstances the hands usually move after a while, each operator believing in most cases that his or her hand is being pushed by the other. If the experiment is persevered in, writing not infrequently results.

As the 'editor' explains, the communications which M and N receive are in three groups: the 'book-letters' from personal friends; those purporting to come from 'angels'; and, thirdly, letters from spirits, brought by the 'angels' to tell their stories, and illustrate the angels' teachings. The spirits are not all good ones, and quite often very unpleasant; in fact, devils.

A number of the exhortations, particularly from the angels, predictably, urge the couple to lead a more spiritual life. M is criticized for a lack of patience which spoils 'receptivity', but N does better and is told that she is growing more 'mystic every day'. The sex of M and N is specified and it sounds, from what the angels say, as if William was not quite so convinced as Evelyn. Some of the messages are more practical: 'You are not to put your strength into foolish dinner parties;' and there is even a naughty one from a famous painter: 'I am Monsieur Watteau, a French Artist. I painted far better than your friend and deserved my reputation. I am quite in the dark, and am not rewarded for my life of trial . . . Poor fools, why not eat, drink, and be merry.' An unpleasant spirit tells them that they are not going to live long, but they are reassured by an angel: 'The spirit who wrote is not highly developed. Much is hidden from her sight; you will not die until your work is done.'

Names of people known to the two recipients of the letters have been altered so that we cannot know who 'Mary' was who wrote: 'I poisoned my husband.' However, there is a curious letter from Professor Sidgwick of Cambridge, dated 7 August 1893,[14] in answer to a letter from De Morgan. Sidgwick, a leading light in the Society For Psychical Research and one of the society's first presidents, was asked if he thought it advisable to ask for an exhumation order on the grounds that a medium had been told that someone had been poisoned with arsenic. *The Results Of An Experiment* was published in 1909 and the professor's letter is sixteen years earlier, but we are told that the experiments in automatic writing were carried out over many years, so it is possible that Mary's poor husband was indeed poisoned! Sidgwick's reply was eminently sensible and cautious. He did not think that De Morgan's idea was feasible; it was doubtful whether the grave and coffin would be identifiable and they would probably be made to look ridiculous. Nothing was done.

It is difficult to date most of these automatic letters, but there are references in some of them to such events as the death of Queen Victoria and the Boer War. Many of the beliefs and Swedenborg's teachings expressed in this book have been shown[15] to have influenced Evelyn's painting, but it is difficult to trace any similar effect on William's novels.

There is no doubt about Sophia's intense interest and belief in spiritualism, but it is refreshing, despite her rather humourless character, to find that she did not seem to take offence at William's irreverent reaction to some of her experiences. For example,[16] Sophia returning from a walk saying: 'I have been in Battersea Park and had a terrible shock – I came face to face with William's Wraith!' 'Just one more of Ma's bogies,' was William's comment. His sister Mary, credited with extraordinary powers of fortune-telling, was also sceptical. A discussion about spiritualism was taking place in a room full of earnest believers who were telling of their personal experiences when she decided to throw a large amount of cold water on the conversation:

> I was at a seance recently and there were seven people present. Each of them had recently lost a relation, and they had come to communicate with the deceased. There was materialisation, and each of the seven persons at once recognised it to be the relation he or she had lost. They all began to quarrel when everyone else claimed it, and in the end became violently abusive. I saw in it only the medium dressed up!

Despite Mary's scepticism, Mrs Stirling gives some striking examples of her alleged powers. Laura Hertford – the artist who had objected to William's kiln at 40 Fitzroy Square in the 1870s – gave a small party there which included Mary, her sister Annie, and William. A Mr Sidgwick, who had never met Mary before, had his hand read and was taken aback when she told him that he ought not to be there, and that he had very nearly died recently, which was apparently quite true. Again, on another occasion Mary read the hand of a house surgeon from University College Hospital, and stopped in mid stream, and could not be persuaded to continue. When he left she foretold that his fiancée would die in a boating accident at sea, something he would witness from shore and that he, too, would die from drowning – both events went on to happen as foretold. These stories, which are necessarily second or even third hand, do not prove anything about

palmistry or clairvoyance but do point to the De Morgan family's fascination with such subjects – although as we have seen the younger generation,
Mary and William, did not treat these topics with the profound seriousness
of their mother.

Sophia published two other books, both mentioned earlier: one a
memoir[17] of Augustus, and the other a book of reminiscences.[18] Both were
informative and clearly written. In her reminiscences there is almost no
mention of her family but this may very well be due to the painful tragedy
of the early deaths of most of her children. Much space is given to her
various activities in the social reform field and to the very large number of
distinguished people she had met during her long life. Some she became
acquainted with through her father William Frend, others through friends
such as Lady Byron,[19] who was involved with Sophia in prison reform,
women's education, and women's suffrage. Sophia's life of Augustus is
mainly an account of his professional activities as a Professor of
Mathematics. She tells in detail of the two occasions when Augustus
resigned on matters of principle. As we have seen, he went back to the
college on the first occasion, having won his case, but not on the second
when his career came to a premature end. It seems, from Sophia's account,
as if he were entirely in the right but it was nevertheless a sad end to a brilliant academic career.

Mary was the only other member of the younger generation to write and
have works published. She wrote three children's books. The first was entitled On A Pincushion and was published in 1876, with illustrations by her
brother; the second The Necklace Of Princess Fiorimonde (1886) had pictures
by Walter Crane; her last story for children, The Windfairies, illustrated by
Olive Cockerell, came out in 1900 and was dedicated to Burne-Jones's
three grandchildren, Angela, Dennis and Clare Mackail. For the most part
they are fairy stories of kings and queens, princesses and wicked witches,
readable, and embellished with excellent if traditional illustrations.

More interesting than these children's stories, charming though they are,
is Mary's one adult novel, called A Choice Of Chance – a title suggested by
William and, it must be admitted, not a great selling one. T. Fisher Unwin
published it under the pen-name of William Dodson in 1887 and there is
no record that it enjoyed much success with the reading public or review-
ers. It is a very melodramatic story. Audrey Dalrymple, bought up as a

wealthy young lady with wealthy parents, lives with her father and, later, her mother who dies quite young. She finds out fairly soon after her supposed mother's death that a rough gypsy-like character she had met as a very young girl was in fact her mother. This lady had earlier been wronged by a very respectable man, whom Audrey knew as her uncle. She also discovered she had a half-brother, Ruben, who was very much from the lower classes. There are the usual elements in a melodrama of this sort – a murder, for instance. Ruben is accused of this crime, tried and condemned, but at the eleventh hour a half-crazy boy called Nat confesses on his deathbed to having committed the deed. Audrey herself sobs her way through all these various tribulations and ends up inevitably marrying a nice boy of impeccable lineage who is none the less undeterred by Audrey's dubious parentage. It must be admitted that Mary's novel does not stand comparison with her brother's. The characters are cardboard, and the heroine with her quite extraordinary *naïveté* and her ability to burst into tears at the slighest excuse does not engage the reader's sympathy. There is no tension during the 470 pages of the two-volume novel. Much of the story is set in grand houses in London or the country, but it does come to life when Audrey persuades a friend, Clara, who does social work in the slums of London's East End, to take her there to see if they can trace some people who were kind to Audrey's mother and her brother when he was little. Mary knew about slums, and Clara, who has no illusions about the East End, sounds rather like the author – brusque, direct, and understandably irritated by the swooning Audrey, whose only idea of helping the poor is to dole out money which, as Clara points out, will be spent on booze at the first opportunity. It is an earnest, romantic run-of-the-mill novel with none of William's lightness of touch or humour and one is not surprised that the experiment was not repeated, or if it was that she found no other publisher.

Of course all these family activities – literary and otherwise – do not explain how William De Morgan, after thirty-five years as a ceramic artist, turned himself so suddenly into a best-selling novelist. But it was a family in which writing was practised, and members of it regularly managed to get books published. More important, I am sure, De Morgan remembered his father remarking years before that his son might be able to succeed as a writer. In any case, novel-writing was what he turned to when the pottery eventually ran out of money for the last time, and he was no longer able to pay the workmen. He recalled later on in his life that in 1901 he had written two chapters of a novel:

> Just to see what I could do. I always loved grubby little boys, and I thought I would like to write a story of a grubby little boy. I began and got interested in him. But when I had read over what I had written, I was so little impressed with the result that I nearly burnt it: in any case I put it away in a drawer and forgot all about it. Later in the year, when we were going out to Florence, it accidentally came with us amongst a great mass of business paper.[20]

When these pages were cast aside by William to be burned, keen-eyed Evelyn noticed the manuscript and kept it. William had retired to bed in Florence, suffering at the turn his business life had taken, from depression rather than from influenza. Evelyn suggested he might like to continue his story and gave him a pencil but no paper. The book therefore was continued in a washing-book and some scrap paper which happened to be handy. But he wrote, as he said later, only for entertainment and occupation, and, at that stage, with no thought of publication.

Chapter 8

Publication and unexpected success of *Joseph Vance*.

DE MORGAN'S NOVELS, when anybody in the last fifty years has bothered to remember them, have had a very bad press, while (particularly since the Second World War) his pottery has increasingly attracted admiring atten-tion. Consider, for example, a very typically dismissive paragraph by Sarah Howell in her article *The World of Interiors* (March, 1989) in a notice of the De Morgan exhibition at the Victoria & Albert Museum:

> Like poor Edward Lear still better known for his limericks than for his landscapes, William de Morgan used to be famous for a minor talent. At the age of sixty-eight he retired to Florence for his health and became a best-selling writer. The Edwardians loved his now unreadable novels which for some time eclipsed the fame of his orig-inal pots and tiles.

On his part, the more sympathetic Jon Catleugh comments[1] that De Morgan's novels reflect his father's passion for Dickens and today make very heavy reading. William Gaunt and Clayton-Stamm confuse De Morgan's first and last novels[2] and Bevis Hillier (in the *Daily Express* of 24 April 1982) perpetuates the mistake. The one outstanding contrary opinion is that of Sir William Haley in *The Times Literary Supplement* of 9 July 1954, on the occasion of the then most recent reprint of one of the novels, *Joseph Vance*, by the Oxford University Press in World's Classics. Haley, a man of wide cultivation (known best as Director General of the BBC), had obviously read all the nine novels, and had enjoyed them. Of De Morgan's writing generally, Haley observes:

> It is a squalid, splendid, hopeful, scuffling, unrancorous world. It is the world before Marx, or Spengler, or Freud. It is a world in which good and bad are seen for what they are. De Morgan had nothing to offer to either the lower culture or the higher criticism. He was, as we have seen before, a naively simple man by modern literary standards, an early primitive, his only vision was human nature as he saw it: his only aim to give enjoyment.

De Morgan's own vivid phrase to describe his novels was 'early Victorian and suburban'. Following his lead, some commentators have taken for granted that all the books are set in the mid-nineteenth century. It is not quite accurate. There is one historical novel of the seventeenth century, one partly set in Renaissance Italy, and some novels set nearer to 1900 than to 1850. Not all settings are suburban by any means; equally important are grand country houses and sordid metropolitan slums.

De Morgan's first five novels were published by William Heinemann in successive years from 1906 to 1909: *Joseph Vance* 1906, *Alice-For-Short* 1907, *Somehow Good* 1908, *It Can Never Happen Again* 1909, and finally a shorter one and the only true historical novel, *An Affair of Dishonour*, 1909. The odd *A Likely Story* followed in 1911, and the last completed novel, *When Ghost Meets Ghost*, 1914, reverts to the classic De Morgan type. At the time of his death in 1917 he left two unfinished novels which Evelyn completed, *The Old Madhouse* (published 1917) and *The Old Man's Youth* (1921), both appearing posthumously.

The first book, *Joseph Vance*, did not find a publisher immediately. A friend of the De Morgans, Walter Shaw Sparrow, undertook as they were in Italy to approach publishers with the typed, but very long narrative. Shaw Sparrow was helped by Mrs Maisie Dawson who owned the typing firm. Hodder & Stoughton read the typescript first and rejected it, saying not only was it far too long, but even if the poor author were to cut it by half, it would still be unpublishable. Shaw Sparrow, explaining the grounds for rejection to De Morgan, softened the blow by saying:[3]

> the first three chapters caused 'the reader' to believe that the book was a find, and he still thinks that Mr. De Morgan will hit the mark throughout a humorous, Barry-Paine-like[4] book, having a story. The humorous books now passing out of vogue have no story. Messrs H & S would welcome a love story written with humour. The present book, they tell me, is much too long and too much in the round-about style fashionable in Thackeray's time.

Understandably deterred by this rejection De Morgan put the typescript aside and started on another novel which became *Alice-For-Short*. Luckily for him, Mrs Dowson sent the bulky typescript of *Joseph Vance* to the publishers Lawrence & Bullen, but again De Morgan, when he heard nothing immediately, gave up hope.

The time had come for them to return to London and he, as usual, returned to England by sea; Mrs Stirling tells us that William spent much of the voyage on the deck playing chess with a Chinese gentleman who could speak no English, and of course William no Chinese. The usual problems on return to England faced them in the shape of no servants, and when they did eventually find a cook she turned out to be a drunkard. William wrote to their friend Mrs Dowson: 'I have been longing to ask you to talk about things, but our Household has bolted or drinks; and this blessed day I have been making the beds and answering the bell, and emptying the slops – Lord have mercy upon us miserable sinners!' Evelyn's view on the lack of help[5] was pungent: 'We have been back a weary month, nothing but drunken cooks tumbling about like nine pins, no studies, no work, no peace, stodgy British incapacity at every turn, soaked in beer.' They did find another cook, who was satisfactory until she too returned home one evening incapably drunk. How they must have regretted the easy and comfortable life of Florence. However, on 5 July a letter came from Lawrence, the publisher, which made all well:

Dear Sir,

I have very nearly finished *Joe Vance*. The book is too long, and yet I wish it were twice the length.

If I had plenty of money I would publish it without hesitation, so pray do not let it ever be said that the book passed through my hands and I refused it.

It must be published by one of the great firms who can afford to advertise it properly for it understanding. After the Marie Corellis and Hall Caines it is like a breath of pure sea air. Whether, the publishers are so soaked with bad English and melodramatic twaddle that they will refuse *Joe* I cannot say, but if they don't fall in love with the doctor and Lossie and forgive Joe for all his faults then they must be either fools or knaves, or both. I should very much like to have a talk with you about the whole matter . . .[6]

De Morgan and Mr Lawrence met and Lawrence duly took the huge type-script to William Heinemann in his Bedford Street office and told the formidable publisher that he must read it. After an initial reluctance he did so, evidently liked what he read, undertook to publish the book in England, and arranged for its publication in the United States by Henry Holt. This all happened before the De Morgans' return to Florence in October 1905. The original typescript ran to 500,000 words, as John St John tells us in his history of the firm of Heinemann,[7] and although the author agreed to cut some 20–30,000 words it remained a long novel at 528 pages. The cuts were painful to De Morgan; he particularly regretted the removal of the love affairs of the snobbish and ambitious Vi, Lossie's sister. Mrs Stirling quotes good examples[8] of the author's attention to narrative detail. He worried about such things: 'I am especially anxious about improbability; authors do make such frightful blunders! There ought to be a profession of literary men's blunders, censors, who could be paid by them at so much a blunder detected.' He was saved from one such minor blunder by Mrs Mackail, Burne-Jones's daughter, who had read the manuscript. She went to see him to tell him: 'You have said that the butcher left the dripping at the door, and you see butchers don't leave dripping at doors!' Not perhaps a world-shaking literary mistake, but worthy of correction.

Joseph Vance (modestly subtitled *An Ill-written Autobiography*) was dedicated to Horatio Lucas – the friend and tenant in Fitzroy Square who had encouraged the young De Morgan to try his hand at the making of stained glass and praised his first tile.[8] There are two main themes to the story, the rise and fall of Joe's father, Christopher, and the lifelong love of Joe for Lossie Thorpe. Christopher Vance, Joe's father, is by general agreement the author's most successful comic figure and outstanding even when set against other similar characters in late Victorian and Edwardian fiction. The novel starts with promising briskness:

> My Father and Mother never could come to a clear understanding about what had disagreed with my Father the day he lost his situation at Fothergill's.
>
> My Father thought it was the sausage and mashed potatoes he had for lunch at the Rose & Crown, at fourpence, and as much mustard and pepper as you liked. My Mother thought it was the beer.
>
> There was something to be said for my Mother's view on the score of quantity.
>
> 'Everything', she said 'I bring to figures, and my aunt Elizabeth Hannah taught me to it'. And sure enough figures did show that my Father, who had a shilling and three pence in his pocket when he left home at six thirty in the morning, must have spent eightpence on beer or lost some of it, – Because if we allow a penny for the 'bus and two pence for a 'arf an ounce of barker which he bought (I do not like to give you the exact words) at a tobacconists with a haemorrhage on his way home, there's the price of two quarts of ale left, put it how you may, – 'And your father always had a weak head', said my Mother in after years, in the many times over she told the story.
>
> Anyhow something must have disagreed with him or he wouldn't have called Mr. Wotherspoon, the head clerk at Fothergill's, an old herring gut when he told him to put his trolley somewhere else, and not leave it in the orfice door.

After dinner on the Saturday following, Christopher having been sacked, Joe goes for a walk with his father, mainly to prevent him from having more than a pint at the Roebuck. Dad goes into another pub with seven year old Joe and explains that as it isn't the Roebuck he can drink as much as he likes. He quarrels with a sweep, a well-known brawler called Gun, who wins all his fights by butting his opponent in the stomach. Poor Christopher is laid out and taken to hospital. Meanwhile, Joe, a frightened onlooker, sees Gun being taken away by the police and throws a glass bottle at him which blinds him in one eye – Joe is not caught.

Christopher is not dead, as Joe fears, but is of course out of work when he leaves hospital. A true original, he sets up as a builder, explaining that a builder doesn't have to know anything practical about plumbing, carpentry and so on: all he has to do is employ people who do. His first client, having seen his noticeboard outside the house, is Dr Thorpe – later to become a major character in the book – who has three children, including the beautiful Lossie with whom Joe immediately falls in love. There is another daughter, Vi, whose story the author had to cut considerably, and there is a son, Joey. Joey is a little younger than Joe, and a thoroughly bad lot. Eventually he will land Joe Vance in trouble.

De Morgan quite often in his stories invents characters of both sexes who are born into poor, even slum backgrounds but succeed in bettering themselves, generally with the help of a middle-class patron (Alice in his second novel is typical). In Joe's case, it is the good Dr Thorpe who notices that the little boy has a most unusual aptitude for geometry and arranges for him to go to a private school. Unpleasant though the school is, with a sadistic headmaster and a lot of bullying, Joe does well, goes to Oxford, and eventually becomes a successful engineer. The gradual emergence of his talent bears, as has been said, a close resemblance to Augustus De Morgan's experience as a little boy.[9] Joe's adoration of the doctor's daughter Lossie lasts until he is at Oxford and it is a traumatic experience for him when Lossie gets married to a gallant soldier.

Christopher Vance makes a lot of money in his building business, but drink, in the form of whisky, is his downfall. His factory is burned down and it is discovered that in a drunken moment he has neglected to pay the insurance premium. Poor Joe partially recovers from his hopeless adoration for the beautiful Lossie and gets married to Janie, a rather pallid, hazel-eyed girl with much good sense. They are very happy but on a sea journey to the Mediterranean for a holiday they are shipwrecked and Janie is drowned. Joe in despair gets Lossie's brother Beppino (i.e. Joey) out of a scrape but as a result of Beppino's duplicity is falsely believed by Lossie to be guilty of

Three brothers, Edward, William and George (top).
Sophia Elizabeth De Morgan in old age, 1886 (left).
Augustus De Morgan (right).

Portrait of William De Morgan, 1886.

Portrait of William De Morgan by Evelyn in coloured chalks, 1907.

Photograph of William Morris and Edward
Burne-Jones, shows them in the garden of
The Grange, Fulham, Burne-Jones' home.

William and Evelyn sitting back to back.

The Vale, Chelsea, where De Morgan lived till 1910 when it was pulled down.

William and Evelyn leaving Italy for the last time. Taken in Venice in 1914.

Evelyn De Morgan.

appalling behaviour. Off Joe goes as an engineer and consultant to South America, and it is only many years later on his return to England that Lossie, now a widow, her husband having been killed in India, learns the truth about her brother's treachery. Old Christopher has died, Beppino has met a timely end (on his honeymoon), and to the reader's relief, Lossie and Joe are reunited, older and wiser.

Joseph Vance is a typical De Morgan story, what Henry James called a 'great baggy monster', a rambling account of two families, one comfortable suburban, middle class, living in Poplar Villa in Hampstead and the other the Vance family, rising above their labouring background through the extraordinary talents of old Christopher Vance, a humorous and cunning man, who can barely read or write. A devoted family man he is shattered by the early death of Joe's mother and loved by his only son. Not for the last time in De Morgan's novels the evils of drink are underlined, Christopher never really gives up the bottle despite the best efforts of his family and friends.

Janie, Joe's wife, was De Morgan's favourite heroine, but Lossie Thorpe is a much more interesting creation. We meet her first when Joe and his father arrived at the Thorpe house to have a look at the drains:

A good many things then occurred outside the range of my experience. It transpired that the Master was in his study and musn't be worried; but that a lady whose name I didn't catch would attend shortly
to give directions. This was confirmed by a real young lady (I had
never seen one at home before) who said from the end of a passage that
Aunt would come in a minute. I wondered whether all the young
ladies at home were beings as glorious and enthralling as this one, and
thought how jolly it must be if they were. She seemed about fifteen,
and had her apron or skirt full of apples or pears. I found after that
they were early pears, and they were being stewed. I have since smelt
stewing pears and the smell always brings back this young lady
passing through a streak of morning sun that got in at the edge of the
yellow blind behind her. If I had been older I should have fallen
desperately in love but I was too young to know how to do that; so I
did the nearest approach to it that I was capable of, which consisted
mainly of substituting the expectation of her next appearance for

every other possible anticipation in life. I forgot discomfort about the imperfections of pumps. My feeling was one of thirst for a second dose of a girl standing in a sunglint at the end of a passage, mixed with self congratulation at having found anything so jolly to tell Mother about.[10]

Lossie is beautiful, kind, rather spoiled and wholly unconscious of the effect the news of her marriage has on Joe. She is also far too quick to accept Joe's guilt over the Beppino affair even though everyone else in the narrative knows Beppino is an unscrupulous womanizer, and when it suits him a liar and a cheat, and an appalling, pretentious would-be poet. Joe's admiration for Lossie is understandable but she herself is less convincing than some other De Morgan heroines.

The supernatural is not so prominent in *Joseph Vance* as in some of the other novels but there is a good deal of serious discussion of the possibility of life after death between Dr Thorpe, his great friend Professor Absalom, and Joe. The author himself said that the amalgam of the characters of the doctor and the professor was close to the character of his father Augustus, and one might well suppose that the opinions expressed in Chapter Forty must have been very like those of Augustus De Morgan. They certainly do not conflict with what Augustus wrote in his preface to his wife's book. The elder De Morgan's views on spiritualism seem to be reflected in a long evening's discussion after dinner one night in Poplar Villa between Joe, Janie, Thorpe, and Absalom:[11]

I expressed just now my mistrust of what is called Spiritualism [says Thorpe] – (very absurdly, as it deprives us of a word the reverse of materialism. I want the word Spiritualist to describe myself, and can't use it because of Mrs. Guppy and the Davenport brothers). But I'm going to say a good word even for this sort of thing. I owe it a trifle for a message said to come from Voltaire's ghost. It was asked 'are you not now convinced of another world?' and rapped out 'there *is* no other world – Death is only an incident in life'. He was a suggestive ghost at any rate . . .

Well, before then I shall have to disclaim any idea of settling the question of the Origin of Evil. That remains exactly what it was to me before, a question not needing discussion until the Balance Sheet of the Universe is audited. As soon as we know the total evil and total good we may think this question, which seems to us now so important, a metaphysical curiosity. For the logical puzzle remains the same, even if we suppose our Universe to be only one among millions, and the only evil in the whole one isolated stomach ache. The owner of the stomach will be just as unable to see why an All-wise and All-powerful God created his ache as we are why great fleas should have little fleas upon their backs to bite 'em, and little fleas have lesser fleas and so ad infinitum.[12]

The 'great fleas' remark is, of course, a direct echo from Augustus. And finally: "'The end of life', said the doctor, "is beyond its powers of knowledge. Death is a change that occurs at its beginnings. The highest good is the growth of the Soul, and the greatest man is he who rejoices most in great fulfilment of the will of God.'"

Plots were not De Morgan's strong point as a novelist. It seems evident he did not know how his stories were going to develop when he started his books. He let his characters dictate what happened to them and to the plot. As is so often the case this can turn out to be a successful way to write a novel, and on the whole it succeeded in *Joseph Vance*. The reason one wants to go on reading the novel is not because one admires the careful working out of the story, but because the characters — at least the more important ones — hold one's attention. De Morgan is also very skilful in constructing vivid backgrounds. Poplar Villa and the tiny workman's cottages where Joe is brought up are equally convincing. Characterization is all-important in a De Morgan novel, and in Christopher Vance the author has invented a truly comic and tragic figure. With him we have the first example of De Morgan's uncanny gift for cockney dialogue. One remembers that the Pre-Raphaelites and De Morgan,[13] had the odd habit of writing letters to each other in a strange cockney idiom, particularly De Morgan and Burne-Jones, and to contemporary eyes it might look like the middle classes showing how patronizing they could be to the working-classes. It would be unjust to level this criticism against the use of the vernacular in De Morgan's novels. This dialogue is free of any hint of condescension, and he is equally successful in his treatment of the pretentious upper classes of society.

There is a danger in a novel like *Joseph Vance*: when you have one character who is by far the most convincing in the story, to kill him off before
the end of the book with over 150 pages to go[14] may result in the reader
feeling let down. Surviving characters are a little shadowy in comparison.
The other problem De Morgan had in *Joseph Vance* was how to make sure,
unless the book was going to end on a very sad note, that Lossie and Joe
could get together in amity if not in wedlock. The answer, of course, was
first to kill off Lossie's husband, General Duprez, in India, and then to lose
Janie in the shipwreck off the coast of Portugal. Finally, even though Joe
disappears to South America for twenty long years, it is essential that
Lossie, through the chance discovery of a missing letter,[15] should realize
how mistaken and at fault she has been in jumping to the conclusion that
Joe has deceived her over the Beppino affair. It was bad luck that the general
died, because Joe had taken him into his confidence and these two upright
men had, with an excess of delicacy, decided to keep from Lossie the full
extent of the dead Beppino's perfidy. Otherwise no doubt Hugh Duprez
could have avoided such unjust behaviour on the part of his wife.

There has been a tendency to dismiss De Morgan's novels as sub-
standard Dickens,[16] implying that most of them are filled with nostalgia for
mid nineteenth century England, particularly London. This I suspect is an
easy generalization made by people who have not actually read them. Some
of the stories as has been said are set firmly in and about 1900 and they are
not as we will see too difficult to date. *Joseph Vance* starts with Joe aged seven
in the mid century, but it follows his fortunes through school-days, university, working life, marriage, and widowhood, with twenty years away
from England in the Americas, so quite a lot of the action must logically
take place in the late nineteenth century.

De Morgan was defensive[17] about his use of coincidence in the development of his plots: his attitude was much like Dickens's, answering the same
objection – namely that there is plenty of coincidence in real life, so why not
in fiction. Although it does not play a large part in *Joseph Vance*, it certainly
does in some other works, notably in *Somehow Good* where the entire plot
depends on a chance meeting in the 'tuppenny tube'. Highly unlikely; but
most readers, by Chapter Two, are sufficiently charmed by the author's
storytelling skills to accept the improbability.

Even while he was correcting proofs of his first novel, the author was hard at work on other stories. Writing to Jack Mackail to congratulate him on his appointment as Professor of Poetry at Oxford University, he says:[18]

> Mary, as you know is in Egypt. Accounts of her read well and are, I hope, authentic. Probably she will be back before I can send *Joseph* out to her – as he takes so long in publishing. Why, here have I actually completed *two* more stories and the proofs of *Joe* only half corrected! I discovered frightful blunders in him – but there! What does it matter? As far as I can make out, modern fiction consists almost entirely of solecisms!

Heinemann was not initially optimistic about the chances of this long first novel. Gladstone's daughter Mrs Drew saw an early copy and wrote[19] to the publishers to say perversely how remarkable it was but that she hoped that the print would be better in the second edition because she could 'recommend no friend over forty to read it'. In reply Heinemann said: 'I'm glad to you like the novel, but with regard to the print, it is very unlikely that a second edition will be called for.' The reception given to this novel certainly surprised both author and publisher. *The Spectator*[20] led with a very complimentary review comparing *Joseph Vance* with the work of Dickens, Thackeray and George Eliot, and then after these heady compliments:

> It is refreshing to find that one stalwart champion of the older school survives. Mr. William De Morgan follows, even in its lesser mannerisms, the method of Dickens and Thackeray. Slowly and patiently he builds up, not an incident or career, or even the whole career of one man, or woman, but the whole careers of a large circle of friends. He gives a true and complete picture of certain forms of life . . . but we have never for a moment a doubt about the reality of the story he tells . . . the book is a remarkable novel – a fine novel but by whatever standard we judge it . . . every character down to the humblest has the stamp of a genuine humanity.

The reception in America, where the book was published by Holt, was equally good. An influential academic, Lionel Phelps a professor of English at Yale University, wrote:[21]

To a highly nervous and irritably impatient reading public, a man whose name had no commercial value in literature, gravely offered in the year of grace 1906 an 'ill written autobiography' of two hundred and eighty thousand words! Well, the result is what might *not* have been expected. If ever a confirmed optimist had reason to feel justification of his faith Mr. De Morgan must have seen it in the reception given to his first novel . . . *Joseph Vance* is not so much a beautifully written or exquisitely constructed novel as it is an encyclopaedia of life. We meet real people, we hear delightful conversation, and the tremendously interesting personality of the author is everywhere apparent . . . It vibrates with the echoes of a long gallery crowded with pictures.

Reaction from friends was equally pleasing: Jane Morris:[22]

Dear Bill —
I don't think I've ever written you a letter before, but this is such a very grand occasion that I feel I must put pen to paper, and say how happy your book has made me. I have not laughed so much for many a long year. Lossie is delightful, I had to stop reading when she'd gone to India; but started afresh when I realised that there was more of Mr. Vance to come. What a dear he is! — I can't write half what is in my mind to say in praise of the book, letter writing being a lost art with me now.
    May you give us many more books is my earnest wish.
Yours, affectionately,
JANE MORRIS.

Professor Mackail wrote:[23]

CHER ET GRAND MAITRE, — have you read the flaming advertisement of Joseph that Heinemann is putting out? I have just had the exquisite joy of reading it, in huge letters on half a column of the Athenaeum. In case of any awkwardness with Them Above I think you ought to go at once and drop off one of your best tiles into the Arno (the Mugnone would no doubt be handier, but there would be

a greater risk of its being fished out and returned to you like the ring
of Polycrates). Read and blush –

JOSEPH VANCE

Universally proclaimed

The greatest novel of

The day.

I think it was mean of him to drop his voice on the last word. *Age*
would have rounded it off better and been less trouble to the printers
to set up.

Some day I hope to see a list showing the sums paid to authors for
works of fiction somewhat as follows (the first two items are real
facts):

	£	s	
Mrs. Humphry Ward.........	12,000	0	0
Winston Churchill............	8,000	0	0
J.W. Mackail	5	6	8
W. De Morgan	25,000	0	0

One of his oldest friends, Ralph, Earl of Lovelace, whom he first knew
when they were children together, wrote:[24]

> *July 1906,*
> *Ockham Park, Ripley, Surrey*
>
> My dear De Morgan – your interesting and delightful book arrived
> last week just as I was starting for London whence I returned to the
> midst of a party here which has only left this morning, so somewhow
> I never found a moment to write even a line of thanks together with
> much appreciation of the three or four opening chapters which I read
> at breakfast the morning Joey Vance came here.
>
> My first impression was like that from *Treasure Island* or *Man Of
> Mark*, a somewhat startled amusement at the outrageous company of
> the fighting circles you introduce one to – not unmixed with sympa-
> thy for the throwing of the bottle which drops so miraculously into
> the horrible sweep's eye. It made me think of the Irish account of a
> scrimmage, 'I dropped my stick on Pym's head and unfortunately he
> dies'.

I shall now be able to continue to improve my acquaintance with the charming Miss Lossie and talk to you about her and your other creations by the time you and Mrs. De Morgan come here.

It is sad to learn that very shortly after the earl wrote his letter he died, but he none the less had told De Morgan that he had read the whole book. One of the most unexpected letters was from an American called Joseph Vance,[25] also an author, and this led to a lengthy correspondence and eventually a meeting in Europe. Even with all this sudden success he did not forget to send an early copy to Mrs Maisie Dowson who had been so helpful in organizing the typing and placing of the book.

There is an excellent essay by Julia Cartwright[26] which has a good piece about De Morgan at this time. She wrote:

It was at this interesting moment in De Morgan's career, in the summer of 1906, that I had the good fortune to meet him at a country house, where he was staying with one of his oldest friends. We had often met before, generally at Burne-Jones's house, and then when I sat by his side at dinner we recalled those happy times and sighed for the days and friends that were no more . . . towards the end of dinner he dropped his voice and whispered he had a secret to tell me 'the fact is' he said 'I have perpetrated a crime or a folly – whichever you choose to call it by – writing a novel, which just been published, and what is more wonderful is that I have in my pocket a flattering review of the book from today's Spectator!'. He went on to tell me how the story of *Joseph Vance* had grown into being: how, when he was ill and away in Florence, a rheumatic hand disabled him from drawing so he took to scribbling instead and began to jot down ideas that came into his head on scraps of paper; how his wife encouraged him to go on with the story; and how he became interested first of all in the character of Christopher Vance, a drunken old builder, and then in that of his heroine, 'Lossie', until the actual writing became a pleasure and the book took its present shape. The speaker's earnestness and animation I remember excited Lord Carlisle's curiosity and after dinner he asked me if what he had caught of our conversation could be true and De Morgan had really written a novel. There was no denying the fact, and soon we were all reading *Joseph Vance* and the friendly review which had given the author so much satisfaction.

The 1908 edition of the work records in the prelims that subsequent to the first edition published in 1906, there were reprints in September of that year; May, August and November (twice) 1907; and March, May and November 1908. From the first, the success of the book was phenomenal, and the girls from the office where the manuscript was typed became so much absorbed in the story that they forgot to go on with their work. The critics were unanimous in their chorus of praise, despite the unusual length of the book, which at first seemed likely to prove a stumbling-block. Mr Punch pronounced *Joseph Vance* to be quite the best novel he had read for a long time and the public on both sides of the Atlantic hailed the advent of a new star on the literary horizon.

Joseph Vance was probably the most successful of all De Morgan's novels. Not necessarily the best, but certainly the longest lived. A bestseller by any standards, although there are, sadly, very few records from the Heinemann archives as to sales figures or earnings over the years. Together with two other De Morgan novels[27] it was reprinted in 1919 in the cheap Nelson Classics and also in 1954 by Oxford University Press in the World's Classics. Surprisingly it was also adapted by the BBC and broadcast as a serial on radio in 1969.[28]

For the first time in their married lives Evelyn and William could stop worrying about money, but the sudden success of this new career does not seem to have changed them or their way of life. Until 1914 they made their annual migration to Italy and Evelyn continued to paint, although she hardly made any effort to sell her paintings, and William continued to produce a formidable number of words each year.

Chapter 9

Publication of second novel, *Alice-For-Short* – Sands End
factory closed but manufacture continued by some of the
designers.

DE MORGAN ENCOUNTERED no trouble in finding a publisher for his
second novel *Alice-For-Short*. Heinemann published it in England in June
1907 and Holt in America in the same year. William Heinemann had a
remarkably successful novelist on his hands judging by the reception, both
critical and commercial, of *Joseph Vance*. Nor was there any falling-off in
the second novel, either in respect of the author's story-telling powers or his
ability to create memorable characters. His skills are well described in the
Bookman of 1910 in respect of his first two works:

> He cannot even see a shivering old crone serving out a ha'p'orth of
> baked chestnuts over her charcoal fire without reflecting that those
> skinny claw-like hands were once the beautiful hands of a young girl;
> he is never content to sketch the least significant of his characters in
> outline only, he must needs give you the whole man and the whole
> woman by deliberately linking up their todays with their yesterdays,
> so that you know their dispositions, the environments that shaped
> them, the motives that actuate them, and will guess how they will
> behave in a given crisis before the crisis is upon them.

His mood at this period of his life was a mixture of sadness at the collapse of his pottery and surprise at the unexpected turn of his writing career.

In a letter in 1907,[1] the year *Alice* was published, De Morgan wrote to Lady Burne-Jones:

It is so strange to sit here in Florence to look out at the Duomo and St. Lorenzo, and then go back to 'washing chintz in the Wandle'.[2] When I saw that place first in '81 it was all arranged that I should make tiles and pots there. Now the tiles and pots have vanished like a dream – a very insolvent dream – and I have turned turtle and am afloat on a sea of Literature. Which is rumness, ain't it? As the pot boy said at the Fellowship Porters.

I have seen nothing of the ex-factory, and all the paraphernalia of all the old processes are packed away in the garden here. Will they ever be bought out again, I wonder?

Georgiana Burne-Jones wrote in reply:[3]

There is something infinitely comfortable in the idea of all the men and the furnaces and the 'works' generally that stood between you and the world having vanished, and just your Self is left speaking exactly as you wish, by means of a bottle of ink a pen and a sheet of paper.

It must have been a relief to friends of the De Morgans that by 1907 there were no more money worries and no more crises arising from the insolvency of the Fulham pottery, which was still limping on. William had a growing number of letters from admirers of his first novel and a continuing correspondence had developed with his hero's namesake in the United States. Just before publication of *Alice* William wrote to Vance:[4]

I have told Heinemann to post you a copy of my forthcomer as soon as it forthcomes. *Alice-For-Short* is the title, with the sub-title A Dichronism, which I hope will explain itself to whoever succeed in wading through 5305 mortal pages of print. It is an odd attempt to weave events over a century apart into consecutive narrative by means of cataleptics and ghosts, and such like.

Your namesake had had a fair circulation in England up to
Christmas. Whether he has died out since then I know not, and shall
hardly dare to ask Heinemann when I get back, for fear of a long face
of disappointment. The effect of *Alice* on Joe may be good.

Alice is a long novel, 563 pages, and has a complicated plot, although the
main threads of the story are fairly straightforward from the very opening
sentences:

> In the January in which this story begins there was a dense fog in
> London, and a hard frost. And there was also a little girl of six in a
> street in Soho, where the fog was as thick and the frost as hard as any,
> where else in the metropolis. The little girl was bringing home the beer
> from the Duke of Clarence's Head at the corner to an old house that
> had been built in the days of her great-great-grandfathers. She did not
> like bringing it; and though her eyes were blue and she was a nice little
> girl, she could almost have found it in her heart to stop and drink some
> of it on the way. But she was afraid of her mother. So she staggered
> on with her large jug, and nobody offered to help her.

Alice is bullied by some nasty, unthinking, small boys. The jug falls on to
the pavement and breaks. She is terrified of what her mother will do to her,
but is rescued by a kind gentleman, Charles Heath, a struggling artist who
has a studio in the house where Alice's parents act as caretakers, and in
which her father carries on a not very profitable business as a tailor. The
Kavenaghs occupy a dark and repellent basement. Mr Heath takes her
home and pays drunken mum for the broken jug which is in fact quite a collector's piece. Some days later when Alice's parents have one of their
drunken quarrels, while poor little Alice lies in bed terrified, Mr Kavenagh
cannot take any more and hits his wife over the head with a heavy piece of
metal. The police are called and Kavenagh, thinking that he has killed his
wife, take poison and kills himself. Alice's mother is taken to hospital; she
is alive, but only just. Charles Heath, who is from a very wealthy background, is on the scene, he tells the police that he will look after the poor
little girl, and takes her to his family home in Hyde Park Gardens. His sister
Peggy, warm-hearted and beautiful, falls for the grubby-faced waif, and as

[126]

the mother dies in hospital and none of the Kavenagh family care about Alice the Heath family adopt the orphan. The meeting of Charles and Alice on that foggy night in Soho is a extraordinary piece of luck for the girl as, suddenly, she is transferred from squalor to a kind and wealthy middle-class family. One did not have to bother much about adoption laws in those days (the mid 1860s, as best one can judge).

De Morgan offers us a fine picture of a Victorian family: Mr Heath, the father, a kind, bumbling silk merchant in the City of London; his wife the vague mother of a large family who has very little control over it; and Partridge who is a mixture of housekeeper and governess; she it is who really runs the house kindly and efficiently and who takes Alice under her wing. The household is a large one and there is evidence of plenty of money. A butler, footman, coachman, endless servants and kitchen staff give the family a very comfortable, carefree life. It is all a far cry from the Soho cellars of Alice's previous existence.

That house where Charles and his art-student friend Mr Jerrythought have their studios,[6] is, as has been noted, a mixture of 40 Fitzroy Square and the big ballroom in Great Marlborough Street. The cellars where the Kavenagh family lived are described in vivid detail. Filfth, darkness, damp and stray cats, horrifying ghosts and endless drunken bickering between her parents had been Alice's lot:[7]

It was difficult to define where the cellarage ended and the basement that was other than cellarage began; both were so dark and damp and smelt so of varieties of decay. There was more fungus, no doubt, in the coal-cellar and the dust-'ole than in the pantry or the 'ousekeeper's room, but even that was rather a matter of guesswork, and you couldn't really tell without a light. And there was none — at least, it was only when mother lighted the Paraffin lamp you could see any-thing at all . . . So poor Miss Kavenagh passed her small new life, mostly weeping, in the darkness and the fungus growths, cut off from upstairs by a swing-door at the top of the kitchen flight, and unsus-pected by the world above.

Although no one believes her, in the beginning of the story Alice evidently saw some very frightening things in the basement, a lady with a dress with red spots on it, and a sinister man in red with a long knife in his hand. Her one solace during this miserable phase of her existence was a little kitten she had befriended; she was allowed to take it with her to Hyde Park Gardens.

Alice's ghosts are, in fact, seen later by both Charles and Mr Jerrythought. The 'lady with the spots' turns out to be the spectre of a girl who was murdered by the man with the knife and buried in the cellar. This all happened in the previous century, after a drunken party in the house. When the landlord has to find new tenants for the ground floor and base- ment he lets the premises to a couple of men who run a business making stained glass for churches, Mr Pope and Mr Chappell, a couple of cockney craftsmen. They are obliged to refurbish the ground floor and the cellars and when their bricklayer digs up one of the cellars, he finds some bones iden- tified as human by Charles with his knowledge of anatomy from his life- class studies. To the disgust of the bricklayer the newly laid floor has to be taken up again, and the body of the poor murdered girl is found still in the ball dress with a spotted pattern which she was wearing on the fatal night. One would expect this part of the story to be gruesome, but in De Morgan's hands it becomes something akin to black farce.

There is an immensely complicated history linking the dead girl with Alice's mother's family, and there is a ring which the dying Mrs Kavenagh gives to Peggy and which supplies the clue to the identity of the girl in the cellar. One has the feeling that the author does not really expect his reader to follow all the intricacies of the plot, which is just as well. One is content to be carried along with De Morgan's good humoured story-telling.

Charles Heath, as the author has told us,[8] shares some biographical characteristics with De Morgan. He is an art student at the Academy Schools, a very generous-hearted but lazy man who, the reader knows from the beginning, will never be a successful painter. Very much later in his life, he is encouraged by his sister Peggy to give up his painting and turn his hand to writing. He is immediately successful, but, irritatingly, we are not told what he wrote. His rather weak character and his wealthy family make him an obvious target for what was known at the time as a 'designing woman'. Sure enough, along comes the abominable Lavinia Straker, who sits for Charles as a model, though a very respectable one – that is, fully clothed. Half French, a very good singer, and to Charles immediately attractive, she is desperate for his money to satisfy the needs of a grasping mother and a hopeless and criminal father and brother. Peggy, from the beginning, has her doubts about Miss Straker, and Charles's family are deeply shocked when he eventually decides to marry her, having been duped into a proposal by the cunning Lavinia. She writes a calculatedly duplicitous letter to Charles suggesting that they should never see each other again; this has the desired contrary effect and sends him off to the country to seek her:[9] 'We have said that we make no pretence of under-standing Miss Straker. But we wish that it should be noted that if she *did* intend to bring about this result, no more skilful manipulation could have been resorted to. It might have failed completely with another man than poor simple, chivalrous Charley.'

Charles's father is furious; he cuts off most of his son's allowance and will not speak to him. Inevitably, after some years of marriage and one sur-viving son, Pierre, Lavinia is unfaithful and makes little attempt to hide her affair from her husband. Divorce follows, with Charles left in charge of their son. He feels the social disgrace keenly. There is absolutely no doubt where the author's sympathies lie, but the reader of the 1990s may feel some sympathy for Lavinia. Unprincipled she may be, but Charles is grown up and should have known better, especially as he knew something of her appalling family. Some years later, the Heath family hear that Lavinia has died and it is obvious to everybody that Alice (by now an attractive and intelligent young woman) must marry Charles. None the less they go on regarding each other as brother and sister. Peggy and her distinguished husband, Sir Rupert Johnson, a famous authority on diseases of the brain, are exasperated.

When Charles studied at the Academy Schools there was a shabby old man, (based on a real character)[10] called Verrinder, a 'life student', as they were known, who was an object of ridicule to the other unthinking young students. Charles, typically, is civil to him, and Verrinder invites the young man to his lodging to see a picture which turns out to be a portrait of the murdered girl in the cellar. When Verrinder was a young man, just married, his young wife fell downstairs, hit her head, and has been unconscious ever since; she has not said a word or recognized her husband. From the window of his lodgings he can see Bedlam, the asylum where his wife is kept; he still hopes that one day she will come out of her coma, even after sixty years. The poor man eventually dies of an overdose of chloral and never knows that with the encouragement of Sir Rupert Johnson, a surgeon at the hospital carries out a trepanning operation on old Kate. She regains consciousness, still of course thinking that she is a young married woman preparing a nice cup of tea for her husband who has left the house for ten minutes. Alice, who has had some nursing experience, volunteers to help look after the old girl and to help her come to terms with the fact that she is now an old woman and that her husband is dead. There is a bad moment when Kate sees herself in the mirror for the first time.

This is good dramatic stuff, but medically, in the light of today's knowledge, a little suspect. However, De Morgan did get in touch with a famous authority on the brain and lunacy, Sir James Crichton-Browne, who wrote to the author:[11]

Prolonged trance and subliminal periods of existence have often been employed in fiction, generally, I think, in a way that does not commend itself to the medical mind. The truth is, such matters are often more wonderful than anything that imagination has conceived. Had I time I could send you some curious cases of trance dug out from old medical literature. I suppose you have heard of Astley Cooper's case in which a naval officer who suffered a depression of the skull from a grape shot in an action in the Mediterranean at the moment when he was issuing an order remained totally unconscious for many months, in which state he was brought home, and who, when operated on in London and the depressed bone being raised, completed the order he had been uttering when he was struck down many months before. He took up his conscious life at the exact moment when it had been interrupted.

One has to remember that at the time of this story, between 1870 and 1890, there was very little known about lunacy and its causes, and even less about the brain and injuries to it. In the case of the unfortunate naval officer he had been unconscious for only a few months, while fictional Mrs Verrinder was in a coma for very many years.

The old lady, now recalled to consciousness, provides clues as to the identity of the murdered woman. Mr Verrinder, when a young man, had worked for an Academician in 40 – Street and remembered a portrait of the woman, who was named Phyllis Cartwright. This information ties up many loose strands of the plot. Old Kate becomes very fond of both Alice and Charles and before she dies makes them promise that they will marry. Sensibly enough they feel they cannot disregard such a request!

Alice-For-Short is a strange book. One can easily criticize it for being too long, too wordy, with too many over-complicated sub-plots very often only loosely connected. De Morgan is neither a literary stylist nor a social crusader. His sole interest is in the play of character; the ordinary people you might see, whether in Clapham, Bayswater or Soho. They range from denizens of the slums to residents of Hyde Park Gardens. As noted earlier, some critics have dwelt on what they consider to be similarities between De Morgan's and Charles Dickens's fiction. De Morgan of course was aware of the comparison[12] and we know from his recorded comments that his family were avid readers of Dickens's novels.[13] There are none the less great differences between the two writers. De Morgan was keen to record the world of London as he remembered it in the mid nineteenth century and, in some of the other novels, as he saw it later at the turn of the century. There is a strong feeling of nostalgia in the first two novels and in some of the later work for the London of the 1850s with its fogs and its dampness; it is the now-disappeared world before the motor car and the telephone, both of which modern inventions he detested. All this is Dickensian enough, but there is very little in De Morgan's work of the other novelist's passionate attacks on cruelty and social injustice and not very much of the teeming underworld and sub-cultures portrayed so vividly in Mayhew's record of Dickens's London. There is compassion for poor little Alice, and for shabby old Verrinder vainly waiting for his wife to speak and recognize him, but almost no bitterness of the kind one finds in later authors such as H.G. Wells, and certainly none of the deep-seated anger so evident in George Gissing's *New Grub Street*, or the early novels of George Moore (let alone Emile Zola). It is interesting to compare the parting of Charles and Lavinia with the extraordinary scene in the Gissing novel, the final conversation between Edwin Reardon and his wife Amy, where neither of them can rescue the situation from emotional catastrophe. Nothing in De Morgan's work matches that intensity of feeling which Gissing achieves, but at such moments one can understand why the former writer was more immediately popular.

De Morgan, in his frequent authorial interventions, has very little good to say about the unfortunate Lavinia Straker and only a mild sympathy for Charles, whose weakness of character has led him into such a hopeless marriage. On the other hand, while underlining the evils of drink, De Morgan is humanely understanding about the circumstances which have led Alice's parents down the slippery alcoholic slope. Her father had been a respectable and moderately successful tailor, and her mother, the daughter of a publican, has forsworn alcohol, having seen the effect of it on her own father. Too many children of the marriage, and business going down hill have led them to the gin bottle. The money gone, the marriage is soured, and Alice, the only child still at home, is neglected. And that is how we meet this pathetic couple. The evils of drink are very apparent in De Morgan's novels. The Kavenaghs and old Christopher Vance with his love of whisky are only three among a number of De Morgan's characters whose lives are ruined by the demon drink, a vice according to the author mainly to be found among the lower classes.

Ghosts and the supernatural are very much a part of the plot machinery of *Alice*, although not much space is given to the activities of mediums or researchers about whom De Morgan knew so much. There is an interesting paragraph[14] in which views are put not dissimilar from those of his father, Augustus:

Psychical Research requires at least one votary of diabolical tenacity of purpose to keep the life in it. Almost every living human creature had some measure of interest in Ghosts and Bogies, but it is a measure that is very apt to run out after say twenty minutes sitting at an unresponsive table, with your little fingers in contact with you neighbours' to keep up the current; or after maybe sleeping one night in an haunted house and not seeing a grey woman; or covering a quire of foolscap with planchette writing from your co-querist's first husband and the finding that she is *Miss* (where you thought for certain that she was *Mrs*) Smith; or being told that young Blank had confessed that it was he pushed the table, just to show what awful asses the Company (including yourself) were . . . Let us all do honour to those who (according to the testimony of their scientific opponents) have passed through long periods of patient research watching for spectres that never come; weighing mediums in *vacuo* and finding that they weigh exactly what you would expect; grappling with other mediums who worm their way out of the cabinet in the dark; and getting smudged by materialisations with vermilion and lamp-black superposed on the medium for test purposes. Never mind if I put some of these points wrongly: join me in admiration of the persistent philosophy that recognises the fact that no amount of negative evidence absolutely proves that anything whatever isn't due to any cause we chose to invent a name for.

This novel isn't 'London suburban' so much as genteel London, and at the bottom end of the social scale, down-at-heel Soho. There is scope for gentle irony whether writing about the Heath family or London cockneys. For instance, a comment on one of the Heath children: '"One often thinks of things in cabs," said Archibald, the eldest brother. He was not considered a genius, so he had been assigned a position of responsibility in his father's business.' One feels rather sorry for the silk trade.

The cockney dialogue in *Joseph Vance* was entertaining, and there is rather more of it on show in *Alice*. De Morgan's cockney is very different from Dickens's version; perhaps the nearest to it is to be found in W.W. Jacobs's delightful stories of Thames-side life with the night watchman and the seamen of Wapping and Limehouse. Mr Pope,[15] of Pope and Chappell, the stained-glass firm, who take over the Kavenagh's basement, provides a good example of the speech of a self-educated man – basically a cockney with a smattering of education. For example, the two partners are incensed: they have gone ahead without permission and installed a kiln in one of the cellars, and a sacked workman informs the district surveyor; they are had up before the magistrate, who fines them and makes them resite the kiln. The indignant Mr Pope:

On the other 'and Mr. Chappell, . . . the number of footins had nothing to do with the slatin' we've got over it. What this Official 'Umbug really objected to was that he was losin' a fif'teen-shilling fee. Do you suppose he'd not have passed those footins if he'd had notice? He's been slatin' us to keep up his salary. That's what *we've* been slated for. And do you suppose that magistrate feller won't get his commission off the job? Of course he will! I know'em. They're all alike. 'Appen to know the expressin 'fishy', Mr. Heath? Meanin' untrust worthy, doubtful, unreliable. Well – of course you do! But you don't know the entomology of it? It's short for official, that's it is . . . But I'm havin' my revenge on him! See this 'ead I'm paintin'? Well – I'm makin' it like that district surveyor as ever I can get it . . . 'Ead of Judas Iscariot. I like the idear.

No one would deny that *Alice* is a ragbag of a novel, but it is highly read able, and through the twists and turns of the story one is constantly aware of the presiding character of De Morgan himself. Wryly humorous, kindly, but with a remarkably sharp eye when it comes to human failings. One wonders when and how, during his thirty-five years as a ceramic designer, he had picked up such a wide-ranging insight into all the different levels of London life. Perhaps much of his knowledge came from listening to his workmen while he was quietly working out his designs for pots and plates in his factory.

Chapter 10

De Morgan and his publishers, Heinemann – their contracts
– publication of *Somehow Good* in 1908 and *It Can Never
Happen Again* in 1909.

THERE IS a photograph,[1] undated, of William Heinemann standing on a pedestal with a kneeling figure each side of him. Edmond Gosse and William De Morgan paying homage to their publisher. Today, one suspects, authors in such a posture would be imploring their publisher to pay them bigger advances, but this certainly would not have been the case as far as De Morgan was concerned. The contracts[2] for his nine novels carry no advances but, as was usual in those days, high royalties going up to 25% of the published price on home sales. Not much correspondence has survived between De Morgan and Heinemann but it appears to have been a good relationship. What letters there are strike the reader as friendly, even when the author is being pressed to shorten an over-long book. It must have been difficult for Heinemann to keep a sensible published price for a book of 528 pages (*Somehow Good*) or, even longer, 799 pages (*It Can Never Happen Again*). The published price of De Morgan's first three books was six shillings, a standard amount for one-volume novels. De Morgan complained that the difficulty was not only the cutting but making sure that afterwards the book still made sense.[3] Alterations often meant adding as well as taking away pages.

Never a good business man, it is doubtful whether De Morgan would have kept a close eye on his annual royalty statements. He was only too delighted to find that when he wanted money all he had to do was to ask his publishers for a cheque for a thousand pounds and along it came.[4] He wrote to Heinemann:[5]

> You mentioned that I might apply to you for an advance, but we didn't name any amount, and I feel a little puzzled when I try to make up my mind how much to ask for. Would you solve the problem for me by sending me whatever sum you think the circumstances warrant, at any such time as you may find to be convenient to you.

He showed a similarly cavalier attitude to the family finances. Being urged by a friend to consult a stockbroker about some securities which were losing their value, he said: 'I don't believe in those chaps stockbrokers. They are dangerous. My idea is – if you have money in an investment, *keep it there*. To alter an investment seems to me something like tampering with the Constitution of the British Empire.'

There are no royalty statements extant so we do not know what total earnings would have been in any one year, nor do we know how many copies each book sold. The numbers must have been impressive, if only judging from the reprints quoted in the fly-leaves of books. It was a far cry from the days when De Morgan could not find the money to pay his workmen. William Heinemann must have been delighted that in 1905 he had taken the risk, albeit a little unwillingly, to publish a very long first novel by an unknown author in his late sixties. The contracts are very straightfor-ward, as in the early 1900s very few rights were involved: home and 'col-onial' sales, American sales and continental rights. The only author's comment we have on a contract is in a letter to Sidney Pawling[6] of Heinemann about the agreement for *Joseph Vance*. De Morgan wanted it to be made clear that no version 'dramatic or otherwise' might be authorised contrary to his wish and judgement. He adds: 'I am rather fussy about Joe and the stage (if ever) because I feel that it is a story capable of being so hor-ribly ill-dramatised.' (In fact Joe was the only work to be dramatized, for radio, long after the author's death.)

We have no record of any serious disagreement between author and pub-lisher. Attempts to woo authors away from their regular publisher are nothing new in the history of publishing, and there are many instances of writers succumbing to the lure of the promise of huge advances. A famous case is that of George Eliot, although she returned to the faithful Blackwood. There is one letter from De Morgan in Italy dated 5 March 1908 to an unknown correspondent. It is heavily corrected but worth quoting:[7]

> Dear Sir,
> Your letter reads to me as though I had failed to make it clear that any negotiation for publication of any work of mine would depend on its final rejection by W. Heinemann. I think I recollect writing to you that I would place a particular MS with you if I found I could make no satisfactory arrangement with his firm.
> Heinemann is I believe willing to undertake this novelette on my terms. But I am in no hurry at present to publish anything further, and shall defer talking to him on the subject till my return to London in June.
> Should he then be less willing to undertake this story, or should he prefer another, I will if I decide on publishing this, place it with you for disposal.

Then there is an addition to the letter: 'It occurs to me that any publisher ready with an offer from a MS of mine without first reading would probably apply to me directly, as I am easily accessible. In the meanwhile it occurs to me that announcement of a desire to receive offers is premature.' This seems likely to be a letter to a literary agent who has been fishing for a very profitable client, but one cannot tell, particularly as the letter, with all its alterations, is probably a draft. Nor does one know what the 'novelette' referred to is.

De Morgan's third novel *Somehow Good* (dedicated to M.D.W. from W.D.M.)[8] was published in London in 1908 by Heinemann and in the United States by Henry Holt and Co. De Morgan wrote to Heinemann[9] very appreciatively after publication:

> Yours is a very gratifying letter indeed — I had no idea that I was so wealthy! However I, of course, don't really know what the circula-

tion of either book has been, either in England or America; It is all curiously and surprisingly satisfactory.

The reviews are quite taking me aback. The Pall Mall I thought a particularly intelligent one. I see with a good deal of pleasure that the unpleasant part of the story takes its proper place as a mere essential to the plot. A good many readers will remain in the dark about it.

The origin of the plot of *Somehow Good* is explained by the author in a letter evidently written some time later:[10]

I had written a tale, which I liked and my wife didn't; and she said to me, 'Why can't you write a story with an ordinary beginning?' I said, 'What sort?' She said, 'Well, for instance, "*It was his last tuppence and he spent it on the tuppenny tube.*" Said I, "An admirable beginning". I put my story in hand straight away, and began writing what is now chapter II of the book. Chapter I was written long after to square it all up.

Somehow Good is wholly suburban. Set in about 1900,[11] there are no grand country houses and no Dickensian slums. Apart from the annual migra‐ tion to the seaside for the summer holiday, most of the action takes place in Krakatoa Villa[12] near Shepherd's Bush station, and in a rather superior house in what the author calls Ladbroke Grove Road.[13] The plot relies on one stupendous coincidence, which the reader has to swallow, and which occurs in the second chapter. A young and inexperienced girl, Rosalind, goes out to India to marry her childhood sweetheart, and while her husband is away on business she is seduced by a wicked colonel, a well‐known lib‐ ertine. When the young husband learns what has happened and it is clear that there is a baby on the way, they have a violent quarrel and he deserts her. She is rescued from a terrible fate by an old gentleman who knows the background to the story. 'The old major', as he is known, arranges for mother and child to return to England. The mother, Rosalind, has been left a legacy which enables her to bring up her daughter, Sally, provided she changes her name to Nightingale.

Sally, by now newly grown up, travelling on the tuppenny tube one day, gets into conversation with a stranger, having accidentally trodden on his foot. He tells her that he has known the name Nightingale in the past. A coin is dropped, and when the man tries to find it under the seat, there is a violent flash, and he gets a severe shock. He is helped out on to the platform, where it is apparent that he has lost his memory. Luckily, on the platform is young Dr Vereker, Sally's family doctor, who is in love with her, and they get the stranger into a cab and take him to Krakatoa Villa to recover. Sally's mother is horrified until she sees the man and the reader fairly quickly appre⁄ hends that he is the long⁄lost husband, who has come from New York to London on business. He is a wealthy man – but of course having lost his memory he has to find himself a job and move out of Sally's home. Within two years Rosalind and 'Fenwick' (for that is the name tattooed on his arm) become fond of each other and get married. The reader soon discovers the details of Fenwick's life. Suspense forms around the questions that will be asked when Fenwick gets his memory back. What will he think of Sally? Has he perhaps got another wife somewhere? Apart from Rosalind Nightingale, the only person who knows the whole truth is the old major, the faithful family friend, who sagely keeps his own counsel.

Life in Krakatoa Villa is by no means uncultured. Chamber music is performed on a regular basis with Sally on the viola, Dr Vereker (cello), Sally's friend Laetitia (violin) and a very brilliant young fiddle player, Julius Bradshaw, with his Strad. Poor Julius, much in love with Laetitia, has to give up his career as a soloist as he suffers badly from nerves; he has a job in a draper's shop, which puts him well below the others in the social scale. He is woundingly referred to as a 'counter⁄jumper'. He only recovers his nerve when he and Laetitia elope and get married. Julius's mother⁄in⁄ law who is heavily disapproving, is yet another of De Morgan's unfair por⁄ traits of middle⁄aged mothers. Music plays a prominent part in the story, and the details to start with are very (and I suspect, deliberately) inaccurate. This is one of the author's jokes, as later on the narrator displays a detailed knowledge of Beethoven's violin sonatas, particularly the Kreutzer.

Half⁄way through the book the family migrate to the sea⁄side for their summer holiday. The book gives us a delightful and obviously first⁄hand picture of what a modest middle⁄class holiday at the sea⁄side was like. St Sennans⁄on⁄Sea, very unfashionable, is clearly Hastings.[14]

St Sennans⁄on⁄Sea consists of two parts – the new and the old. The old part is a dear old place, and the new part is beastly. So Sally says

and she must know, because this is her third visit. The old part con'
sists of Mrs. Iggulden's and the houses we have described on either
side of her, and maybe two dozen more wooden or black'brick build'
ings of the same sort; also of the beach and its interesting lines of
breakwater that are so very jolly to jump off or to lie down and read
novels under in the sea smell. Only not too near the drains, if you
know it . . . You may tramp along the sea front quite near up to where
the fishing luggers lie, each with a capstan all to itself, under the little
extra old town the re'tanned fishing'nets live in, in houses that are like
sail'less windmill'tops whose plank walls have almost merged their
outlines in innumerable coats of tar, laid by long generations back of
the forefathers of the men in oil'cloth head'and'shoulders hats who
repair their nets for ever in the Channel wind unless you want a boat
to'day . . . There is an aroma of the Norman Conquest and of
Domesday Book about the old town. Research will soon find out, if
she looks sharp that there is nothing Norman in the place except the
old arch in the amorphous church tower, and a castle in the distance
on the flats.

There is a description of the circulating library, where apart from some toys
and beach paraphernalia there is a bookcase containing works by Mrs
Radcliffe, Sir Walter Scott, Bulwer Lytton, Currer Bell, 'well even Fanny
Burney, if you come to that. There was certainly a copy of Frankenstein
and fifty years ago our flesh was so compliant as to creep during its perusal.
It certainly wouldn't now.'
    Much of the denouement of the story takes place at the sea'side. Summer
holidays were obviously long ones in those days. The often'spurned
Conrad Vereker appears and is eventually accepted as a likely husband by
the mercurial Sally. The news of the elopement of Julius and Laetitia is
broken in a letter from the runaway bride. Above all, in a somewhat melo'
dramatic way Fenwick gets his memory back. He has had a number of dis'
turbing flash'backs to his previous life, and the return of his memory is
helped by an extraordinary machine on the pier which gives people electric
shocks. Very upset by his memories of India and what had happened there
he goes back on the pier early in the morning and slips into the sea. He is a
strong and athletic man, but cannot swim. Sally, who can, rescues him but

nearly drowns herself, dragged down, as she is, by her dress. Vereker, luckily, is at hand to revive her, and Fenwick accepts the somewhat odd situation with regard to his twice-married wife and the daughter who, of course, is not his.

If one had to judge the book on its plot only there would be little to recommend it. But as is the case with the two previous novels, and indeed with the fourth, *It Can Never Happen Again*, it is the characterization, the storytelling, and indeed the background (Edwardian west London and St Sennans-on-Sea) which render the book so readable. Sally is another of De Morgan's teenage heroines who, from numerous letters quoted in Mrs Stirling's book, so delighted his readers. Elderly ladies, as has been noted, do not fare so well. Laetitia's mother is an arch-snob and the bane of her family. Dr Vereker's mother (he is incidentally an only child) is appallingly possessive and demanding, and her beloved son, who it must be admitted is a little feeble, is much too considerate towards his parent. She is described by the malevolent author as 'a gilt spectacled lob worm'. She appears at the seaside with her son and is horrified at what she considers lax morals. She holds forth on the subject of her son:[15]

You were very snappish and peevish with me just now, Conrad, without waiting to hear what I had to say. But I overlook it. I am your mother. If you had waited, I would have told you that I have no fault whatever to find with Miss Nightingale's bathing dress, It is, no doubt, strictly '*en régle*'. Nor can I say, in these days, what I think of girls practising exercises that in my day were thought unwomanly. All is changed now, and I am old-fashioned. But this I do say, that had your father, or your great-uncle, Dr. Everett Gayler, been told forty years ago that a time would come that it would be thought no disgrace for an *English* girl to jump off a boat with an *unmarried* man in it . . . My dear, I am sure that the latter would have made one of those acrid and biting remarks for which he was celebrated in his own circle, and which have even, I believe, been repeated by royalty.

And so on. One can hear that inexorable maternal voice only too well. Or again:

Had I been asked – had you consulted me, my dear – I should certainly have advised that Mr. Fenwick should have been accompanied
by another married man, certainly not by a young single gentleman.
The man himself – I am referring to the man in the boat – would have
done quite well, whether married or single. Boatmen are seldom
unmarried, though frequently tattooed with ladies' names when they
have been in the navy. You see something to laugh at Conrad? I'm
your mother. But I am used to it.

It is perhaps a fault on De Morgans's part to disclose to the reader so early
on Fenwick's identity. The resolution of the story depends so much on what
will bring back Fenwick's memory and it really does to have to be either
another shock or a bang on the head. The sub-plots – Sally's relationship
with Vereker, the elopement, and even the sad death of the old major (a very
Dickensian scene) – are insufficient to prevent the book sagging in the
middle. Maybe William Heinemann could have tried harder to get the
author to engage in a little pruning, but this is not easy to achieve with a
successful writer, as De Morgan was and knew himself to be.[16]

It was an extraordinary achievement, by 1908, to have published three
long successful novels. The way of life that Evelyn and William had established on the strength of his new earnings, between Italy and England, was
now free from anxiety. William, indeed, found it easier to write in Florence
where there were fewer interruptions and Evelyn worked hard meanwhile at
her painting, though she still had no desire to sell or exhibit any of her work.
However, in August 1908 Evelyn's uncle, Roddam Spencer Stanhope, died
and even though his widow stayed on at the Villa Nuti, Florence was never
quite the same for the De Morgans. The old man's death was extraordinarily peaceful; he had just finished a picture on which he had been working
and died in his sleep the same night.[17] De Morgan commented: 'How glad
I should be to go across to the other side in the same way – write (as it is
writing now) up to the last hour or day, and then get away from this painful
flesh – and leave as good a memory behind as may be, though few of us may
succeed in leaving as good a one as his – and so many to treasure it.'

In addition to this personal loss, the De Morgans had to contend with a
number of earthquakes in Florence. Evelyn wrote to Janey Morris in
January 1909:[18]

How kind of you to write! Yes, we are both all right, but nervous after our earthquake, it was a sharp shock and coming on top of the Messina horrors produced a considerable panic.

We were asleep, but the noise woke me, then came the shaking and swaying of the room, and we both sprang up and dressed in less than five minutes. We were at the top of a very high house so we had the full benefit of the shaking. We and some Russian friends spent the night partly out of doors and partly sitting in my studio (which is on the ground floor), with all the doors open, fearing another shock that might bring the house down. Some people slept through it, but a great many turned out and spent the night in the streets. No harm was done, but at Bologna the Palazzo Publico was injured, and a lady died of fright. It has not done my nerves any good, and we tremble if a door bangs.

The new book, De Morgan was obliged to report to Heinemann,[19] was not going well. It was not only the effect of the earthquake; the author did not rate his new novel as good as its predecessors, and as early as January 1908 he considered the work to have no plot and he did not know how it would turn out. Later, he reported to his publisher that he did not like it even when he had got 237,000 words written:

I'm going very slowly, even when at work. My impression is that in practice I go at the rate of 1000 words per diem.

However, I hope this and the revision of the whole will run concurrently with a big final delay, viz: the needful time for reading it aloud to Mrs. De M. She, you see, is a very strong character, and when she wakes up, makes me read all through from her last recollection. But this final read-through is a *sine qua non*; and if deferred till the proofs, it would be letting a most valuable discrepancy-detective loose on the work just a few hours too late, so to speak. Also reading the whole aloud is my own final revision . . . So when it comes to plausible print, I overlook things.

I have got interested in the wind-up and She also – emphatically, which is satisfactory; so I am a good deal reconciled to it – think much better of it than I did . . . Thanks for the agreement. I won't sign it yet. 'Blind Jim's' life is sufficiently precarious without having a signed agreement to kill him!.

The book had to be finished without too much delay because Heinemann wanted to publish it before the new Hall Caine came out. Various titles[20] were discussed, but in the end they agreed on *It Can Never Happen Again* and at the author's insistence the book was put out in two unwieldy volumes, the only time this was done. As a result the book was boycotted by four libraries, including the powerful Mudie's. Heinemann wanted to include a frontispiece in each volume with different portraits of the author by his wife. She objected to the second one, which is the well known depic- tion of William holding a large vase with some of his novels behind him. The first volume has an earlier portrait, painted in 1893.

This fourth novel is not only the longest novel De Morgan wrote, but is arguably his most ambitious. The characters in it are drawn from three widely different sections of society in the England of the early 1900s. First of all there is the writer, Alfred Challis, and his sad wife, Marianne, who live in suburban Wimbledon, then the Arkroyds in their grand country house, Royd; and lastly the inhabitants of slummy Tallack Street.

There are two main threads, only loosely connected, as so often with De Morgan's stories. The first is the story of Blind Jim and his little daughter Lizarann (plenty of Dickensian pathos here). Jim, a merchant seaman, has lost his sight in an accident. When he arrives home to the appalling Tallack Street, a decaying London slum, he finds that his young wife has just given birth to a baby girl, and is dying. His sister, Mrs Steptoe, and her drunken husband, Bob, give shelter to Jim and his little daughter, but very grudg- ingly. All poor Jim can do is to beg and sell matches, guided each day to his pitch by Lizarann whom he calls his pilot. Bob is not a bad man when he is occasionally sober, but his wife 'was a fine study of the effect of exasperating circumstances on an uncertain temper',[21] and father and little girl suffer accordingly. A very rich family, the Arkroyds take a very lofty interest in Tallack Street and occasionally pay a visit to the poor inhabitants and patronize them.

The Arkroyds and their splendid country house provide an important background to much of the story. Large house parties are part of the life- style and one of the people invited is an up-and-coming novelist, Alfred

Challis, who writes under the name of Titus Scroop. He is of a very different class from the Arkroyds and his home in Wimbledon is very modest.
Marianne, his wife, is much too shy and jealous of her husband's smart
friends to go to Royd. As Challis's career prospers, so the marriage deteri-
orates. The situation is not helped by a relationship which develops between
Alfred and the young, beautiful and unscrupulous Judith Arkroyd. The
connection between Royd and Tallack Street is strengthened when the local
vicar, in the country, goes to London to take over the parish in which Jim
and Lizarann live. The clergyman intervenes when Bob Steptoe finally
hits the bottle once too often, get the DTs, and kills himself after trying to
throttle his wife (always, for obvious reasons, called Aunt Stingy by
Lizarann, but not to her face). The Rev Athelstan Taylor is a good character, an unorthodox and muscular Christian. When old Jim is knocked
over by a cart and loses a leg, and his little daughter, out in the snow looking
for him, contracts pneumonia, the kind-hearted Athelstan takes them to the
country to recuperate near Royd.

The affair between Challis and Judith Arkroyd is made complicated
because Challis has married his deceased wife's sister which was illegal at
that time, so technically this marriage could be considered void. The
couple, who are seriously considering eloping, are awaiting a bill to go
through parliament. Little wonder that De Morgan found it a difficult
book to write. Compared with the previous novel, *Somehow Good*, there is
a lot more to unravel, but he copes, very typically, with accident and coincidence playing a large part in the plot. Jim is again knocked down, this
time by one of those smelly new inventions, a Panhard[22] motor car;
Lizarann finally succumbs to TB; and Challis gets a severe bang on the
head in the same accident in which Jim is killed. When he comes to, he
cannot remember anything that has happened to him in the last eighteen
months, which of course includes Judith and their plans to elope. His only
wish is to be with his estranged wife, Marianne. She appears at Royd at the
opportune moment, having seen a piece in the paper about the famous
author who has been involved in a serious car accident. Judith sees sense, in
her cool, arrogant way, and gets married to a duke which, as everybody
agrees, will suit her much better.

It is a complicated plot, but the reader remains involved and interested
because of the characters. They come to life, whether from the slums of

Tallack Street, suburban Wimbledon or lordly Royd. Of particular interest in this novel are the main female protagonists, Marianne, her wicked friend Charlotte Eldridge, Judith, Aunt Stingy, and little Lizarann herself, who provides the tragic element. Judith becomes more and more unlikeable as the story develops and it becomes plain that despite her great charm and beauty, she is cold and calculating, and too fond of her own power. Poor Challis has no chance once she has decided that he is worthy of her attention. The reader is enlightened as to her character when she makes it quite plain that she is not in the slighest bit interested in the fate of old Jim after the accident, even though she has been a passenger in the car which knocked him down.

One feels sorry for Marianne, if rather exasperated with her. She is not very intelligent, and rather narrowminded, and hates the idea of meeting her husband's rich and intellectual friends. All might have been well between the couple but for Marianne's mother, who is depicted as a spiteful old religious maniac, and, more importantly, Marianne's best friend, Charlotte Eldridge. Charlotte is a memorable mischiefmaker who manages to poison her friend's mind with telling halfsentences of innuendo: 'Mrs. John Eldridge possessed in the very highest degree the faculty of making it understood, by slight inflections and modulations of voice, by pauses in the right place, by gestures the shrewdest eyesight could not swear to, though the dullest could never remain in ignorance of them, that a lady and gentleman were engaging her attention.' Challis and Judith, of course.[23]

Mrs Steptoe, Aunt Stingy, is not a subtle portrait, but a very convincing one; she is the poor, whining and cruel product of a Victorian slum. The author's treatment of Lizarann is sentimental, but this is a fault which it is difficult to avoid when describing the death of the little girl from TB. She is not unlike the little Alice in the second novel.

Royd is one of the grandest of the country houses which the author describes in his novels; full of servants, from butler down to chambermaids. Neither the family nor the guests at their grand house parties are treated very kindly. The baronet, head of the family, is the most likeable; a kindly man immersed in the history of the Middle Ages. His wife is vague and an arrant snob, their only son is more likeable than Judith or her sister, but the guests, for the most part, are portrayed by the author as intolerable bores — partic

ularly a pompous MP and a marvellous caricature of a German philosopher, Graubosch. His masterpiece is called *Divagationes Indagatoris*. The following quotation is a fair example in translation of author's style: 'The
Thinker of the Future will do well to turn his attention to the construction
of a language expressly adapted to deal with the Unknown and the
Infinite.' And so on.

The picture of a rather grand Edwardian country house is a detailed one
and, one would think, drawn from personal experience. This book, indeed,
has a dedication at the beginning: 'Not in respect of anything its pages
contain, but solely in remembrance of two long concurrent lives and an
uninterrupted friendship, this book is dedicated by its author to the memory
of Ralph Earl of Lovelace.' This old friend had a large house and estate in
Surrey, Ockham Park, and a house in Swan Walk, Chelsea. The De
Morgans were invited to house parties in the country by the Lovelaces, but
one hopes with better company than at Royd.

Despite the author's doubts about the novel, it was on the whole well
received by the critics and his readers were faithful as long as he wrote novels
like his first four. There were splendid reviews in *The Morning Post* and *The
Spectator*, and, most gratifyingly, in the *Athenaeum*: 'His mind is broad, his
experience catholic, and his taste fine. He has wide human sympathy, a
sense of comedy, and a pungent feeling for tragedy. His people are alive, and
depict themselves. His episodes are amusing or pathetic, or both, or merely
interesting. He holds his readers.'

Chapter 11

Move from The Vale to Old Church Street, Chelsea – the
publication of his only historical novel *An Affair of Dishonour*
in 1910, and *A Likely Story* in 1911.

BETWEEN 1906 and 1909 De Morgan had had four long novels published
and one can hardly blame him for wanting a change in the type of novel he
was writing. He and Evelyn were having a difficult time quite apart from
earthquakes and the death of Evelyn's uncle in Florence. The lease of their
house in The Vale was coming to an end and the landlord wanted to pull
down the three old houses and develop the site. So that meant moving house
for the first time since they were married. Eventually they found two houses
in Old Church Street, Chelsea, which they knocked into one. Unlike most
of the buildings in which De Morgan lived and worked, both houses are
still there and they are remarkably handsome.

The three tenants[1] of the three houses in The Vale decided to have a
memorable party as a send-off and there is an engaging if flowery description of the occasion by Mrs Stirling:[2]

> . . . conditions looked hopeless for an entertainment designed to be
> partly *al fresco*, for it was a niggardly summer of continuous and
> torrential rain; yet when the important date arrived a day of
> unclouded sunshine faded into a night of balmy breezes and glim-
> mering stars.

And as darkness fell, the Vale, like a victim adorned for the sacrifice, took on a new beauty. All carriages were stopped at the prosaic King's Road, and the guests wandered a-foot into an unexpected fairyland. Old Chelsea Pensioners in their scarlet coats guarded the lane, which was festooned with glowing lanterns; and at its end the three householders received in the centre of the roadway under trees gemmed with fairy lamps. There, all around, brickwork and foliage were alike sparkling with points of flame. Wherever the eye turned, the illumination was repeated with artistic effect, the colours blended softly, the lines of twinkling fire swaying in the breeze, and creating down spangled vistas an impression of limitless space.

There was music, different sorts in the three houses, and supper in the old deer park at the bottom of the lane, which was also doomed.

De Morgan wrote to Heinemann:[3] 'I passed the evening in such a hopeless bewilderment in a huge throng, that we might very easily have both been in it unknown to each other. It was like Cremorne.[4] *It Can Never Happen Again* because we go out at Christmas.' In his novel *The Old Man's Youth*, De Morgan, through the eyes of his hero Eustace John, describes a final visit to the old house:

The last time I saw the place . . . though it remained then an oasis in the desert of bricks and mortar that grew and grew throughout the whole of our occupancy, the signs of approaching doom were upon it. The entrance gateway swung helpless on one hinge, and it seemed no one's business to repair it. The lane was defiled with filth and discarded journalism, and the trees were dead or dying. The gardens remained, but a weed unfamiliar to me, that I never knew the right name of overran them, and the standard rose trees were a thing of the past . . .

A further misfortune befell the De Morgans. William, through his friend and correspondent in America, Professor Lionel Phelps, had received a most flattering invitation to go to Yale University to receive an honorary degree, but he had to write to Phelps to say that he could not possibly come. In May 1910,[5] he says:

[149]

Did I write to you of our misfortune of last Autumn? Not in full, anyhow. It came about thus: – we were just leaving our old home, which was on the point of being pulled down, when my wife met with an accident, fell down in the street, and was brought home with a dislocated shoulder – The case was most grievously mismanaged, and months of trying anxiety have followed during which I have done little or no work. She may never be fit for a visit to the States, and I should not come without her. Neither am I over fit myself, just at present – it may pass off. I am only 70, so far, and a good many folk live another decade or two, after that.

The damaged shoulder took some months to recover, with the help of a Swedish masseuse, and Evelyn was able to get back to her painting. He adds:

There is a house, standing chaotic, in Chelsea (England) waiting to be got into order. A nice confusion we have been in,[6] with the old home of 20 years broken up, ruction with builders of a new one, broken limbs – such a combination! . . . A short book of mine – only 400 pages of 350 words each – will appear in August, say. It is an experiment for me – quite unlike all the others. I couldn't tell at first what period it would turn out. It decided on the Restoration – and is handicapped by its author's ignorance of that date. However, that wont matter for readers who know less – and those who are really well up in Pepys and Evelyn will have to be forgiving – I have altered historical fact to suit the story, more than once. I shall be curious to see the result.

The novel he refers to is *An Affair of Dishonour*[7] and is indeed an historical romance set in the reign of Charles II. It was published in 1910. Not unexpectedly the reviews were mixed and De Morgan's faithful readers were a little dismayed that they had not got the mixture as before. The reasons for their reaction are not too hard to find.

Sir Oliver Raydon, a thoroughly dissolute and corrupt country squire, seduces Lucinda, the beautiful daughter of a neighbouring landowner, and her father challenges the wicked Sir Oliver to a duel. Lucinda's father is killed, and Oliver is desperate that Lucinda should not hear about it. He takes her away to a remote house called Kipps Manor,[8] in Suffolk just north of Southwold. Oliver, unlike his usual self, is becoming quite fond of Lucinda. While there they witness a great sea battle, the battle of Sole Bay, between the Dutch and the English, and also a violent storm. A lot of wreckage and some dead bodies are washed ashore and also a wounded seaman who, by an extraordinary coincidence, turns out to be Lucinda's brother who has been in America. He is temporarily blinded, so that he cannot recognize his sister. Still Lucinda does not know of her father's death, until the secret is broken to her through one of Oliver's discarded mistresses. The grief-stricken girl flees back to her old home pursued by Oliver, and he is forced to fight a duel with the brother, whose sight has been restored and who has been told of what has happened to his father.

Oliver is wounded when he falls on his own sword during an attack of epilepsy, to which he is prone. He is also a sleepwalker, and going out on to his terrace at dead of night thinks he sees the ghost of his dead mother whose accusatory figure sometimes appears before him. He falls to his death, having a few days before married Lucinda – his first wife, who had left him, having conveniently died of the plague in London. Lucinda, rather unexpectedly, had agreed to a marriage, being still fond of the appalling Oliver and having found that she was expecting a child.

The author himself wrote: 'But such of Mr De Morgan's readers as consider Porky Owls or Lizarann[9] or their equivalent de Rigueur, had better skip this book and wait for the next. It is an experiment of the author's and may prove too great a trial for their patience.' Unfortunately for them, the next book although partly a return to early 'Victorian and Suburban' turned out to be something of an experiment too.

Reviews were mixed but not all the British ones were hostile. Ellis in the *Fortnightly Review*, wrote:

Possibly his finest work. It is not an historical romance in the ordinary sense of the word . . . it is an historical picture of the time it relates to, and I know of no other work of fiction in this category except Esmond, which has so much atmosphere about it, for the characters not only speak and act but think in the manner of their period . . . it is like a bizarre dream from the past.

Most of the other critics were not so kind. Mrs Stirling maintains that this novel sold better than his previous ones, but there is, unfortunately, no way of checking this as the publishers have no information. Judging from the excerpts the author quotes from the American reviews in the rather curious 'An Apology In Confidence', at the end of *A Likely Story*, the critics were very hostile: 'Probably written years ago, and found in an old desk,' was not the most unpleasant review!

The book, despite what Mr Ellis says about it, does not succeed. In his previous four books, it is obvious where his strengths lie. No one can very well defend his plots, least of all De Morgan himself, nor can one ignore the large number of coincidences that help the plots along in many of the stories, but what one misses in this novel are the things he is good at. There is no humour. There is no opportunity to use his outstanding gift for dia-logue, particularly his own special brand of cockney. Historical novels always present a real problem when it comes to deciding how the charac-ters will speak – whether to go for a pastiche of, in this case, seventeenth-century speech (pseudo-Congreve), the speech of today, or worst of all a made-up language full of gadzooks and tushery. The problem is not solved in this story. Here is a typical sample of a conversation between Oliver and Lucinda. He has just told her that they are going away. 'What journey, Oliver mine? I know of no journey.' And he replies, 'Because I have not told of it, thou fairest of wenches! I tell thee now, that thou mayst know it.'[10]

It does not help that one cannot believe in Lucinda's love for Oliver; this is mainly due to the fact that Oliver is made into a stage villain with his stilted speech, his diabolical sneers and his impressive list of innocent girls seduced and discarded. It is sadly a relief to the reader when he finally falls backward off his own terrace and cracks his head open.

De Morgan was writing under considerable difficulties at this time. Before they could move into their new house, they stayed in the Sussex Hotel in Queen's Gate, seriously worried by the injury to Evelyn's shoulder – at one time they really thought that she would be unable to paint again. All the same, he never should have decided to write an historical novel. As De Morgan admitted himself, historical facts were not particularly impor-tant to him. When it was pointed out to him that there were two battles of Sole Bay, he confessed that he was not really clear which one he meant to refer to: 'Of course my story used history as it liked . . . the fact is that I have always taken full advantage of the painter's and the poet's *quid liber audendi* – and I shall continue on the same lines. What is history if one cannot pervert it in fiction? After all one does the same in Fact.' He did not repeat the experiment although, as we shall see, the next novel was partly set in the past.

Both Evelyn and William were modest and retiring people. Public appearances obviously sent him into a panic. In November 1910 he was invited to be the guest of honour at a dinner given by the Society of Authors and then found to his horror that he was expected to give a speech; he agreed to go but asked his wife not to be present in case he broke down in the course of his talk. After the ordeal he wrote[11] to his brother-in-law, Spencer Pickering.

Dear Spencer –

The dinner was just like any other huge dinner, except sometimes the grub *is* good, and other places are no criterion of the Criterion where it is always bad.

I had misapprehended my importance in the concern and found myself painfully conspicuous. I am not used to the SKY.

I think my speech was a failure, but it was so ill delivered that people may think it would have been good if they could have heard it. It will come out complete in *The Author*[12] – that is, a faked version of it, as near as I could recollect, with some things I meant to say and forgot.

I'm very glad Evelyn didn't go – I should have busted up altogether.

I complained to one or two friends in the audience, after, of them not making a row when I stuttered, to drown my confusion. But they said, 'We were so anxious to hear what you were going to say!'

Evelyn says I oughtn't to have burnt a feeble portrait of myself in a top hat in the Graphic – but have sent it on – but really even the patience of a Saint has its limits. I'm a Saint (I'm something else if I'm not).

[153]

A few authors dislike publicity and hate giving interviews. William was certainly one of these. One of the few published interviews we have is with Bram Stoker (a prolific writer in other fields as well as the author of *Dracula*). This appeared in *The World's Work*, in the July 1908 issue, when the De Morgans were still in the Vale. It contains some good photographs taken by William Heineman of the author posing rather formally in Florence, and a picture of No. 1 The Vale which looks like a comfortable country villa, as of course it was. A very sympathetic piece, it does not tell us anything very new about the author, despite being good on the house in The Vale:

> a fairly old one, all ramshackle, with some queer little rooms and alcoves made in the process of 'improvements' at various times. It is just such a house as should be found in a quiet suburb. Attached to it is a large studio used by Mrs. De Morgan who in her maiden name of Evelyn Pickering, made a distinguished success with her pictures, as she has done ever since . . . Before I came away I asked Mr. De Morgan to tell me something of his method of work.
>
> 'I make no scenario. I just go on finding as one often does, such inspiration as is necessary from my pen. I find that the mere holding of a pen makes me think. The pen ever seems to have some conscious, ness of its own. It can certainly begin the work. Then I forget all about it, and go on wheresoever thought or the characters lead me. I think I work best in Florence where it is always quiet and where there is something stimulating in the air. It is certainly stimulating to the nerves; perhaps it is to the intellect also. I work there all the winter through. My time for beginning work is after breakfast. I work all day, off and on, and sometimes a little in the evening. Weather does not effect me as all my work is done in doors.'

The move to 127 Old Church Street, Chelsea, eventually took place in the autumn of 1910. When someone showed sympathy to De Morgan for the loss of their house in The Vale, he remarked:[13] 'We have decided not to take that view at all. We walk there sometimes and are very much interested in what is going on. The mulberry trees belonging to our old garden are still standing.' A pleasanter picture than the one painted by Eustace John in the last novel.

The Christmas of 1910 was the first they spent in England for many years. At long last, his health was giving him no cause for anxiety, but he had not been able to write anything for several months, mainly owing to the move and the time that they had had to spend in the Sussex Hotel. This did not seem to upset him unduly. 'A really good thing! As during the last five years I have published over a million and a quarter words!' During 1911 he had been doing some work on a long novel which would eventually be his last finished novel, *When Ghost Meets Ghost*. It was giving him some difficulty, and at Heinemann's request he produced a shorter book which was published in 1911, at first called Bianca and, finally, *A Likely Story*. He wrote: 'Compared with Joe it is a mere anecdote, to my thinking, the shortness of the story should cover a multitude of sins.' It is certainly one of the author's shorter books, a mere 344 pages.[14]

There are three main threads to the story. One is the troubled marriage of Reginald, a young artist and restorer, and his wife Euphemia. Through a ridiculous misunderstanding when they are visited by the upper classes, in the person of Madelaine Upwell and the handsome young army officer Captain Jack Calverley, Euphemia takes offence at a remark made by Reginald to their awful slatternly maid Sairah, and flounces off to go and stay with her Aunt Priscilla. Madelaine's romance with the dashing Jack is cut short because his regiment is ordered to South Africa; it is the time of the Boer War, which conveniently dates the story.

The young couple had paid a visit to Reginald in his studio as he was restoring a picture of a beautiful young girl, obviously painted by an accomplished Italian artist of the fifteenth century. The picture is restored and safely delivered to the stately home of Madelaine's family and hung in the place of honour in the drawing-room. One evening the family is out to dinner, and an old family friend, Mr Pelly, an antiquarian and linguist, is half asleep in front of the fire. The picture begins to speak, much to his amazement, and bit by bit the girl in the portrait tells the story of how the picture came to be painted. The girl, Maddelena, was married off by her father to a very rich and repulsive old count who, according to her, combined all the worst attributes of the devil. He commissioned a brilliant young artist to paint her portrait and he turned out to be a childhood sweetheart. The inevitable happens and they were caught having a chaste kiss. The young man was badly hurt and consigned to a nasty dungeon where he spent six months, until the old man was killed by an ex-lover and he escapes and they live happily ever after. The story does not emerge from the picture all at once but it is filled in from an old manuscript that Mr Pelly has.

The peculiar fact is that the picture, even a copy of it, can speak, and so it does, to Euphemia. This comes to the ears of a dreadful friend of hers who is deeply interested in psychic research. This gives the author a good opportunity to show how bogus most of the so-called psychical research was at that time. It does not seem as if William was nearly so convinced of the importance of such research as we are told that Evelyn and as we have seen Sophia De Morgan were. The earnest group who investigate the talking picture come to the conclusion that it must be 'self induced hypno- sis'.

'As to the actual story,' De Morgan said, 'I seriously thought of calling it an Experiment In Nonsense.' Well, one does have the feeling that the author really did not take it very seriously himself. The good things in the book are not Italy four hundred years ago; the old Count is a cardboard villain and one knows that it will turn out all right for the lovers. Madelaine and her soldier are not very important to the plot. He comes back from South Africa minus an arm, having been posted missing, presumed killed. The story really comes alive when it deals with the rift between Reginald and his wife. Some of this is very funny, particularly the character of the aunt. The more the aunt presses her to go back to Reginald, as it is her duty so to do, the more she won't:

> Nothing irritated this injured wife more than to be reminded of fem- inine subordination to man as seen from an hierarchical standpoint. So when her Aunt quoted St. Paul – under the impression that extra- ordinary man's correspondence so frequently produces, that she was quoting His Master – her natural irritation at his oriental views of the woman question only confirmed her in her obduracy, and left her more determined than ever in her resentment against a husband who had read St. Paul very carelessly if at all, and who took no interest in churches apart from their Music and Architecture.[15]

In the end it is the picture, or rather a copy of it, which gives Euphemia the good advice to return to her husband, helped by the rich Madelaine.

Curiously, De Morgan's favourite character in the book is the awful housemaid, Sairah; not a very kind portriat, but perhaps he was remembering the experiences of Evelyn and himself with the procession of drunken and half-witted cooks and housemaids which they both complain about in letters to friends.

He had set himself a very difficult task in this book, and it is not surprising that he does not succeed in making a satisfactory story out of two such disparate elements as quattrocento Italy and London suburbia of the early 1900s. There is an attempt to draw a parallel between the Italian love affair and Madelaine and Jack, in that the young artist lost his arm in the noisome dungeon and Jack Calverley left his arm behind in South Africa. The historical Italian part of the book is commonplace, and could have been written by any number of late Victorian or Edwardian popular period novelists, but South London suburbia is unmistakably De Morgan at his best.

Chapter 12

Last completed novel, *When Ghost Meets Ghost*, published
1914 – has difficulties writing it.

A Likely Story was published in 1911 and it was not until 1914 that the next
novel, *When Ghost Meets Ghost*, came out. An unusually long gap, but this
mammoth book[1] gave the author a good deal of trouble. Also he was reaching an age when death seems not only possible, but, maybe, not too far off.
Thoughts on the subject in letters to friends were, despite his good health,
quite frequent, although anxieties about his back seem to have disappeared:

> I shall burn out without spitting and fizzing, I hope . . . Still, it's one
> of the quarrels I have with my Creator that, with all the unlimited
> resources of Omnipotence, He could not contrive some less awkward
> and repulsive way of winding up Life than Death. And to make
> matters worse, one is decently interred. It is no use pretending that
> God did not make undertakers, because they have just as good a claim
> to be considered His Creatures as Members Of Society!'[2]

And, again, he wrote:

> I long ago gave up playing the slightest attention to diseases' names.
> There are really only two sorts, those that kill, and those that permit

of a *modus vivendi*. I prefer the first. The *modus* never a comfortable one for their . . . client – suppose we say – however satisfactory to themselves. But what fun it would be to be a pain in the head of somebody one hated! How one would come on, get worse, and never yield to treatment!

William and Evelyn were delighted to get a copy of their old friend Henry Holiday's[3] reminiscences, and William wrote to him:

It's very strange to read at this length of time such clear recollections of that old Welsh period – which a life full of troubles has since made misty. There have been seven deaths in my family since then, and though some have not been definitely tragic, there has been an element of Aeschylean tragedy in the story.

However, nothing comes near poor Simeon[4] in tragedy.

He was also made very sad by the news which reached him in Florence, in early 1914, of the death of William Morris's wife, Jane. Her daughter May had written a moving letter to him:

> *Kelmscott Manor*
> *Lechlade*
> *6 Feb: 1914*

My dear William

I forgot what I told Evelyn in writing: it was sudden – absolutely unforeseen – beautiful and serene like her whole life. I had just come from a happy little visit to her, and we were making plans for the summer *here*. And here I shall live with their memories.

Old friend, if you could help my passionate hope for something beyond the clouds that shut us in, to a belief in it, you would help me to pass the remaining years in some serenity.

I'm never going to *show* grief but the loss is so overwhelming, the sense of emptiness so uncontrollable that the world all seems to have shrunk away into unreality.

Yet I am going to try to get back to work next week.

I see your book is soon out. We were speaking about it together the other day.

With love to both and thanks for your kind words.

Yours affectionately,

MAY MORRIS

He wrote her a letter which is worth quoting at some length as it not only shows William's shining honesty but also his lasting faith in his father Augustus's wisdom. The letter[5] from his house in the Via Milton, in Florence, reads:

My Dear May, –

How I do wish I could write a word to put heart into a old friend – so old a friend! – face to face with Death. I grieve to have nothing to say, that I am at liberty to say, beyond that my own belief is fixed, that this life is an instalment of a larger and longer one.

I know – or think – your enquiry to mean – 'Has this belief been founded on mere reason, or on some confirmatory experience?' My answer is that some small experience I have had of apparent communication with folk on the other side must have *some* weight in turning the scale so decidedly. But it may have been very small. I suspect that the lifelong faith of the strongest consecutive reasoner I ever knew – my father – had more to do with it than anything else.

If the few things I have met with, that have any value, could be told without involving others than myself, I would gladly write them to you. But they would amount to very little all said and done. I don't think that from all my experience I could produce anything so much to the purpose as the incidents described in my father's preface[6] to my mother's *From Matter To Spirit*, which you may have read. These incidents need to be read – to see their force – with a much closer attention than is commonly given to things in print.

Perhaps we shall die and after all be none the wiser as to what Death means, and Life. But it does not recommend itself to my understanding. Intense curiosity, and the hope that life is a dream we wake from, rather than Death a sleep we fall into – those are my mental conditions.

The voice and opinions of William De Morgan come over clearly, as well as his father's opinions. The reasoning in the letter recalls the discussions in *Joseph Vance* between Dr Thorpe and Professor Absalom.

Apart from the reflections on immortality, William was wrestling with his new, and very long, novel and complaining bitterly to his publisher of his problems:

> One volume is past praying for! But by all means let us pray! I think I shall take to writing Magazine Serials with lots of Pirates and Revolvers . . . It can never pay you at six bob. It is really the equiva-lent of three six-bobbers . . . It is too long for its merits . . . I really think this awful book had better be hung up until some way presents itself of dealing with it . . . You know what *I* should do – I should print a shilling sample and issue the remainder if called for.

There is another despairing letter to Heinemann of 12 July 1913, in which he suggested that the whole book might be rewritten – he had apparently fin-ished it – with another subject. His publisher had obviously been urging some cuts and William is defending some of the characters whom he thinks are essential to the story. 'Come to dinner!' he writes. 'It would give my wife the opportunity of showing the courage of her opinions that that blessed book of mine won't bear splitting.' However, at long last the book was fin-ished and to Joseph Vance, the American author and friend, he wrote in November: 'I have just completed a long nightmare of about 400,000 words. I will send you a copy when it comes out. But you musn't read mine because I read yours! – That wouldn't be fair measure. Sample the first 100,000.' From what one can gather from the extracts from De Morgan's letters to the publisher there had been some discussion about the possibility of publishing in two volumes[7] but it was in the end published in one volume ('The book too big and the print too small,' complained the author), with a two-volume edition printed at the author's expense for his personal use.

When Ghost Meets Ghost is long, 892 pages, but its reception was good. It was back to the characters and background which De Morgan's readers liked. Even the author thought it might be a success; he wrote to Heinemann from Florence to say that the librarian there was sending out every copy with a printed request that it should be returned within three days. The publisher somewhat acidly made the comment that Viesseux, the librarian, must be a humorist if he gave his clients only three days to read this particular book. The novel went into several impressions, and its immediate sales were a considerable relief to the author. Reviews were encouraging, particular the one in *The Times*.

Frank Swinnerton, in his *Swinnerton: An Autobiography*, has some interesting comments on the novels published immediately before the First World War. The readers of a literary periodical voted that the greatest living novelist in 1914 was Thomas Hardy, followed by H.G. Wells, Joseph Conrad, Henry James, George Moore and Arnold Bennett (bracketed), J.M. Barrie, Rudyard Kipling, Charles Garvice, and William De Morgan. They voted that the best novel published in 1914 was Joseph Conrad's *Chance*, but among the other twenty titles was *When Ghost Meets Ghost*, and also, one is glad to see, Frank Swinnerton's own book, *On The Staircase*. The only odd name in the list is that of Charles Garvice, a very obscure novelist, poet and journalist.

Most of the story is set in the mid 1850s, and there is a real feeling of nostalgia both for the vanished London which the author had known in his youth, and the London of Dickens. There were horse-drawn fire engines, and Euston and Marylebone Roads had still to be built. There is also a reference to the famous butting sweep who plays an important part in the beginning of *Joseph Vance*, and how he was eventually overcome by one of the characters in the present book, Moses Wardle. Unusually, a definite date is given at the beginning of the story – for the building of a sewer in North London, September, 1853. Candles are used, even in the grand houses, as gas had yet to be laid on, and, curiously, cigarettes are mentioned as newcomers to the social scene as opposed to pipes and cigars.

Not surprisingly, with De Morgan as the author, and a novel of almost 900 pages, the plot is extremely complicated and the author was sorry for the critics who had to cope:

What an arduous task, it must be to get up a review of 900 pages! I don't wonder critics object to the length. I have read one review, a long newspaper column of small print, embodying a careful analysis of the story, and wondered how much the writer, poor fellow, got for it! Certainly it should have been £5 – I suspect it was nearer £2

The basis of the plot concerns two sisters, daughters of a miller, in Essex in the early part of the nineteenth century. One of them, Maisie, is seduced by the son of the local squire, Thornton Deverill, and inevitably has a baby. Thornton marries her but shortly after is convicted of forgery and is transported to Van Diemen's Land.[8] He is eventually paroled and tells his wife to join him, which Maisie does, leaving her child with her sister; the little boy dies young. The cunning Deverill tells his wife that her sister in England has died, and lies to the sister in Essex that her twin in Australia had died. This is of course to get his hands on some family money. However, he dies and back to England goes Maisie with her boy, born in Van Diemen's Land, who turns out to be worse than his convict father, commits various crimes and is transported to Norfolk Island.[9] The two sisters are in their old age when the novel opens in the 1850s. One is living in the country and the other in a poor part of London, in Sapp's Court just off the Tottenham Court Road, but neither has any idea that her twin is still alive. The book opens on what the author rather curiously calls Chapter 0:

> Some fifty years ago there still remained, in a street reachable after enquiry by turning to the left out of Tottenham Court Road, a rather picturesque Court with an archway; which I the writer of this story, could not find when I tried to locate it the other day. I hunted for it a good deal, and ended by coming away in despair and going for rest and refreshment to a new-born tea shop, where a number of young ladies had lost their individuality, and the one who brought my tea was callous to me and mine because you pay at the desk. But she had an orderly soul, for she turned over the lump of sugar that had a little butter on it, so as to lie on the buttery side and look more tidy-like.

In the court live two small children, Dave and Dolly Wardle, orphans brought up by their Aunt M'riar and her brother, Moses, known to everyone as Mo, a gentle giant of a man who had been a renowned heavyweight prize-fighter. These two small children are the connecting link between Sapp's Court and a grand house in the country, Ancaster Towers. Dave has an accident, and a rich charity worker arranges for him to recuperate when he is out of hospital in the village near the big house. By coincidence, and this is a very convenient one for the plot, one of the two old sisters lives there, the other one being a tenant of the Wardles in Sapp's Court. The daughter of the noble earl who owns the Towers, Lady Gwen, takes a great interest in young Dave. She is beautiful, intelligent and generous-hearted, but also supremely self-confident and, not unusual for her class, very arro-gant. The author is more critical than in his other novels of the feudal aspect of rural England in the mid fifties. The villagers treat the grand folk in the big house with not only respect but subservience, and the number of 'my ladies' which are addressed to Lady Gwen when she goes visiting get a little tedious. There is not much nostalgia here for the good old days, rather a sense of relief that that kind of life has gone. A really sinister element to the story is provided by the return of young Deverill to England from Norfolk Island. He is wanted by the police for the murder of a policeman. He tracks his mother down but she dies before he can extort money from her, and then finds that his wife, Aunt M'riar lives in Sapp's Court. He gets some money out of her but when trying to escape out of the court meets old Mo. The old man has a bad heart, but evading a knife-thrust knocks young Deverill over and kills him, only to die himself half an hour later. A dramatic scene and a good climax to the story.

De Morgan had obviously taken a lot of trouble in researching the back-ground to convict life for those transported to Australia. There is a moving scene when young Polly (Aunt M'riar) tries to catch a last glimpse of Deverill before he sails away on one of the transports on the Medway, and a chilling account by Deverill of the cruelties practised in the penal colony. It was not difficult to identify someone who had come back from transporta-tion; they had a peculiar way of walking called the Derby Roll, a result of working in chain-gangs.

Dave Wardle is of course one of those small boys with a cheeky expres-sion and a dirty face who always appealed to the author, but Uncle Mo is perhaps the most memorable and original character in the book. Not a very practical man, but universally respected for his fame as one of the giants of the bare-fisted boxing world and for his obvious good nature. When he retired he put all his hard-earned money into a pub but of course lost it by giving too many free drinks to all his friends. He is still very welcome in the local boozer and there is a good sample of conversation between Moses and

Billy, one of the regulars, on foreign policy. It should be explained that it is the time of Crimean War. Billy is holding forth:

This afternoon he was eloquent on foreign policy. Closing one eye to accentuate the shrewd vision of the other, and shaking his head continuously to express the steadiness and persistency of his convic, tions, he indicted Louis Napoleon as the *bête noire* of European poli, tics. 'Don't let yourself be took, Mr. Moses', he said, 'by any of these here noospapers. They're a bad lot. This here Nicholas, He's a Rooshian – so him I say nothin about. Nor yet these there Turkeys – them and their Constant Eye No Pulls!' – this with great scorn. 'none of 'em no better, I lay, than Goard A'mighty see fit to make 'e, so it ain't, so as you might say, their own fault, not in a manner of speak, ing. But his Louis Sneapoleon, he's your sly customer. He's as bad as the whole lot boiled up together in a stoo! Don't you be took in by him, Mr. Moses. Calls himself a Coodytar! I call him . . . etcetera de rigueur as some of old Billy's comparisons were unsavoury.

'Can't foller you all the way down the lane, Willy,um', said Uncle Mo, who could hardly be expected to identify Billy's variant of Coup d'Etat. 'Ain't he our ally?'

That's the p'int, Mr. Moses, the very p'int to not lose sight on, or where are we? He's got hisself made our ally for to get between him and the Rooshians, What he's a,driving at is to get us to fight his battles for him, and him to sit snug and accoomulate cucumbers like King Solomans.[10]

This novel is not only back to the kind of story which De Morgan was good at, but it is also quite up to the standard of his early books. It was obvi, ously a relief to his readers that he had not embarked on another historical novel.

Chapter 13

Return from Florence for the last time, they settle down for
good in Old Church Street, Chelsea – outbreak of war and
effect on William – much energy devoted to inventions to
help war effort – two novels started but left unfinished, to be
completed by Evelyn after William's death in 1917.

FLORENCE HAD NEVER BEEN the same for the De Morgans after the death
of Roddam Spencer Stanhope. In addition, as we have seen, William's
health had ceased to be a worry, so that it was not too much of a wrench to
turn their backs on the Via Milton and live in London all the year round.
Before returning in the first half of 1914, they took a short holiday in
Venice. There is an excellent photograph of William and Evelyn in a
gondola on the Grand Canal, looking remarkably comfortable, with their
luggage piled up on the boat, Evelyn wearing an amazing hat and William,
in his tweeds, looking like an English country gentleman up in town for the
day. They must have been on their way to the station, as it was, of course,
in the halcyon days before fast motor boats. Not surprisingly, though, they
missed Italy. Julia Cartwright tells of meeting William in front of a newly
built Roman Catholic church in Chelsea, in Cheyne Row:

> The door stood open and we saw the priest within reciting the office
> of Benediction, the clouds of incense rising heavenwards and the
> gleam of silver and lighted candles on the altar. 'Ah!', he said, 'I like
> that and it makes me feel I am at home again!' And it flashed upon
> him that this church stood on the exact spot where his first pottery kiln

had been set up, in the garden of Orange House; and so, as he said, 'it really was his home'.

Evelyn's paintings which she had completed in Florence had arrived safely back in England and they could settle down in Old Church St, working away at their painting and writing. In fact William had already started work on two books at the beginning of 1914, neither of which he was destined to finish. The outbreak of the First World War in August unsettled him so much that in the next two and a half years he found it very difficult to concentrate on his writing. The comfortable world of London which he had written about so engagingly in his novels was fast disappearing and the horrors of the Western Front were only too real. He showed a rather unexpected bellicosity in his letters to his friends. To Professor Phelps[1] in America he wrote:

I have received your book and am glad to see it, and grateful. It is a pleasure to look forward to when the light breaks – at present one cannot read or write for the guns. Not that one hears them here, except metaphorically. But they are audible at Ramsgate.

I am sorry to say that I am barbarous by nature and catch myself gloating over slaughter – slaughter of Germans, of course! Half of these men I should have liked – a tenth of these men I should have loved. It is sickening – but . . .

A friend has just left me who maintains that the Germans never do anything that is not in strict accordance with international law. Then a devil might break loose, and yet comply with international law!

And to his friend, Scott-Moncrieff, he wrote: 'What a hideous time this! Shall we ever be at peace again? I am sick of it, and only feel if I could kill two junkers, I should die content! I wonder if any pacifist ever made an oration on the top of a reinforced concrete block made in peace-time to bombard London. Really Germany is the devil!' Very war-like sentiment for such a gentle peace-loving man, but the virulent anti-German sentiments which he expressed were very common in England at this time. Evelyn managed to continue her painting, although her subjects became grimmer, but William, in his study below the studio in Old Church Street, found for the first time in his writing career that it was very difficult to con-centrate on his novels. Instead, his thoughts turned to experiments which might be of help to the war effort. According to his wife and Mrs Stirling he spent a great deal of his time at the Polytechnic[2] where he was allowed space to work on inventions which he thought might contribute to aero-plane and submarine defence. He sent many schemes to the War Office and Admiralty, but they disappeared without trace, and his wife regretted after-wards that so much time 'was stolen from literature'. As far as we know nobody ever followed up William's suggestions. I wonder what their Lordships at the Admiralty made of the following idea?

> The object of this letter is to show that our submarines may be handled so as to neutralise enemy submarines, and thus re-assimilate the relation of fleets on the water to that which held good before the new arm came into existence.
>
> Suppose a submarine to be connected with a ship by a telephone wire, its movements can be directed from shipboard so long as its whereabouts is known. This may be determined by a float (say a piece of coloured cloth) which will remain visible at some distance even from the ship's deck and further still from the ship's rigging.
>
> The methods of handling it would be identical with those now in use when the vessel is independent, with the exception that she would not have to keep her periscope above the surface. Her commander would really be on the ship's deck, with a full view of the surround-ing water.

There then follows a very long and complicated description of a new system of communication between ship and submarine which the author is convinced will revolutionize the war at sea. It must have bemused some clerk in the Admiralty.

The Polytechnic also must have regretted his presence there when he created an explosion in one of the public rooms which blew out all the windows. After that he was politely asked to leave. 'Innocently expecting the hydrogen to burn like a Christian', he wrote, 'with a lambent flame, scarcely visible by daylight, we put a match to the hydrogen bottle. It busted with a loud report and blew out a lot of glass . . . Mr. Skinner, the Principle at the Polytechnic, tells me that Dewar made a lot of experiments on the knack hydrogen has of escaping. Really, Jack Sheppard and Montechristo are not in it![3] There was still a great deal of the schoolboy with his chemistry set in the grown-up William and one is reminded of the disastrous first firing of his kiln in Chelsea, which resulted in an explosion and the destruction of a whole firing of tiles.

Julia Cartwright[4] tells how, even in the first two and a half years of the war, when the casualty lists and the grim news from the Western Front must have been enough to depress anyone, William never lost his enthusiasm and optimism:

> He took a keen interest in an exhibition of his wife's symbolic paintings dealing with subjects suggested by the war, which was held in Chelsea last spring [1916] and was very proud of the substantial sum which it realised for the English and Italian Red Cross Societies. All through these anxious months his familiar figure was frequently to be seen in the streets of Chelsea. You met him in the morning doing his own marketing and carrying provisions home, and later in the dusk of evening he was constantly to be seen setting out on a rapid walk along the embankment. Often you caught sight of him stopping at a street corner to exchange greetings with some old inhabitant or engaged in earnest conversation with a soldier in khaki just back from the front. The tall figure was slightly bowed with advancing years, and Time had whitened the locks and beard that were once a rich brown, but the brisk, alert step and clear blue eyes with their frank, kindly glance, were still the same as ever.

Of the two books which were published posthumously, and which Evelyn completed, *The Old Madhouse* is the less successful and interesting. Published in 1919, it contains 'A Few Last Words To The Reader' by Evelyn which are certainly worth quoting. She writes:

> I feel that a short explanation might be welcome to the readers of this unfinished novel, in order that they may understand how the notes as to the proposed ending of the story come to be really what my husband had intended and not merely a matter of surmise on my part.

[169]

When my husband started on one of his novels, he did so without making any definite plot.[5] He created his characters and then waited for them to act and evolve their own plot. In this way the puppets in the show became real living personalities to him, and he waited, as he expressed it, 'to see what they would do next.'

It was his usual practice to read out aloud to me every Sunday evening all he had written during the week. When the novel was completed we read it aloud again straight through from the beginning to the end, so that he might judge of how the story came as a whole, omitting or adding parts as he considered necessary. This process of weeding or elaborating was not always left until the completion of the story, but he relied on being able to do it before giving his work to the public.

As the story was always read to me while in progress I too got to believe in the reality of the characters, and found myself thinking of them as real live people, and I have frequently asked him when he came down to lunch, or had finished writing for the day, such a question, as for instance, 'Well, have they quarrelled yet?' and he would reply, as the case might be, 'No, I don't know if they will come to quarrel; after all, I must wait and see if they do.' However, towards the end of the book when an intelligible winding-up of the story became imperative, the plot was taken up and carefully considered, all the straggling threads gathered together and finalities agreed upon, though latitude was always allowed for details to sharpen themselves after their own fashion.

Thus it happened on that last Friday night in December, when my husband laid down his pen in the middle of a sentence never to be completed,[6] he had told me as much as he knew himself of what the ending of the book was to be. I am therefore able to give a short synopsis of his ideas, and furthermore to assure the reader that not one word has been altered in the manuscript. It is exactly as my husband left it; even in places where I knew he had intended to make some slight alteration, I have left it as it was written.

My husband's writing was wonderfully clear and distinct, with very few erasures. He considered that he wrote very slowly, but judging by the amount of work he got through, this cannot be regarded as having been the fact. He never made rough copies and practically finished as he went; everything was so complete that he found even a slight alteration in the text would often let him in for as much work as the writing of a whole chapter would have given him.[7]

Latterly he found that he did his best writing after tea, but he never could be persuaded to give up the traditional working hours of the artist, with the result that he usually spent the whole day in his study, not allowing himself a short walk before dinner . . .

The Old Madhouse has two main threads to its plot. The first tells the story of two friends Frederick Cartaret and Charles Snaith, close friends from school, who when they both get married resolve to buy a shabby old house called the Cedars (known locally as the Old Madhouse because it had been a private lunatic asylum) and divide it between them. The second concerns Fred's guardian, his uncle Dr Cartaret, a formidable headmaster, who has to give his consent first and goes to inspect the house. He is shown in by the caretaker, who sees him enter the front door, but he never reappears and is never seen again alive. We have to wait until the end of the book to find out the answer to the riddle.

The friends' plans for the house are upset when Fred quarrels with his fiancée, Cintra, who is understandably jealous of Charles's Lucy, attractive and on the make. Lucy has only married Charles because he might inherit, and when she finds out that this will not happen she ensnares the weak Fred and they elope to the Continent, leaving poor Charles with a small baby. Lucy divorces Charles and marries Fred, but soon gets tired of him and embarks on a life as an unscrupulous adventuress. Fred, full of remorse, makes it up with his old school chum and emigrates to Canada. Charles gets married again to a much more sensible girl. It is a very moral story.

The mystery of the missing headmaster is resolved when a trapdoor is uncovered in a passage in the Old Madhouse; that opens into a well and the body of Dr Cartaret is found at the bottom of it, half eaten by rats. Before that, his ghost has been seen in the house and has actually appeared to Charles and they have a long talk together before the old man finally disappears.

As perhaps can be seen from this fairly brief summary of the plot, this is not a very satisfactory novel. The reader's interest in the disappearance of Dr Cartaret wanes over more than five hundred pages and the two main characters, Charles and Fred, are very cardboard. Lucy, the wicked, beautiful temptress, is more fun; perhaps an easier character to bring to life, and she does develop as the story goes on. But the book lacks the very real virtues that one finds in most of De Morgan's other novels. Apart from the almost total lack of humour the story is simply not strong enough to engage the reader's attention throughout a very long novel. Evelyn contributed ten pages at the end of the book, as well as her afterword, and she does succeed in tying up the loose ends. The date of the story is easy to establish; the motor car has appeared on the scene, although as there are not many of them on the streets it is safe for the younger characters in the book to cycle to see their friends on cycles with Sturmer-Archer gears. Not using the author's own invention, of which he was so proud.

De Morgan's last book to be published, *The Old Man's Youth* (1921), presented Evelyn with a bigger problem than *The Old Madhouse*. There were quite a number of gaps in the manuscript which she had to fill in as well as adding chapters at the end to finish off the story. Out of forty-eight chapters, fourteen are by Evelyn, written to make the book more intelligible. Perhaps she contributed too much in the way she underlines the point of the story, making it more obvious than the author might have liked. As Evelyn died in 1919, she never saw the book published. This, of course, is the novel which De Morgan himself said contained a lot of autobiography. According to him, he thought of the basic idea at the time that he was writing *Joseph Vance* – an old man in hospital telling the story of his life – but did not go back to the story until after 1914.

The old man, the narrator Eustace John Pascoe, dying in the Chelsea Infirmary, is treated very kindly by the nurses and doctors but does not get on with the parson; like William and his father Augustus, he has a poor opinion of ministers and the established Church.

Eustace John was brought up with his three sisters in a large house in Mecklenburgh Square. His father, kind and irresolute, works for the Inland Revenue. His mother Caecilia, a silly, petulant and neurotic woman, depends heavily on Endicott's Mixture, otherwise known as laudanum, and mainly consisting of opium. She is not fond of her only son. Because of her ill health, a housekeeper is appointed called Helen Evans, a bright, embittered girl who hates Mrs Pascoe. Mr Pascoe discovers two antique vases in the attic which he sells for a lot of money, but loses it all when he unwisely invests in a bank which fails. His wife dies from an overdose of her medicine given to her deliberately by Helen. 'Miss Evans took the glass in one hand, and the bottle in the other, but the hand that held the bottle shook, and an ugly gleam flashed in her beautiful eyes.' No one much regrets the death of the tiresome lady, but murder has been committed and one of the daughters and a servant with the extraordinary name of Varnish have a very good idea who is guilty.

The family, having lost most of their money, move to Chelsea to a house which, as we have seen, was very much like 1 The Vale. Mr Pascoe makes a wounding discovery during the move, when he discovers a letter, never posted, from his late wife 'to her first and only love'. De Morgan writes: 'The heartwhole allegiance of twenty long years snapped and broke.' It is no surprise when, not long after the move, Pascoe marries Helen the house-keeper, much to the fury of the eldest girl Roberta and the implacable Varnish, but despite their suspicions nothing can be proved against the murderess of the first Mrs Pascoe. Very nice for Helen, but she does suffer from a very guilty conscience which gives her sleepless nights and an addic-tion to all those appalling patent medicines, many of them containing opium, which one could buy over the counter from any chemist. The book is in fact a considerable indictment of the irresponsible and uncontrolled sale of these lethal concoctions. The date of the earlier part of the story is made plain when Eustace John's best friend joins the army and gets killed in India; it is the late 1850's, the time of the Indian Mutiny.

Eustace John, like the author, decides to study painting. 'Another land-mark which had painful consequences for me in after life, was my discov-ery that I had no genius for the Fine Arts.' The parallels between the author's and Eustace John's career are obvious. Slocum's studio is very like Cary's, and he goes on to the Academy Schools. The account also has echoes of Alice-For-Short. Eustace John is not much good as a painter but has a talent, not for ceramics, but for book illustration. He emigrates to Australia with his childhood sweetheart, but when she dies comes back to England as a dying old man. The final five short chapters written by Evelyn are rather weak, but do tie up the loose ends. The Chelsea house has gone, and as Mr Pascoe has died, Helen retires to a convent where she is thought to be saintly and when she tries to confess her sin of murder they will not believe her and think that it is delirium.

Basically this novel has a strong plot and had De Morgan had a chance to finish it and tidy it up, it would have been one of his most successful. His only truly wicked female character, Helen, led into murder by a bitter personality and a deep-seated envy of Caecilia Pascoe, the first wife, is impressive. The father is interesting, particularly in his relationship with his only son; he is humorous, understanding and affectionate, also a rotten businessman. One imagines that William De Morgan would have been such a father if he had had children, but one is under no illusion that the evil Helen or the first Mrs Pascoe bear any resemblance to Evelyn.

The end of 1916 found William well and in good spirits. Julia Cartwright describes him:

> The last time I saw him he was singularly bright and hopeful. He had thoroughly enjoyed a short September holiday at Lyme Regis, and was eloquent on the beauties of the Dorset and Devon coast. And he spoke with the utmost confidence of the coming campaign on the Western front next spring. For him there could be no doubt as to the final issue of the struggle. The devil was let loose for a while and all the powers of evils were ranged against us in the battle, but right must conquer in the end, he felt convinced, and the hour of victory, he believed, was not far off.

William's death came about quite unexpectedly. His sister-in-law Mrs Stirling tells us that William and Evelyn went to lunch with them on Christmas day 1916 and he was in very good spirits, full of energy and good talk. On Boxing Day, the Stirlings went to Old Church Street to spend the evening with the De Morgans and found a strange officer there from the Western Front, having tea. Mrs Stirling does not mention him by name, but in fact[7] he was the Hon Maurice Baring, the journalist and novelist and a member of a very rich and smart set in pre-war London. At that time, in his forties, volunteering for active service, he became first of all ADC to Henderson, the officer commanding the Royal Flying Corps, and then

ADC to the formidable Trenchard. He had read *Joseph Vance* and wanted to meet the author. Evelyn had written to Baring postponing the visit, but he never got the letter. Mrs Stirling describes what happened:

We sat on through the dusk, the room lit only by dim candles and the ruddy gleam of the fire. As desultory talk rose and fell, it transpired that the officer was in the Air Force, and William eagerly seized upon the opportunity thus afforded to gain information on a problem con-nected with his new flying machine which had baffled him. 'I wish you would look at a model of an aeroplane I am constructing', he said. 'Come to my study – the light is better there for seeing it.' The two men left the room. For half an hour they were shut up in close proximity in William's little sitting-room; then they returned; and the stranger said good-bye.

Out in the hall we heard them talking. William had discovered connecting links among acquaintances common to them both, and was plying his new friend with questions concerning these. The stranger's final answer came with a note of melancholy: 'My father is dead, my mother is dead; my aunt whom you remember is dead – everyone connected with me is dead. Good-bye'. And as William came back into the room he observed quaintly in reference to the visitor's last remark, 'Well that's a nice cheerful state of affairs – *Every one connected with him is dead!* I thought, under the circumstances, there was only one thing to be done – so I gave him a copy of *When Ghost Meets Ghost!*'.

That was on Tuesday. On the following Friday evening, December 29, William feeling strangely tired, laid down his pen in the middle of an unfinished sentence in the *The Old Madhouse*. By the morning he was ill; before nightfall he was raving in the delirium of trench fever. For seventeen days that continued; and during all that time he believed he was a wounded soldier in a hospital in France. With piteous reiteration he kept imploring that someone would take him back to his home – to his wife, while, she poor soul, sat, a frozen image of grief, waiting for the one moment of recognition, the one word of farewell which was never granted. On the seventeenth day he found rest; and she was left to face a darkened world with a broken heart.

Two days before William died, Evelyn had written a short note to her niece Molly.[8] She had not given up hope, but was discouraging visitors as William had to be kept quiet. She was helped by two nurses, as well as the doctor, and refers to the illness as 'trench fever, in common parlance gastric influenza'.

It was a sad end, and Mrs Stirling's account is a moving one, but there are two odd things about it. It was strange to refer to Baring as 'the stranger'. He must have been known, at least by name, to both the De Morgans and the Stirlings, not only as member of an aristocratic banking family but also as a writer. Also, surely Mrs Stirling makes a mistake when she refers to the cause of William's death as being trench fever. Both a local paper and Julia Cartwright refer to influenza, which seems more likely. Trench fever, which affected thousands in the First World War, was rarely fatal, though it left people ill for months; the organism which caused the disease was carried by lice, common amongst men in the appalling conditions of the trenches. Maurice Baring did not serve in the trenches and there is no mention in a recent biography[9] that he ever caught this very unpleasant illness. In a book which was published in 1956, *The Merry Wives Of Battersea And The Gossip Of Three Decades*, Mrs Stirling explains why she did not mention the visitor by name. Quite simply she did not want Baring to feel 'guilty', if indeed it was he who passed on the infection to De Morgan.

The funeral took place on the 20 January 1917 at Chelsea Old Church, and William was buried in Brookwood Cemetery in Surrey. The headstone was designed and modelled by Evelyn and carved in marble under the supervision of Sir George Frampton.[10] There are two figures, representing Grief and Joy, and two intertwined hearts in the pediment of the stone. A sentence is inscribed quoting from the automatic writing,[11] one of the letters from angels: 'Sorrow is only of earth; the life of the Spirit is joy.'

Evelyn received a large number of letters from relations and friends and, of course, admirers from all over the world. There is a very moving letter from one of the De Morgans oldest friends, Lady Burne-Jones:[12]

My poor dear girl (always that to me)
The news of your bereavement only reached me this morning, and is hard to believe. Yours was one of the blessed marriages, and it will never end, but the pain of this separation cannot be expressed either

by you or your friends. I only write to say that I have heard of it, and I am with you at heart.

I long to know something of you – and shall do so in time . . . at such a time, however, details have ceased to be important – all is swallowed up in the tremendous fact.

The thought of trench fever and its seeking a victim here is tragic among a thousand tragedies. I heard that he took the war very much to heart . . .

I have a treasured remembrance of the last time I saw him when I was cheered to see him looking better and younger than when we had met before . . . His immovable friendship is in no way dimmed to me by death – as it never was by distance of time or place; for me he cannot die, but still lives, amongst memories that nothing can wipe out. And for this I am very thankful.

For all the long years of our unchanging friendship I thank God; and for how much more must you have to return thanks, – none but yourself knows. In these terrible days it is beautiful to feel that the best things remain unchanged, and that Love is the key to the world.

My dear, forgive these stumbling words – but it touches me to the heart for you.
Always your affectionate old friend,
G. BURNE-JONES.

One of his oldest friends,[13] from the days when they were both art students together, wrote to Evelyn:

How sad it all is! How I feel for you in the loss of your companion, and such a gentle one, for so many years . . . He never grew old, he changed nothing since I first knew him fifty-six years ago. I expect, with his ups and downs counted, he had a very happy life, such simple characters usually have.

Maurice Hewlett wrote to her:

I value everything I remember of him. I feel myself the better man for having known him. As for his books, they are part of himself, and I have almost them part of myself; they are unique, as all books must be which faithfully express so rare a spirit as his. Those who love them will not let them die; and the number of their lovers will increase.

Unless Mrs Stirling left out references to his life as a potter, it is interesting that immediately after his death, William was mainly remembered as a novelist.

On 11 July 1918, some eighteen months after his death, a group of his old friends met at Chelsea Old Church, for the unveiling of a monument – a tablet, designed by his old partner Halsey Ricardo, with wording by Reginald Blunt, author and historian of Chelsea, and, of course, his business manager at Sands End. May Morris spoke, and particularly referred to the great friendship between her father and De Morgan and their dream of reviving rural handicrafts in the Cotswolds and starting a factory there in which they would both work. Edmund Gosse[14] followed her and talked about the novels with a good insight into their quality. He is worth quoting:

I am very much struck with the tranquillity of De Morgan's novels. There seems no stress in them, no anxiety. They move in a social world where the family is not challenged, where religion is quietly respected, where property enjoys all its rights, and where the army scarcely seems to exist. What leisure for reflection, what long hours extended in an easy chair! De Morgan seems to be so calmly assured of the stability of the social order that even those errors and those paradoxes which he observes will not avail to disturb his equilibrium. What a storm of social rebellion blows under the smiling surface of Dickens! What revolt against social convention in Meredith! What sullen resignation to fate in the vast romances of Thomas Hardy! – William De Morgan has no belief in the approach of a catastrophe ... His temperament, whether in his writing or his art, presented an image of serene confidence in humanity not found elsewhere. His style ignored the French manner altogether; he did not teach, he talked, and that leisurely, with a pervading, tranquil optimism. His books had uniformity and a vivid individuality, although qualities such as form and construction were matters of indifference to their

Fireplace in a dining room in a house designed by Norman Shaw, 1879.

Vase with lustre decoration, c.1890; and a vase and cover with Persian decoration, c. 1890.

Three vases with lustre decoration; top two c.1890, below c.1885.

Two dishes from the 'Sunset and Moonlight' suite with lustre decoration, c.1900.

Dish with Persian decoration, c.1890.

Dish with Persian decoration,
c.1890 (top), Bowl with lustre decoration c.1890 (middle), and Ewer
with Persian decoration, c.1890
(right).

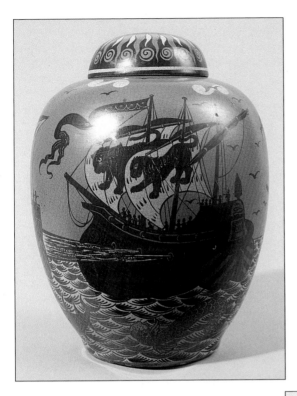

Vase and cover with lustre decoration (above) and Vase with Persian
decoration (right), both c.1890.

Vase with Persian decoration,
c.1890 (top), Vase design and Vase
with lustre decoration, c.1890 (middle and bottom), showing the way
in which De Morgan adapted his
designs for different pots.

author. He was a true artist, and in these iron times we do well to remember his gentle, loving and loveable individuality.

Evelyn did not live very long after William's death, although she continued to paint right up to the end. She died on the 2 May 1919, and was buried in Brookwood Cemetery, next to her husband, under the monument she had designed.

Chapter 14

Evelyn's death in 1919 – De Morgan's posthumous
reproduction both as a potter and as a novelist.

THERE WAS AN OBITUARY of De Morgan in *The Times* of 17 January
1917, headed 'Novelist and Potter'. The writer gave an accurate outline of
De Morgan's life and work but devoted more space to his career as a novelist:

> His novels were thoroughly Victorian in their spirit, method and
> detail. He followed the old tradition of leisurely development, with
> all the particulars fully filled in, leaving nothing to his reader's
> imagination and little to his powers of perception. Nice-minded,
> genially humorous, and pleasantly sentimental, he had nothing in
> him of the modern novelist's anxiety about life or passion for the truth,
> however ugly . . . writing to please himself, he wrote as he pleased; so
> that even the least momentous of his very many pages has the interest
> of his peculiar quality.

The posthumous publication of the two novels in 1919 and 1921 was
noticed by the critics, some of whom were sorry that they had not been left
in their incomplete state. There are no records in the Heinemann archives
to tell us how many copies the books sold, but the publishers printed 10,000

of *The Old Madhouse* and 5,000 copies of *The Old Man's Youth*,[1] which was published in America under its original title of *The Old Man's Youth and The Young Man's Old Age*. It was meant to be published in two volumes. Evelyn was not alive to see the publication of the second book, or to sign the con-tract for it, which is in the name of Mary De Morgan, one of the three nephews and nieces to whom Evelyn left the literary copyrights. The other two were Campbell De Morgan and Millicent Antrobus.

The next revival of interest in De Morgan's novels was occasioned by the publication of Mrs Stirling's biography, *William De Morgan and his Wife*.[2] Orlo Williams in *The Times Literary Supplement* of 22 June 1922 wrote a long article on the novels, pinpointing what made them so popular, the characters, which readers found so memorable, De Morgan's extraordinary command of cockney dialogue, which Williams considers more convinc-ing than Dickens's and what he calls an 'engaging serenity, which irradi-ated the whole of his literary work, making even its less successful passages tolerable, and holding an impatient reader contented, while, with absorbed deliberation, he lingers over every detail of his elaborate and melodramatic constructions'. He is critical of Mrs Stirling's book, pointing out how dis-orderly she is in her chronology, leaving the reader hopelessly confused, and also saying how disappointed he was in the portrait of William and even more so of her sister, Evelyn: 'This is not a biography, the composition of which, on the principle of bouillabaisse, becomes exasperating when one is made aware by momentary succulence that some of the ingredients were succulent.' As I have said, for a biographer her book is tantalizing in the glimpses it gives of the chief characters, but exasperating in that there is a total absence of notes on sources, while most of the letters she quotes from, many of them undated, seem to have vanished. But of course her book is an invaluable quarry even if one has to be very cautious of the quality of the product.

The Times Literary Supplement celebrated the centenary of De Morgan's birth with an article in the 18 November 1939 issue in which the writer commends *Joseph Vance*. By the outbreak of the Second World War most of his books must have gone out of print, perhaps with the exception of the three early titles which had been reprinted in cheap editions by Nelson. Oxford University Press World's Classics republished *Joseph Vance* in 1954 and this was the occasion for Sir William Haley's very thoughtful and knowledgeable essay on De Morgan's work – mentioned in Chapter Eight – perhaps the best piece on the novels to have been written. Haley is not uncritical; he refers to De Morgan's style as 'a controlled garrulity'. He was not good at plots; he was a novelist of character and situation. One must also agree with Haley that the first four novels are probably the best; that the huge *When Ghost Meets Ghost* has much in it that is memorable, although it is too long and complicated. It is fascinating to read a list of some of the books which Haley mentions that appeared just before and just after the publication of *Joseph Vance*:

> The English novel reader had been offered *Kipps*, *The Lake*, *Sacred and Profane Love*, and Upton Sinclair's *The Jungle*. In the twelve months or so after came *In The Days Of The Comet*, *Puck of Pook's Hill*, *Sir Nigel*, *Chippinge*, *The Passing of The Third Floor Back*, *Hills and The Sea*, and Miss Rose Macaulay's *Abbots Verney*. Modernism was not perhaps yet with the Edwardians, but it was breaking through. And into the midst of it there erupted this remarkable throw-back to the 'early Victorian and suburban', (the description is De Morgan's own).

The description is a little misleading because, as we have seen some of the novels are set at the end of the nineteenth century, and others earlier.

A.C. Ward wrote an introduction to the 1954 edition of *Joseph Vance* describing De Morgan's achievements:

> To become an immediately popular and intellectual novelist with a first book of the immense length of over 250,000 words written in his sixties after a life-time of entirely different work; to follow with eight more long novels which, together, caused reputable critics to place him with Dickens and Thackery, Meredith and Hardy; such was William De Morgan's unparalleled achievement in the years preceding his death in 1917 at the age of seventy seven.

Ward making thoughtful comparison between Dickens and De Morgan. He acknowledges the latter to be inferior to Dickens in comic invention and the ability to bring to life creatures of fantastic improbability. He also lacks

Dickens's social indignation, but he is perhaps better at controlling emotional situations and at sentiment without excess. Better, also, at portraying
women, and finally: 'If the structure of a novel is determined by the degree
in which its characters seem to become part and parcel of the lives of its
readers, Joseph Vance is a great novel.'

Plenty of evidence has been given that De Morgan was in no doubt what
he owed to Dickens. In some notes dated 4 January 1912, for the Dickens
Centenary, he wrote:[3]

1) Unhappily I have no personal recollections – I wish it were otherwise.
2) In my opinion I owe Dickens everything that a pupil can owe to a
master – to the head master. Whether I have succeeded in rising above
mere imitation I can't say – I must leave the point to my readers. My
own memory of Charles D is simply one of unmixed gratitude and
plenary acknowledgement of obligation.
3) It is impossible to assign a value to any work without a standard of
comparison. In the case of the two novelists of last century – C.D. &
W.M.T. – there is no such unit among English writers – except
Shakespeare – to make such a comparison would be presumptuous,
unless one had given to it the study of a lifetime.

Humour always appeals most to its own age – Keeping this in view,
I should say Dickens's humour showed a exceptional vitality – I meet
people now and then who deny it, but have not found their own
samples of humour, produced at request, the reverse of exhilarating.

I think there can be no doubt which is his greatest book. But autobiographical parallel is such a powerful engine in fiction that it is
scarcely fair to place his other works in competition with it. Conceive
the difficulties of writing the *Tale of Two Cities*, against *David
Copperfield*.

For many years now, none of De Morgan's novels have been available except
in second-hand bookshops and libraries, but his pottery has had a very
different history. We saw in earlier chapters that after the Fulham pottery in
Sands End finally closed down, the two Passenger brothers, Frank Iles and
F.L. Ewbank started up their own firm at 162 Brompton Road, and were

allowed to use his designs as long as it was made clear that the products had not originated with De Morgan himself. Without him there the quality of the pottery deteriorated. Fred Passenger went on to work when he was an old man, with the Bushey Heath pottery, which was started in 1923 by Mrs Ida Perrin. It is only too easy to see what a difference there is between the work produced at Bushey Heath and the pots produced at Sands End.

In April 1914, the British government organized an exhibition in Paris of British decorative art, in the Pavillon de Masan at the Louvre. It was a very full survey of all aspects of the Arts and Crafts movement, with a large section given over to the work of William Morris and his collaborators; there were forty examples of William De Morgan's work, both pots and tiles. His influence in the field of lustreware was to be seen in examples by Maw & Co. and Pilkington's factories, who used distinguished designers such as Walter Crane, one of the organizers of the exhibition and President of the Arts and Crafts Exhibition Society in 1914. The exhibition opened, of course, in the year when the First World War began, and all the objects in it spent the war in the museum cellars. By 1919, tastes had changed. There was reaction against ornament in design and against art of any kind which could be classified as 'Victorian'. In June 1924 there was a large exhibition of Chelsea china and pottery at Chelsea Town Hall, with a big section in the catalogue on De Morgan's work by his old friends and col׳ laborators Reginald Blunt and Halsey Ricardo, but by this time his work was out of fashion and he was much better known to the public as a novel׳ ist. Pottery in the 'twenties and 'thirties — handmade 'studio pottery' — depended more for its appeal on simplicity, shape and function, and decora׳ tion was in disfavour.

It is more than a little ironic that while De Morgan's ceramic work is eagerly sought after by collectors, although, as I have said, still not much liked by the potters of the 1990s, his novels have been forgotten except in reference books, and not one of them is in print. He might very well have made a joke out of it, but I am sure that he would be a little disappointed that not more of his inventions had found favour with anybody, except of course for the ones which he had developed for his pottery.

Nevertheless De Morgan has a secure place in the history of English ceramics. His achievements were unique and although he had a consider׳ able influence on some designers none could equal him in his imaginative powers. His novels have been out of fashion for some years now but there is an increasing interest in the achievements of lesser known writers of the late 19th and early 20th centuries and it is quite possible that some enterprising publisher will republish some of De Morgan's novels. It is very rare that someone can be a successful novelist, starting in his late sixties, an artist and an inventor, and, perhaps, equally rare to find someone of such varied talents who is also altogether an admirable and likeable human being.

Appendix A

A Game based on Dante's *Inferno*, invented by De Morgan in 1864

Upon one occasion Jones drew a set of fantastic drawings to show what he termed 'economy for publishers' – that is how one set of pictures could be utilized to illustrate two entirely different tales – and De Morgan and Holiday were deputed each to write a separate interpretation of the designs without seeing what the other had written. Holiday thereupon wrote an extremely ingenious paper purporting to be drawn up by Austen Henry Layard for General Sabine, of the Royal Society, Assyria, giving an account of the further exploration of 'the great Palace of Kouyunjik' and of the unique bas-reliefs and sculptures found therein: while De Morgan, perhaps recalling his recent training under the son of the great translator of Dante, described the drawings as representing a new version of the *Divina Commedia*.

As the earliest specimen of De Morgan's fiction now existing, these verses are of interest; but it must be borne in mind that they were no serious composition, only a carelessly written effusion in a boyish game; while no emphasis is necessary to point the baffling nature of the drawings which they interpret, or the topical character of the interpretation in days when the pre-Raphaelite Brotherhood represented the newest phase of Art, when Literature was still sentimental, and when Fashion decreed that crinolines were *de rigueur*, so that each woman, if not a 'dowdy' or a 'blue,' was confined in a 'stout cage.'

'The following are the fragments of Dante's Inferno which Michael Angelo illustrated. Cary's translation.'

[187]

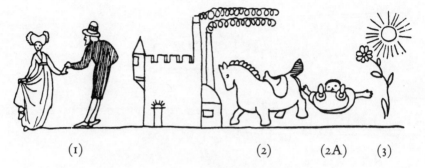

(1)   (2)   (2A)   (3)

'... Then my Guide: –
"Lo, monsters twain [No. 1] beside the Infernal gate
Who circle rotary in hideous dance!
Father are they and daughter, Death and Sin,
Whom Satan passed in Milton. I forget
Its whereabouts i' the poem; but it's there!"

'Then in the brazen lock the key revolved
Courteous. Then I – "Sweet father, what is this Shape?" [No. 2]
And to me he – "Cerberus" ....
Athwart the path it stood, a form to awe
The stoutest [No. 2A], who had fallen on the path[1]
On it beholding. ...

'Now had we left the noonday sunset's ray [No. 3]
Sinister, all a-pause on Cancer's Zone
Betwixt Astrea and the Scorpion's sign
In juxtaposition. There with digit raised
Virgil – "Behold!" I looked and saw a throng
Of Ghosts tumultuous [No. 4], females rushing on
Headlong towards a dungeon. "Who are these,
Sweet pedagogue?" said I; and he to me –

'"The Heroines of Romance, who expiate,
Here in this circle, mawkishness above."
Then we approached, and those sad Shades cried out –
"Alas! Alas! that ever we were bores!"
Then I – "Among ye are there any here
Of Florence, or of any other town

[1] *Footnote by De Morgan.* Michael Angelo appears to have misunderstood this passage, having drawn 'the stoutest' on the path distorted with horror. It is a fine specimen of that foreshortening for which he is remarkable.

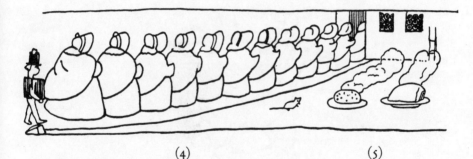

(4)   (5)

In Italy, or out of it?" – "Yea we!" and one – "Yea, I
Was Agatha's Husband's Wife, an awful bore,
A woeful and abominable bore."
"And I was '*Mrs. Halifax, lady*,' cried another.
Then a third and smaller one –
"And I was Muriel in the self-same novel
As she who last addressed thee." Then they all
With one accord, set up a mournful song –
"Go tell Miss Mulock[2] to ha' done, and make
Night hideous with her bores no more!" "And I,"
One other cried, "was Esther Summerson
In Dickens's *Bleak House*, a conscious minx
A mock-meek bore, a moralizing bore.
O should'st thou, Mortal, e'er to earth return,
Implore my Author that he ne'er again
Write sentiment!" She vanished and we passed
Onward . . . . '

'The citroned pudding and the osseous beef' seen in the corner, No. 5, give
scope for a dissertation upon Love contrasted with the action of 'the insignificant
Rat,' who tries –

'To use Free Will according to Free Wont,'

and the poem continues –

'Then in the circle twenty-fifth we moved
And I my Guide bespake – "O Teacher, say
What yonder form betokens?" [No. 6] for beyond
(One from a multitude) a fiend-rid goose

[2] Miss D.M. Mulock (Mrs Craik), author of *John Halifax, Gentleman*, and a very large number of
novels.

(6)

With wing outspread and agonizing cry
Swept o'er the Vast. Then Virgil thus to me –
"O Son, thou seest here the fruit of Sin
Most deadly, Criticism called of Art!
For yonder Goose, a critic erst on Earth
Now pays the price of many an Article
At which an earthly goose might well have sneered."
Then we approached, and to the bird I spake: –
"Wast thou of Florence?" and he "No!" replied;
"Of Marylebone was I. I was an Ass
On Earth, and therefore am a Goose;
I wrote of what I did not understand
For many penny periodicals
And others. Yet, O mortal (shoulds't thou e'er
Return to Marylebone) implore my friends
Not to be horrid humbugs!" . . .

'"In yonder dark abysm," [No. 7] said my guide
"Are punished Blues and Dowdies, they who wore
No crinoline on Earth, and thence looked limp,
Or trod with clumsy foot on toe of male.
The former that I mentioned went cram full
Of History and the Tongues to festive scenes,
And scientific recreations talked
Each to her partner in the dance." And lo!

(8)

Even then a bonnet coal-scuttle I saw
On female, tough and durable, who fled
A ruthless fiend [No. 8]. He with a bristled broom
Swept her, she clinging to the wall with cries
And lamentations, towards a frightful cage
(From which, 'twould seem, she had escaped) and drove
Her in, where she with wailing sank to earth,
While he the devilish engine locked and barred.
Then we approached. That Demon fell and foul
With broom upraised, in act to strike, surveyed
My Teacher, with forbidding mien. But he
With mild rebuke suggested other course.
"Forbear," he said, "for beings twain can play
The game thy mood suggesteth." So he fled.
And the woman from beneath the cage,
"O mortal, for that such thou art I see,
I was on Earth a Dowdy and a Blue
And eke strong-minded. Wherefore I bewail
Hampered by deadly Crinoline, my Sins.
O pity, though thou blame! And O take note
(Alas! Alas! that ever I took notes)

Of my forlornness! Not a book have I
T' inform the stronger-minded! No – not a tome!
Hast thou a Cyclopædia? Perchance
Thou hast, and thou woulds't lend it." . . . '

The next illustration, No. 9, represents the Hell of those: –

'Who are wont to take no sugar in their teas,
O error prime and impious –'

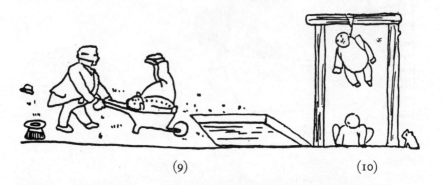

(9)   (10)

(De Morgan himself being wont to indulge in a plentiful supply.) Therein a friend
is seen bearing away one of the offenders in a wheelbarrow to immerse him in a
pool of molasses; while No. 10, a man on a gallows, is said to depict an enemy of
the pre-Raphaelite Brotherhood: –

'"Say, who was't thou on Earth," I said to him
Who swung in midmost air with woeful plaint.
"I was a hanger!" straight he answered me.
"I who once hanged, now hang for evermore.
I hanged my friends upon a line. All P.R.B.'s
I skied, and now myself am skied!" "Explain," said I
And he – "I was of the Academy
Where Plato taught. In thy Square Trafalgar
An Academician I
The Boshite hanged, and skied the P.R.B.
Or altogether fearless to become
In danger of the Council, turned him out."
Then at the gallows base a bitter fiend
With scoff and scorn cried out – "Go hang thyself!
Thou rogue thou."'

In a similar vein many other pictures are explained; and meanwhile Holiday, with well-feigned erudition, discussed them from the standpoint of an excavator and antiquarian. In No. 1 he saw an interesting ancient bas-relief of Bacchus and Ariadne. In the so-called 'Cerberus' he saw 'the fall of Phaeton, and one of the horses galloping off in the direction of Vulcan's forge, leaving the rash youth on the plain.' In the long train of ladies in crinolines and coal-scuttle bonnets, instead of Miss Mulock's sentimental heroines, he saw 'the visitors returning home from Belshazzar's Feast,' the remains of the viands being seen upon the right; while in the lady being attacked by the broom, he saw 'the heroine of an Assyrian fable being swept from the Globe.' Finally, upon the mysterious cage in the corner he discoursed yet more learnedly, having deciphered the ancient characters relating to it which, in phonetic spelling, revealed that it was a mysterious, pre-historic article known as a kri-nu-lin.

Appendix B

Lustre Ware

Paper delivered by William De Morgan to the Society of
Arts on 31 May 1892 and published in their journal on 24
June 1892

The word, 'lustre', in its connection with pottery, has not always been used in its present limited sense, but rather as an equivalent of our word 'glaze'. It has been applied to the glossy surfaces of the Greek, Roman, and Etruscan pottery, although the gloss upon these is comparatively slight. Nevertheless they are lustrous as com-pared with unglazed tile or brick. In a more restricted sense the term may describe any metallic deposit on a glazed surface where the decorative effect depends upon, or is enhanced by, reflected light. But even this definition would be now-a-days dis-allowed by the common understanding of the word, which applies it almost invariably to the special iridescence of Persian, Arabian, Hispano-Moresque, and Italian majolica. This iridescence, the means by which it has been and is obtained, and more especially the means by which I have myself endeavoured to obtain it, form the subject of the following paper. It is a subject which may be treated either historically or technically, but the two lines of treatment interesect at many points, and it is at these points, if at any, that what I have to say may be of interest. I will, therefore, before describing my own experience, give the shortest possible retro-spect of the history of the subject, although in so doing I shall no doubt be going over ground already familiar to many now present.

All investigations seem to converge towards the conclusion that Egypt or Assyria were the earliest nurseries of the art of decorating pottery, which after-wards attained its maturity in Persia. The glazed and coloured terracottas from the palace of Darius, brought from Susa by M. Dieulafoy, and now in the Louvre, show that those who produced them possessed all the materials and almost all the

[194]

processes known to their successors. But there is no apparent knowledge of the lustre process either in these or any other ceramic productions of remote antiquity, although an accidental stain of copper lustre has been detected on an Egyptian vase in the British Museum. The earliest lustres known are those found on frag-ments dug from the ruins of Persian cities, more especially those of the city of Rhé, or Rhages, to which a very great antiquity has been assigned. They have been generally accepted as antedating the destruction of the city 600 years ago. But although Sir R. Murdoch Smith speaks of a possible age of 2000 years for some of them, this is very conjectural; and until we can find proof of the process being in existence in Persia previous to the Arab conquest in 641, its Persian origin cannot be considered beyond a doubt. However ready we may be to ascribe a Persian parentage to the art of the Arabs, we cannot shut our eyes to the fact that the area of Arab conquest in the ninth century is almost exactly co-extensive with the distribution of the manufacture of lustres, so far as it is known to us, in the twelfth. Before the Arab conquest, decorated Persian ware is known to have existed by surviving samples, all without lustre. As soon as our authentic record of lustre-making begins, it is found throughout the conquests of the Arabs, and nowhere else. In 1154, Edrisi, the Arabian geographer, speaks of it as being then made at Calatayud, in Spain, which was at that date a recent conquest of the kings of Arragon from the Saracens. A century before (1040), Nassairi Khosrau testi-fies that they were made at Cairo. These are, I believe, the two earliest trustworthy testimonies to the manufacture of lustred pottery.

Perhaps the safest judgment as to the origin of the process in modern times is that which makes the Arabs the distributors, east and west, of a knowledge trans-mitted to them from Egypt or Assyria. It is stopped in its journey eastward at the borders of the Persian empire, and is conspicuously absent from China and Japan. Its non-appearance in the manufactures of these countries may be accounted for by the nature of the materials already in use. I have tried to get lustres on Chinese and Japanese ware, but have always failed; the glazes appear singularly refractory. Other causes may have helped to prevent the Persian or Arabic process going east-ward. In the other direction, the course of the Arabs, from Cairo to Tangier, has been said to be traceable by the glazed and decorated wall tilings of their build-ings, especially the mosques. No doubt, this is in some sense true, but it has been more than once told so as to convey a false impression that the Saracen invaders of Africa built tile-kilns at every station of importance, and that pottery factories were at work in Spain, if not during the time of the Abbasides, at any rate very soon after the establishment of the Caliphate of Cordova. Wall tiles, beautifully decorated, were placed by the historical imagination on the walls of the great mosque at that town, and by implication at Seville and Toledo also. But the ten-dency of more recent investigation is to ascribe all the surviving examples of Arab wall tiling in Spain to a much later date. However, there might have been wall tiles in the mosque of Abd-el-Rhaman of native manufacture, as fragments of decorated pottery, supposed by some to have been made in Spain about the year 969 A.D. occur in the Museum at Grenada. The construction of the mosque was still going on in the time of the vizier Almansor, who melted up the bells from the shrine of Compostella to make lamps for the mosque, at which he used to work with his own hands. This was in 985. But, if we judge by contemporary descrip/ tions of buildings, these great mosques, and others, such as the palaces of Az/ zahra, at Cordova, were marvels of decoration in marble, gold, and ivory, but were entirely without wall tiling. Moreover, mosques of the same period, at Cairo and elsewhere, are entirely without tile decoration.

The next landmark in the history of the subject is the erection of the Alhambra by the Moorish kings of Granada. The old tiles with which its walls are covered are genuine native *azulejos* of the date of the completion of the building, about 1350. They must be distinguished from those placed in the building when it was restored by Charles V in the sixteenth century. They belong to the same group of manufactures as the great jars which were found full of coin under the building. The well/known one, of which there is a copy by Deck at South Kensington, is still in the Alhambra, and there is a similar one in the museum at Madrid. These and one or two others are the oldest surviving examples of the practice of lustre in Spain. There does not seem to be any need to assume that they were imported from Cairo or Persia, and we may probably ascribe their fabrication to Malaga. The Alhambra tiles may have been made there too, although in view of the compar/ atively simple operations involved in the making and firing of the latter, and the vast quantity required, it might be more reasonable to suppose they were made on the spot. It would have been far easier to build a kiln on the works at Granada than to carry all that weight of tiles over the Sierra Tejada. But the pots were quite another thing. They were made for exportation as well as native consumption, and Ibn/Batoutah, an Arab traveller, found the manufacture in full work at Malaga in 1350.

Time, or rather the want of it, prevents my making more than a passing allu/ sion to the lustred wares of Sicily. There are some examples of what has been called Siculo/Arabian ware to distinguish it from the dark blue pottery covered with small diaper ornament, which is ascribed to Saracenic or Moorish potteries at Calata/girone (about thirty miles from Syracuse), probably of the period of the maturity of the Hispano/Moresque. I believe there is nothing antedating the Norman Conquest of Sicily. But there is documentary proof of the exportation of *faïence* to Sicily from Barcelona, in 1528, which suggests that the manufacture never became firmly rooted. However, we must remember that Sicily had been under the Spanish rule, or misrule, from 1479, and hunting Saracens was a part of their political economy. The desirability of extending the export trade may have accelerated the suppression of the Siculo/Arabs. I am rather surprised that the near coincidence of this date of the Spanish in Sicily with the appearance of lustres in Italy should not have caused the ascription of its Italian origin to these particular potters and no others. It would have been at least as plausible as the other theories.

One of these had its origin from the existence of *bacini*, or *bacili*, with which the walls of certain churches at Pisa and elsewhere are decorated. Marryat, the historian of pottery, ascribed a Saracenic character to these, and framed a theory to account for them which is so picturesque that I wish it were true.

In 1115, the Pisans made a crusade against Nazaredek, the Saracen King of Majorca, whom they overcame after many mishaps by land and sea. They liberated no less than 30,000 Christian captives from his dungeons, and returned home with shiploads of Saracen prisoners, gold and silver, embroidered garments, and decorated crockery, to say nothing of two large porphyry columns, which they afterwards gave to their allies, the Florentines, and which stand on each side of Benvenuto Cellini's Baptistry gates to this day — an eternal testimony to the truth of the story. The decorated bacini in the walls of the churches at Pisa were supposed to have been placed there as trophies, and, indeed, continued to be thought so until Mr Fortnum's examination of them in 1868 settled the matter. He made a close inspection of those on six churches at Pisa, and found only one fragment of Saracenic origin. Marryat had the tale of the crusade — which, no doubt, is good history — from Sismondi, but Sismondi says nothing whatever about the cargo of lustred pots. His chief authority is Laurence of Verona, who wrote a poem about the Crusade. It does not seem to contain any allusion to the *bacini* or kindred subjects, but then my failure to find it in 3000 Latin hexameters is far from conclusive. However, what I rely on is that I have seen no citation from them in Mr Fortnum's writings. Mr Fortnum has been over the ground, and had there been a word about the *bacini* in the poem, he would certainly have found it out. The passage in Marryat's history conveys the impression that he did not look behind Sismondi, and indeed that his conjecture was a mere passing surmise, chiefly based on the *bacini* in the church walls themselves.

Another conjecture, which would have been just as good as the foregoing if the dishes had been Oriental in character, ascribes their origin to the Saracen merchant ships captured by the Pisans at Syracuse or Palermo, at the time of their alliance with the Normans in their invasion of Sicily in the tenth century.

Another, the latest I have met with, is that of M. Mely, who tells us that at Tchakindji in the Caucasus, the armorial bearings of Genoa and Pisa occur on mediæval buildings, and that the mosque of Erivan in that neighbourhood is richly decorated with tiles. He suggests that this may have been the point of contact between West and East which caused Italian pottery. But there is no difficulty in finding ways in which the Italians *might have* learned technical secrets from the Saracens. The difficulty is to connect the actual art, as it appeared first in Italy, with any one of the sources to which it has been ascribed.

Majorca has certainly had the preference hitherto. But we have no actual record till 1442, when one Giovanni di Bernardi, of Uzzano, in a treatise on navigation, speaks of 'the war of Majorca and Minorca, which had then a very large sale in Italy'. To my own thinking, there are two things which account for the promi-nence given to Majorca. One is the story of King Nazaredek and the conjecture Marryat founded on it about the *bacini*. The other is the name majolica, applied to lustred ware at first, and afterwards to all Italian *faïence*. But when we come to look for the first use of the word in the sense of pottery, we are referred to Julius Cæsar Scaliger in the sixteenth century, who says that the recent skill of the Majorca potters has made such clever imitations of Indian (Chinese) pottery, that it is hard to tell them apart, and that these are called after Majorca, all but a letter or so. An antiquity which this record is not entitled to creeps round it in the mind of any unobservant reader when, in close proximity, he reads the line of Dante, in which he speaks of 'l'isola di Cipri ê *maiolica*'. I feel certain that many who have seen this connection of two writers born over 200 years apart, must have run away with the idea that Dante called earthenware majolica.

There is also the testimony to the importation of Spanish-Moorish ware from Valencia to Italy of Escolano, a Spanish writer, who says that Pisa was the port to which the Moors exported their *faïence*, in exchange for that of Italy. This is a very odd statement. If the merchants of that date (before 1600) really brought *faïence* back from Italy, it must have been something of great value, some article of luxury. It is utterly inconceivable that they should bring back freights of cheap serviceable earthenware to a country famous for its crockery since the days of the Romans, when Murviedro was Saguntum. On the other hand, if rare and highly decorated work came from Italy, where is it now? It is well known that the bulk of the fine samples of Hispano-Moresque were found in Italy, having been exported to the Italians as a favourite article. There should have been a few, at least, of corre-sponding samples in Spain of imported Italian ware. However, it is noticeable that testimony of Spanish exports to Italy at an early date should also bear witness to the importation to Spain of Italian ware presumably of equal value. It is also a fact of much importance that, while all this testimony is limited to showing that there was a commercial reciprocity between the Spanish ports and Pisa, the first records of lustred pottery in the north of Italy begin, not at Pisa, but at Pesaro.

Pesaro is a clay centre, and a seat of pottery manufacture from a remote antiq-uity. Passeri, the earliest historian of Majolica, was Vicar-general of Pesaro, and although he writes with some natural partiality for the town, I believe his conclu-sions are generally respected, especially as he had opportunities for inquiring into the earlier manufacture which no longer exists. He places the decoration of the mezza-majolica (as the ware came to be called) as early as the end of the trecento period, and the characteristic *madreperla* lustre towards the end of the quattrocento. He also claims for Pesaro the honour of having produced ruby lustre in 1480. If some of the mezza-majolica at the British Museum is rightly dated, there is no reason why this should not have been the case. At any rate, Pesaro is where we have to look for the Moors, who came and taught the Italians lustre.

Now, Pesaro is a long way from Pisa, and the Apennines are between. It is quite as near Venice, and is a seaport. For every one communication between Pesaro and Pisa in the Middle Ages, there would be a hundred between Pesaro and Venice. And between Venice and Syracuse there would be much more frequent communication than between Valencia and Pisa. If we must have Arabs to teach the Pesarese lustres, why not go to Sicily for them. The fact is, that a mistaken historical clue guided the inquirer to Pisa first, in the case of the twelfth century *bacini*, and it is difficult to get away from it. If another instance of *bacini* – that of the church of Lucera, in Apulia – had attracted attention to the same extent, we probably should now find it equally difficult to get rid of the Moors or Arabs of Calatagirone. For my own part, I do not believe either had anything to do with it, beyond the impulse the circulation of their ware gave to the ingenuity of one of the cleverest races in the world in an age of increasing artistic activity.

I have lately had the satisfaction of finding that this opinion is also expressed in the work of M. Theodore Deck, on 'Ceramics'. M. Deck's opinion ought to have great weight, as he is certainly the most eminent practical potter who has written on the history of the subject.

I have dwelt upon this historical evidence, because it is just one of the points at which the lines of history and technical inquiry intersect. I will now give my version of the other side of the matter.

The technical distinctive feature of Hispano-Moresque ware is that it is invariably on a white ground of glaze rendered opaque by oxide of tin. All the mezza-majolica, the early Pesarese ware, is on the white ground described by Passeri, which had, according to him, been in use since 1300, perhaps earlier. It is not a tin enamel, but a white slip covered with a mixed glaze of lead and alkali, *marzacotto*. Not a single dated example of lustre appears in Italy on a tin enamel till near the end of the fifteenth century, either at Pesaro or elsewhere. Now I can testify, and so can every potter who has ever made lustre, to the facility and certainty with which it can be produced when tin is present in the glaze as compared with other glazes.

That the Italian potters should learn from a Moorish source, and yet get so little clue to the superiority of this white ground that no experiment in its use should survive, and no tradition be handed down, is most improbable. But it becomes more improbable still at the next step in the history of majolica when, about 1475, or perhaps rather earlier, the tin glaze begins to supersede the white slip. The course the Italian potters took then was to use it not as the glaze *par excellence* susceptible to lustre, but as a whiter substitute for the white slip, glazing it over with *marzacotto* precisely as they had glazed the old ground. It might be difficult to pronounce certainly on this point from inspection alone, but there is other testimony. Piccolpasso, in his very explicit description of the Gubbio process and Italian pottery generally, in 1548, leaves no room for doubt. He notices the necessity for glazing the tin glaze thinner than the white *ferra di Vicenza*, or slip. But there is not the slightest hint that the old *marzacotto* glaze was ever discarded.

It may be objected that the tin glaze was unknown, or unobtainable. There is strong evidence to the contrary even as to its use by Italian potters, and the tendency of recent research is to place the date of its adoption earlier and earlier. But apart from this, it was in use in Italy for another purpose long before. Luca della Robbia had had time to mature his method of covering terracotta with it, and to place his two great bas-reliefs above the doors in the Duomo at Florence by the year 1438. So that, however much we strain dates, there is a long period during which the tin enamel was known in Italy, and yet the makers of the mezza-majolica persisted in the use of a ground of their own, while, had they been acting under Moorish instructions, they must certainly have been looking and longing for the more man-ageable Moorish ground. If Luca got his knowledge (as Jacquemart supposed) from the potteries of Faenza or Caffaggiolo, it makes the combination of circum-stances still more puzzling. Faenza is a two days' journey (about seventy miles) for a horseman from Pesaro, certainly not more – and the interchange of *employés* was probably not uncommon.

I believe what I have said would hold good equally whatever view is taken of the exact date of the first Pesarese lustres. The question is a little complicated by the fact that the date of the lustre is not of necessity that of the piece. An unlus-tred piece of *faïence*, 300 years old, could be put through the kiln now, and no human penetration could discover the date of the lustre. *Bacili* made at Pesaro in 1450 may have been lustred at Gubbio in 1550.

I leave this part of the subject with many things unsaid, in order that I may not be forced to omit the next landmark in the history. The bottega at Gubbio, and its connection with Giorgio Andreoli, has been considered as the most important of all from an artist's point of view. Maestro Giorgio was a sculptor, a pupil of Luca Della Robbia, who took to pottery and worked at this bottega, which had already produced some fine lustre work, perhaps as fine in all decorative respects as any which followed. The free use of ruby distinguishes this from the mezza-majolica, and the Maestro Giorgio productions may be again distinguished from it by a varied character in the ruby, and a finer white ground. The aim evidently is a trans-parent ruby to be used as a pigment. To my own thinking, the work throws doubt on its suitability for this purpose. However, there can be none that in his time the colour attained its greatest brilliancy. The dates range from 1418 to 1537, the later examples being by his son and other contemporaries, who carried on the work a little longer. But all lustres disappear from Italian decorative work about 1550, so that a period of 60 years covers the whole production. I have before spoken of the longer life-time of the Hispano-Moresque process, but, in both cases, the dis-appearance was only that it ceased to be used on elaborate work; as certainly in Spain, and possibly in Italy, the practice has never completely died out.

It is more difficult to account for its disappearance so long before the collapse of the arts in the eighteenth century than for the vigorous and successful attempts to out-do the Moorish pottery in the age of Renaissance. It may satisfy some to say that a change of fashion did it; but this is only substituting one phrase for another, and very nearly means nothing at all. A plausible surmise is that its use became incompatible with the careful and dexterous brushwork on fresh-dipped enamel, which reached to such perfection at Castel Durante and Urbino. The greater an artist's success in manipulation, the less is he disposed to incur the risks of an uncertain firing. A lustre-kiln may spoil the whole out-right, or even if the lustres themselves are successful, may only come into existence at the cost of elbowing their neighbours out of it. So long as the material was used for its own sake, and no attempt was made to go beyond its natural limits, all went well, but as soon as the artists began to be discontented with the restrictions its use put upon their opportunities of showing their own dexterity, the lustre colour had to give way. It may have been this, or possibly the demand may have been diminished by the dis-appointment consequent on local mishaps. The death of a furnaceman of special skill might cause a suspension of work, or, what is more likely, a substitute might be found whose failures might lead to a belief that the process depended on some secret which his predecessor had kept to himself. Whatever the cause, or complica-tion of causes, they vanish in 1550, and do not re-appear for 300 years.

The process is not described by Brongniart, who was the great technical author-ity on pottery of fifty years ago; and Salvêtat, who was his successor, makes only a very speculative allusion to its possible character. And in the catalogue of the Great Exhibition of 1851, which is a sort of death register of the arts of antiquity, not a hint of lustred pottery appears. The modern revivals begin with those at the Ginori factory at Doccia, near Florence, and those of Carocci at Gubbio, of which Mr Fortnum speaks very highly. There were some of these in the 1862 Exhibition in London. I have never seen any myself. The best I have seen are those of Cantagalli, at Florence.

In spite of the Doccia and Gubbio reproductions, an impression continued to prevail that the process was a secret. I used to hear it talked about among artists, about twenty-five years ago, as a sort of potters' philosopher's stone. At that date the attempts to reproduce it in England had met with only very partial success, although an Italian had gone the round of the Staffordshire potteries showing how to do it. Even now it is sometimes spoken of as a secret by newspaper writers. My attention was attracted to some very interesting work of Massier, of Cannes, in the last Paris Exhibition, by a newspaper paragraph headed 'Re-discovery of a Lost Art'.

In fact, re-discovery appears to have dogged the footsteps of the lustres from the beginning. I re-discovered them myself in 1874, or thereabouts, and in the course of time some of my *employés* left me, and re-discovered them again somewhere else. I do not think any rediscoveries of this sort contributed in any way to the very general diffusion of the process in the potteries at this moment. Very likely some of them have an earlier record than mine, but the only one I chanced upon when I was in Staffordshire was that of the late Mr Clement Wedgwood, who showed me a number of experiments which would have been successes if the glaze had been suitable, and a small sample shown me by the late Mr Colin Campbell. As far as the technical difficulties of simply evolving a copper or silver lustre go, I see no reason why (as in the case of the Arabs and Italians) every discovery should not be totally unconnected with every other. But there was one thing the Italians found out, when they reproduced the Moorish firings, namely, how to make a strong, and beautiful, and original use of their materials. It may be that the less we say about the modern parallels of their case the better.

Perhaps we may now make a new departure, and consider that the process is as well known as any other process in the arts; at any rate, I will contribute what I can to make it so, by telling all I know of it myself. I got nothing from Piccolpasso, as I did not see the work till long after, nor from any printed information, except the chemical manuals I had read in youth. The clue was furnished by the yellow stain of silver on glass. When overfired this shows iridescence, which is often visible on the opaque yellow visible from the outside on stained glass windows. I tried the stain on Dutch tiles, and found them unsusceptible in the glass kiln, but, in a small gas muffle, I found that both copper and silver gave a lustre when the gas was damped down so as to penetrate the muffle. I pursued my investigation, and, after an interruption, occasioned by setting the house on fire and burning the roof off, I developed the process in Chelsea. This was 1873–4, since which time it has not varied materially, although I have tried many experiments, with a view to improving it.

As we now practise it at Fulham, it is as follows: The pigment consists simply of white clay, mixed with copper scale or oxide of silver, in proportions varying according to the strength of colour we desire to get. It is painted on the already fused glaze with water, and enough gum arabic to harden it for handling and make it work easily – a little lamp black, or other colouring matter, makes it pleasanter to work with. I have tried many additions to this pigment, of infusible white earths such as lime, baryta, or strontia, and other metallic oxides, but without super-seding the first simple mixture. Any infusible clay will answer the purpose, though we have always used kaolin, as the least fusible. In Deck's work on pottery he gives several receipts for lustre pigments, only one of which seems to me to belong to the true process of lustre. The others all contain sulphur, which is not necessary, though it may work very well. The sulphur lustres are akin to the old Swansea lustre, which only requires to be burnt at a low heat without smoke. The sulphur evaporates and leaves a metallic deposit which is not oxidated, or only partly so, by the access of air after the sulphur vapour has left the kiln. I believe all the lustres included in the colour-maker's lists are of this nature, but the results produced in modern ware do not tempt the investigator. The prettiest one I have seen is Burgos lustre, which, however, contains gold. The only ingredient containing sulphur mentioned by Piccolpasso would be the small quantity of vermilion (that is, if *cinabrio* means vermilion), which he adds to his receipt for *oro*. Piccolpasso's recipes are for the diluent clay only, as he says nothing of either copper or silver. But he had them from hearsay, and if he really tried to produce lustre with them without any addition of metal, it quite accounts for no lustres ever appearing at Castel- Durante, where he was master potter. Indeed, it raises the question whether he was not hoaxed by Maestro Cencio, Giorgio's son, who is supposed to have given the information.

The ware, when painted, is packed in a close muffle, which is then raised to a very low red heat, so low, when the ordinary tin enamels are employed, as to be only just visible. A charge of dry wood, sawdust, wood-chips, or, indeed, any combustible free from sulphur, is then introduced into the muffle through an opening level with the floor, a space having been left clear under the ware for its reception. As soon as it has blazed well up, the opening is closed. The flare then chokes down and the combustion of the charge is retarded, the atmosphere in the muffle consisting entirely of reducing smoke. The test pieces will soon begin to show a red or yellow stain, the pigment itself looking black, until it is wiped off to show the stain. This operation must be repeated until the tests look right, when the fires should be drawn and the muffle left to cool.

The difference between this operation and Piccolpasso's is chiefly in the use of the closed muffle, which is rendered necessary by the difference in fuel. The sulphur from coal or coke would injure the glazes where there was no lustre, and would interfere with the process itself. In the Italian process, where wood is the fuel, the wood is packed in a perforated sagger, into which the smoke from the furnace is choked back by closing a damper, or by simply increasing the volume of smoke from the furnace by heaping on brushwood. But the principle of the operation is the same in both cases, and the dangers are the same. The firing may be vitiated in either by any of the following causes. There may be too great heat, or too prolonged heat; the smoke may be too dense, or too attenuated, or not long enough maintained, or the reverse. If more than one of these factors is wrong at the same time, the harm done will be in proportion. Even when the conditions are most closely observed, the results will show unexpected variations. It is impossible to secure uniformity throughout a muffle. Consequently, the size of the ware must be small in proportion to that of the muffle, or a vase might be overdone at the top and underdone at the bottom, while a number of small pots in the same space would have turned out very well, a few of the top ones being uniformly overdone (and perhaps little injured), and a few of the bottom ones underdone, and only wanting a second similar firing. This also makes a longer and slower firing neces- sary with larger ware, and this means more risk.

The different sorts of copper lustre may be classified thus:

1. Opaque metallic copper deposited on the surface of the glaze. The oxide is in this case probably reduced at the moment of deposit. Nearly the same result takes place in the common lustre of the potteries, where the sulphur of the sulphide of copper is driven off by a low heat.

2. Combination of copper suboxide with the glaze without reduction to metal. This is to all intents and purposes the same thing as when glass containing copper is flashed and becomes ruby. The harder the glaze is, and the higher the temperature, the less likely is a deposit of metallic copper.

3. The result of prolonging heat without smoke on No. 1. The deposited copper is thus slowly absorbed into the glaze, becoming ultimately red without lustre, but passing through every intermediate stage.

4. The result of increasing the reducing agent on No. 2. In this case the oxide already in combination is brought back to the state of metal. I believe that all the best lustre should be classed with this or No. 3.

Silver lustres show the same results, but at a lower temperature. So when both lustres are fired together, we may expect Nos. 3 and 4 of silver lustre, with Nos. 1 and 2 of copper.

The ugliest results are when the glazes are overcharged to the point of opacity. But accidents of this sort may be taken advantage of when the designer foresees the result. For instance, great blotches of opaque pale yellow on an inky black background may be very ugly, when an arabesque of fine lines of the same yellow on the same ground might be rather pretty.

I have said that the tin glaze is the most susceptible to lustre, but it does not necessarily give the finest results. The Gubbio lustres are really on superposed *marzacotto*, and possibly the exceptional beauty of some Persian lustre may be due to what is often called a siliceous glaze, which is what I call an alkaline glaze, as all glazes are siliceous. A film of such a glaze over the tin would almost elude any possible means of detecting it, and yet would scarcely be penetrated by the lustre colour, so thin is it.

The best of the first lustres I made on Staffordshire ware were on ironstone or granite. The body was repellent in colour, but the glaze particularly good. Latterly, we have used the common opaque white made with tin. It has also been ugly in colour, being, I believe, made so by the addition of cobalt, to make it whiter, just as the housepainter spoils his beautiful white chalk with French blue. I have tried many experiments with glazes, but I am inclined to think that the way they are fired in the glost oven has as much to do with their adaptability for lustre as their chemical composition.

I have also tried in this past 20 years a vast number of experiments, with the idea of adding to the first simple process of the Arabs. To save others needless work, I will enumerate a few, with my recollection of their results.

1. Reduction by other agents than carbonaceous smoke: by ammonia, by steam in contact with reducing fuel, by coalgas, by vapour of water and glycerine or spirit. None of these gave any new results.

2. The use of copper and silver colours as enamels, or under glaze, and their subsequent reduction by any of these agents. Sometimes there were good results, but the colour was always patchy.

3. The deposit of copper or silver from vapour of the chlorides, ammonium chlorides, or iodides, those portions of the glaze being protected which were to remain white. These experiments might be repeated with advantage. A similar one was the painting of the pattern in a susceptible glaze on a refractory one, and its exposure to vapour containing copper or silver. The suboxide of copper itself vaporises under certain conditions, which is the cause of the flow red colour occur-ring on many examples.

I have, of course, tried endless modifications of the ordinary process, such as using special woods for smoking, sawdust, shavings, paraffin, and othr combust-ibles. Any of these answer the purpose, the application being slightly varied. But nothing material has come of any of these experiments, and the process remains substantially the same as at first. I believe that if there has been any new opening for the application of chemistry, although I might not have followed the clue successfully, I could hardly have missed it altogether.

In conclusion, I may say that I believe we have learned all there is to know of the chemical and mechanical side of the art, as it was known to the ancients. What remains to be discovered in order to produce original work, equal to that of the Renaissance, is not a technical mystery, but the secret of the spirit which animated the fifteenth century not only in Italy, but all through Europe. We have got the materials and many more, but the same causes that forbid the attainment of new beauty with the new ones, have stood between us and the revival of old beauty with the old. In saying this, I do not suppose myself to be going outside a universally accepted truth, or, at any rate, one that is very rarely questioned. Some day there may be a new imagery and a new art. In the meanwhile I can only say that if anyone sees his way to using the materials to good purpose, my experience, which I regard as an entirely chemical and mechanical one, is quite at his disposal.

Appendix C

Marks on William De Morgan ceramics

(The marks are not drawn to scale)

Chelsea period 1872–1881

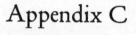

(a) Impressed mark

(b) Impressed mark

(c) Impressed mark

(d) Impressed mark

Merton Abbey period 1882–1888

(e) Impressed mark

(f) Impressed mark

(g) Impressed mark

(h) Impressed mark

Early Fulham period 1888–1897, De Morgan
in partnership with Halsey Ricardo

(i) Impressed mark

(j) Impressed mark

(k) Impressed mark

(l) Impressed mark

(m) Impressed mark

Late Fulham period 1898–1907, De
Morgan in partnership with Iles and the
two Passenger brothers

(n) Impressed mark

(o) Impressed mark

List of places

Where William De Morgan pottery is to be seen

Collections open to the public

Bedford: Cecil Higgins Art Gallery
Birmingham: The City Museum and Art Gallery.
Cambridge: Fitzwilliam Museum.
Cardiff: The Castle Museum.
Devon: Knightshays House.
Italy: Ceramics Museum at Faenza.
London: Fulham Public Library (by appointment).
       Leighton House, Holland Park.
       Old Battersea House (by appointment).
       Richmond Fellowship, 8 Addison Road – The Peacock House –
       (by appointment).
       William Morris Gallery, Walthamstow.
       Victoria and Albert Museum.
Manchester: City museum and Art gallery.
Northumberland: Cargside House.
Norwich: Castle Museum.
Oxfordshire: Kelmscott Manor.
Sussex: Standen.
Wolverhampton: Wrighton Manor.

Sources and References

These abbreviations are used to denote the following works:

Burlington — May Morris, 2 articles in the *Burlington Magazine*, August and September 1917.

Gaunt — William Gaunt and M.D.E. Clayton-Stamm, *William De Morgan*, London, Studio Vista, 1971.

Life's Little Day — *Life's Little Day: Some Tales and Reminiscences*, A.M.W. Stirling, London, Thornton, Butterworth, 1924.

Memoir — Sophia De Morgan, *Memoirs of Augustus De Morgan*, London, Longmans Green, 1882.

Stirling — A.M.W. Stirling, *William De Morgan and His Wife*, London, Thornton, Butterworth, 1922.

William Heinemann — John St John, *William Heinemann: A Century of Publishing 1890–1990*, London, Heinemann, 1990.

Wonderful Village — Reginald Blunt, *The Wonderful Village*, London, Mills & Boon 1918.

Chapter 1

1 There is a very full family tree of the De Morgan family at the back of Mrs Stirling's biography *William De Morgan And His Life* by A.M.W. Stirling. London, Thornton Butterworth, 1922. Hereafter, Stirling.

2 'Drawing mathematics'. Mrs Stirling tells this story and it is very similar to the passage in *Joseph Vance*, London, Heinemann, 1906, when young Joseph's talent is discovered by Dr Thorpe.

3 Augustus's antipathy to organized religion is mentioned by Sophia in her *Memoir of Augustus De Morgan*, London, Longman, Green, 1882. Hereafter, *Memoir*.

4 Sir John Herschel, Bt., 1792–1871, a famous astronomer, and a prominent member of the Royal Society and the Royal Astronomical Society. A lifelong friend of Augustus.

5 Charles Babbage, 1792–1871. Prominent mathematician, well known for his invention of the 'analytical engine', the forerunner of the computer.

6 Lord Brougham and Vaux, 1778–1868. Lord Chancellor and prominent politician. He was one of the moving spirits in the formation of the Society for the Diffusion of Useful Knowledge, and was very much involved in the foundation of London University.

7 Henry Warburton, 1784?–1858. Philosophical radical. One of the leading supporters of Brougham in the foundation of London University and a member of its council in 1827.

8 Thomas Hodgkin, MD, 1798–1866. A physician at Guy's Hospital. Hodgkin's disease is named after him. A member of the Senate of London University until his death. Quoted from an article by him: 'University College, London, Fifty Years Ago', Newcastle-upon-Tyne, *The Northerner*, 1901, vol. i, p. 75.

9 Prof M.J.M. Hill, *Some account of the holders of the Chair of Pure Mathematics*. MS in the library of University College. f. 4.

10 Professors' salaries. The annual Reports of the University of London 1827–34. Also the AGM of the Proprietors for 27 February 1828 and the Report of the Council for February 1833 on the Remuneration of Professors.

11 Obituary of Augustus De Morgan in *Proceedings of the Monthly Notice of the Royal Astronomical Society*, 9 February 1892.

12 For a fuller account of Augustus's two resignations and the reasons for them, see Sophia De Morgan's *Memoir*.

13 This building is still there and is now an hotel. Renumbered 35.

14 Sophia De Morgan, *Memoir*.

15 Dr Reginald Thompson. Very little is known about him, apart from the fact that he collaborated with De Morgan in the Chelsea period on designs, and married one of De Morgan's sisters, Annie. He was a physician in the Brompton Hospital.

16 Lady Byron, the widow of Lord Byron, and mother of Ada, who married De Morgan's childhood friend Lord Lovelace.

17 Elizabeth Fry, 1780–1845. Quaker and prison reformer.

18 In 1889 Sophia wrote a vivid description of the St Pancras Workhouse '40 years Ago'. Printed in the *Englishwoman Magazine*.

19 Stirling, p. 48.

20 Letter to Joseph Vance, the American author, quoted in Stirling, cf Chapter 9 n. 25.

21 Dates from the remaining records of University College School.

22 See letter from William De Morgan to Isabel Sieveking of 1 March 1908 re author as idle student at College. The Lilly Library, Indiana.

23 Letter from Augustus to his son William quoted by Stirling, p. 57.

24 Stirling, p. 57.

25 Sir William Blake Richmond, 1842–1921. This extract is from his preface to Mrs Stirling's biography – unfinished at the time of his death.

26 Henry Holiday. A lifelong friend of the De Morgans. He worked with Morris on stained glass and became well known as a painter, a sculptor and stained-glass designer.

27 Fred Walker 1840–75. Painter specializing in lyrical landscapes.

28 Simeon Solomon. Though acknowledged by his contemporaries at the Academy Schools to have as much if not more talent than any of them, ended his life in penury and alcohol. He also had an unfortunate brush with the law in 1873.

29 Description of Academy Schools quoted in Stirling, p. 58.

Chapter 2

1 The Fitzroy Square house is still there.

2 There is very little connection between the abominable Soho house in *Alice For Short* and the present building. The area looks remarkably clean, innocent, and cat-free.

3 Mrs Siddons' house, whose ballroom was William De Morgan's west-end showroom for some years, has long since gone.

4 There was great enthusiasm but not enough expertise when it came to painting the murals in the Oxford Union. Because the surface of the walls was not pre-pared properly, it was not long before the paintings deteriorated and actually came off the walls. There is very little left of the original murals now.

5 Edward and Georgiana Burne-Jones became and remained very close to the De Morgans, and they lived quite close to each other in Fulham and Chelsea.

6 Dante Gabriel Rossetti, perhaps the most talented of the original PRB, was much admired by his friends and colleagues but proved to be the most difficult of the group. As far as one can gather he was never close to the De Morgans and in any case they would very probably have disapproved of his way of life, particularly his long-standing affair with Janey Morris.

7 Ford Madox Brown, one of the original members of the PRB and a very successful painter, who had a considerable influence on Rossetti.

8 Thomas Woolner was one of the original members of the PRB. Mainly known as a sculptor.

9 Stirling, p. 74.

10 The regal was a kind of reed organ, used in churches and in private houses. Very typical of Morris's eccentric behaviour, but it did not lose him the respect of his friends.

11 Colloquially – 'Go away'.

12 Stirling, p. 75.

13 George Price Boyce was a painter and a friend of Morris and his circle. He kept a diary which has been a useful source for Morris biographers.

14 Philip Webb, architect, was a close associate of Morris for many years. Responsible for Red House and other private houses such as Standen.

15 Morris's ceramics were poor technically.

16 Bodley was one of the leading church architects for whom Morris and his associates provided much stained glass.

17 I am indebted to Jon Catleugh for a list of the five churches which definitely do have stained glass by De Morgan. 1. Layer Marney, Essex: David Window. 2. Rocester, Staffordshire: E. window, St Michael window. 3. Hamborough (St Oswalds): E. window (made by Powells). 4. Gwennap, Cornwall: W. window. 5. Filkins, Oxfordshire: S. Chancel, De Morgan/Lyon.

18 Stirling, p. 77.

19 From Sir William Blake Richmond's introduction to Mrs Stirling's biography.

20 May Morris's two articles in the *Burlington Magazine*. 'Reminiscences of William De Morgan', August and September, 1917. Hereafter, *Burlington*.

21 Encaustic tiles were tiles inlaid with coloured clays which were burnt into the tiles during the firing.

22 An essay in *William De Morgan Tiles*, by Jon Catleugh. Somerset, Richard Dennis, 1983.

23 See Appendix B for complete paper and pp. 73–75 for a discussion of it.

24 Piccolpasso wrote a description of the lustre process in Italy in 1548.

25 Stirling, p. 79.

26 Lucas was a contemporary of De Morgan at University College.

27 May Morris, *Burlington*.

28 Halsey Ricardo was an architect and designer, later a partner in William's firm, and the architect of the Debenham House in London.

29 Stirling, p. 61.

30 He must be referring to the most famous theme in the 'Waldstein' Sonata by Beethoven.

31 Tyssen's diary, quoted at length in Stirling, p. 65.

32 Undated letter from Burne-Jones, quoted in Stirling, p. 71.

33 Herschel letter, Stirling, p. 81.

34 Letter to fellow author in America, Joseph Vance, Stirling, p. 79. See also Chapter 9, n. 25.

Chapter 3

1 May Morris, *Burlington*.

2 Stirling, p. 86.

3 Reginald Blunt, *The Wonderful Village*. London, Mills & Boon, 1918. Hereafter, *Wonderful Village*. Blunt was later to be De Morgan's manager. An historian of Chelsea and its inhabitants.

4 Fred Passenger, despite ill-health, worked for De Morgan for twenty-eight years, and his brother Charles, a cripple, for nearly thirty years. Both of them were expert painters whose initials appear on many pots.

5 Dr Thompson and his wife, Annie, had three children; the three sons, according to Mrs Stirling, were all brilliant.

6 Stirling, p. 87.

7 *Burlington*, 1917.

8 *Wonderful Village*.

9 Stirling, p. 91.

10 *On A Pincushion*, by Mary De Morgan. London, Jackson and Halliday, 1876. Fairy-tales illustrated by William De Morgan.

11 *Burlington*.

12 The Victoria & Albert Museum. They also have a good collection of De Morgan ceramics, and some accounts of the business.

13 Walter Crane (1845–1915), painter, illustrator and designer.

14 For more information on De Morgan's tiles, see Jon Catleugh's *William De Morgan Tiles*, Shepton Beauchamp, Somerset, Richard Dinnis 1983, and also *William De Morgan*, by William Gaunt and M.D.E. Clayton-Stamm, London, Studio Vista, 1971. Hereafter, Gaunt.

15 Stirling, p. 90.

16 Ricardo, architect, and De Morgan's partner.

17 See his comments in his book on De Morgan tiles and the various marks on the pottery.

18 Gaunt, p. 25.

19 Gaunt, p. 24.

20 Sir Richard Burton (1821–90). Traveller and explorer in the Near East. Author and translator of several works from the Arabic.

21 Blunt, *Wonderful Village*.

22 Stirling, p. 103.

23 'Lustre Ware'. Lecture to the Society of Arts on 31 May 1892, and published in their journal 24 June 1892. Printed in full as Appendix B.

24 Catleugh collection.

25 May Morris bought the house in the 1920s.

26 *Life of William Morris* by J.W. Mackail, 2 vols. London, Longman, Green & Co., 1899.

27 *Cormell* Price, known to his friends as Crom. Oxford friend of Morris's and a famous headmaster of the school Westward Ho! immortalized in Rudyard Kipling's *Stalky & Co.*

28 May Morris, *Burlington*.

29 Stirling, p. 122.

30 *Burlington*.

31 Stirling, p. 126.

32 J.W. Mackail, *Life of William Morris.*

33 Bale, quoted in Stirling, p. 127.

Chapter 4

1 Henderson, Philip *William Morris. His Life, Work and Friends*. London, Thames and Hudson, 1967, p. 232.

2 Stocklists and price lists at the V&A.

3 More pots were being thrown in the factory later in his pottery career than in the early Chelsea days.

4 Gaunt, p. 28.

5 Bernard Leach. Known as the father of modern 'studio' pottery. Very influential.

6 Stirling, p. 128.

7 Burne-Jones correspondence. Stirling, p. 131.

8 Univ. London Lib. Pal. Dept.

9 Bale, Stirling, p. 130.

10 The Grosvenor Gallery was opened at 131 Bond Street on 1 May 1877 to show pictures by artists who were disillusioned with the Royal Academy.

11 (John) Roddam Spencer Stanhope was much involved with the painting of the Oxford Union.

12 May Morris, *Burlington*.

13 We do not know which brother.

14 Stirling, pp. 194-95.

15 Stirling, p. 196.

16 Stirling, *Life's Little Day. Some Tales and Other Reminiscences*. London, Thornton, Butterworth, 1924. Hereafter, *Life's Little Day*.

17 His last, unfinished novel, completed by Evelyn and published by Heinemann after his death.

18 James Abbott McNeill Whistler, 1834-1903. American painter who settled in England.

19 Austin Dobson, 1840–1921. Civil Servant, writer of light verse and biographies.

Chapter 5

1 *Memories and Machines: The Pattern of My Life* by Sir Harry S. Ricardo. London, Constable, 1968.
2 Grinding mill: for grinding raw materials, usually for glazes.
3 Pudding mill: for re-constituting clay into a usable texture.
4 Accounts records in the V&A.
5 Written at the request of Mrs Russell Barrington. In Alan Green Bequest papers at Birmingham City Museum and Art Gallery.
6 Grog: finely ground fireclay which prevents shrinking.
7 Gaunt, p. 28.
8 Sands End markings, see note on marks in Appendix C.
9 May Morris, *Burlington*.
10 Examples can be seen at the V&A, Old Battersea House and Cardiff Castle Museum.
11 De Morgan's involvement with the society can be traced from the society's catalogues in the V&A.
12 Bacini or bacili (literally bowls) are lustreware imported into Italy from the Middle East which were until recently mortared into recesses in the exterior walls of churches in Pisa as decoration. They are now replaced by copies, the originals are in the Museo Nazionale, Pisa.
13 The Egyptian report cannot be found in the British Library, although it is catalogued, as the copy was destroyed in the Second World War and not replaced. There is an MS in the manuscript collection (Eg. 3293) which is a rough draft of the published report together with correspondence between De Morgan and the Egyptian Government with regard to the terms and conditions on which he would undertake the work. A copy of the report, published in Cairo by the National Printing Office, can be found in the National Art Library at the V&A (Box V 96 HH): *Report on the Feasibility of the Manufacture of Glazed Pottery in Egypt*.
14 Gaunt, p. 37.

Chapter 6

1 Roddam Spencer Stanhope and asthma, see *Life's Little Day*.
2 *Life's Little Day*.
3 May Morris, *Burlington*.

4 Letter to Burne-Jones. Univ. London Lib. Pal. Section.

5 Method of tile painting. See May Morris, *Burlington*.

6 May Morris, *Burlington*.

7 Cantagalli: A well known and old established family business dating from the fifteenth century and run in De Morgan's time by two brothers, Ulisse and Romeo. Specialized in the production of majolica ware.

8 Stirling, p. 212.

9 May Morris, *Burlington*.

10 Gaunt, p. 35.

11 Iles and other staff. Another letter to Ricardo. Stirling, p. 213.

12 Another letter to Ricardo. Stirling, p. 213.

13 Letter from Iles quoted in Gaunt, p. 40.

14 Letter in Alan Green Bequest – Birmingham City Museum and Art Gallery.

15 10 Feb. 1895. See Gaunt, p. 40.

16 Brer Rabbit. One of the main characters in the Uncle Remus series by Joel Chandler Harris, 1848–1908.

17 Copies of correspondence owned by the De Morgan Foundation.

18 Eric Gill (1882–1940), sculptor and typographer.

19 In an unpublished book of memoirs in the Chelsea Public Library by Reginald Blunt.

20 Letter to Mackail, 1897.

21 The offer from the William Morris firm was typically generous. Would this have been Philip Webb, life-long member of Morris's circle?

22 Letter to Blunt in Stirling, pp. 223–24.

23 Bedford panels. Duke of Bedford's diary at Woburn.

24 Letter to Blunt in Stirling, pp. 223–24.

25 Stirling, p. 224.

26 Gaunt, p. 45.

27 Letter quoted in Stirling p. 225.

28 Fictionary – re Merton Abbey Works.

29 V&A National Art Library.

30 Reginald Blunt, *Wonderful Village*.

31 He was wrong!

32 Prices of De Morgan's pottery. See a fairly recent auction when Sir Andrew Lloyd Webber bought the Wiltshire collection.

33 Most of the collection in the V & A is on view.

34 Debenham House or the Peacock House – occupied by the Richmond Fellowship for mental welfare and rehabilitation.

35 Stirling, p. 229.

36 Investigation and experiment were what he enjoyed most of all, but he went on inventing things.

37 University of London Lib. Pal. Section.

Chapter 7

1 A well-known writer today who started a successful career as an adult novelist late in life is Mary Wesley. De Morgan's contemporary George Du Maurier, another exceptional case, wrote his only three novels towards the end of his life.

2 De Morgan was well acquainted with Dickens's work and also Browning's and quotes from these two writers in his novels. And see discussion in Chapter 14; also Chapter 8 n. 19, Chapter 9 n. 12.

3 Well-known figures who wrote much on spiritualism were, for example, Sir Arthur Conan Doyle and Sir Oliver Lodge, FRS.

4 Sophia was a very serious woman who seemed to lack a sense of humour, perhaps because she had many family tragedies in her long life.

5 *From Matter to Spirit: The Results of Ten Years Experience in Spirit Manifestations. Intended as a Guide to Enquirers* by C.D. with a Preface by A.B. London, Longman, Green, Roberts & Green, 1863. See also Chapter 12 n. 6.

6 Animal magnetism: a curious theory about energy, widely believed in, before the discovery of electricity.

7 *From Matter To Spirit*, p. 91.

8 There is an interesting account by Mrs W.B. Richmond, the wife of the artist, of an investigation into psychic phenomena, carried out in Beavor Lodge, Hammersmith, West London, the Richmond's home. The two investigators were the Secretary of the Society For Psychical Research and Sophia De Morgan. Their efforts led to a lessening of the disturbing occurrences. *William Blake Richmond, An Artist's Life 1842–1921* by Simon Reynolds. Norwich, Michael Russell, 1995, pp. 98–100.

9 See *From Matter To Spirit*, p. 4; also Sophia De Morgan, *Memoir*.

10 See Swedenborg, *Spiritualism And Society*. London, Routledge and Kegan Paul, 1969, pp. 53–54. Also Swedenborg's *Heaven and Hell*, paras 87–115 on doctrine of correspondence.

11 *The Old Man's Youth*, p. 519.

12 Sophia was well acquainted with Swedenborg's work.

13 *The Results Of An Experiment*. London, Simpkin Marshall, Hamilton, Kent & Co., 1909.

14 Professor Sidgwick's letter, University of California, the Bancroft Library.

15 See Chapter 'Evelyn De Morgan And Spiritualism' by Judy Oberhausen in Catherine Gordon's *Evelyn De Morgan Oil Paintings*. London, De Morgan Foundation, 1996.

16 Stirling, p. 107.

17 *Memoir of Augustus De Morgan by his wife Sophia Elizabeth De Morgan*. London, Longman, Green and Co., 1882. (In notes abbreviated to *Memoir*.)

18 *Threescore Years and Ten*. Reminiscences of the late Sophia Elizabeth De Morgan to which are added letters to and from her husband, the late Augustus

De Morgan, and others. Edited by her daughter Mary A. De Morgan. London, Richard Bentley and Son, 1895.

19 Lady Noel Byron. The widow of Lord Byron, and mother of Ada, who married De Morgan's childhood friend Lord Lovelace.

20 Stirling, p. 233.

Chapter 8

1 Catleugh, p. 37.

2 Gaunt, p. 145. De Morgan's ninth, unfinished novel *An Old Man's Youth* is the 'life of an old man dying in the workhouse as told by himself', while *Joseph Vance* is the first person account of Joe's life not remembered in a workhouse.

3 Stirling, p. 237.

4 Barry Paine, 1864–1928. Author of many short stories and novels. Became the leading comic writer in England.

5 Stirling, p. 238 (4 July 1905).

6 Stirling, p. 239.

7 *William Heinemann: A Century of Publishing 1890–1990* by John St John. London, Heinemann, 1990. Hereafter, *William Heinemann*.

8 Stirling, p. 241.

9 Memoir of Augustus.

10 *Joseph Vance*, p. 36.

11 *Joseph Vance*, pp. 375, 378.

12 *A Budget of Paradoxes* by Augustus De Morgan, 1872. Reprinted from the *Athenaum*.

13 See letters between author and Burne-Jones, for an example, see Chapter 2.

14 Christopher Vance's death in *Joseph Vance*, p. 364.

15 The missing letter. See Lossie's letter to Joseph Vance, p. 525.

16 William De Morgan himself said, 'My works are in my own opinion, founded almost entirely on Dickens, with very rare stretches of individuality'. See also Chapter 9 n. 12. Yale University Library.

17 See discussion of coincidence in later novels.

18 Stirling, p. 242.

19 Stirling, p. 247.

20 *Spectator*, Stirling, p. 247.

21 Professor Lyon Phelps, *Essays on Modern Novelists – William De Morgan*. (New York: Macmillan). Quoted in Stirling, p. 247.

22 University of California, Berkeley.

23 Stirling, p. 254.

24 The Earl of Lovelace. He and William saw a lot of each other when they were both boys. His mother, Ada, Countess of Lovelace, who was taught

mathematics by De Morgan's father-in-law, William Frend, was one of the original inventors of the computer.

25 Joseph Vance was a moderately successful popular American novelist.

26 Julia Cartwright. 'William De Morgan, A Reminiscence'. *The Cornhill*. April, 1917.

27 The two other novels reprinted in 1919 in Nelson's cheap editions are *Alice-For-Short* and *It Can Never Happen Again*.

28 Dramatized in thirteen parts by Frederick Bradnum. First instalment, 15 June 1969. See also *Radio Times*.

Chapter 9

1 Letter from Florence. Stirling, p. 276.

2 'Washing chintz in the Wandle.' De Morgan's factory was next door to William Morris's, but there is no evidence that William ever helped his friend in the work of dyeing.

3 Georgiana Burne-Jones's letter, Stirling, p. 276.

4 Stirling, p. 276.

5 *Alice-For-Short*, In fact 563 pages in the Heinemann edition.

6 The house in Fitzroy Square is now a foot hospital, but the building where the shop was in Great Marlborough Street has gone.

7 *Alice-For-Short*, p. 11.

8 Not only the author, but also May Morris in *Burlington*.

9 Charles's letter to Lavinia Straker, author's comment, *Alice-For-Short*, p. 238.

10 An old life student in the Academy Schools whom De Morgan knew.

11 Stirling, p. 285.

12 De Morgan and Dickens. Admitted his debt on a number of occasions and was afraid that the beginning of *Joseph Vance* was too close to his predecessor's writing. Stirling, p. 329, quotation from letter to Prof Phelps. See also Chapter 8 n. 18.

13 Family and Dickens. Stirling, p. 261.

14 The paragraph on ghosts in *Alice*, p. 138; see also p. 309, in the talk with Sister Eulalie.

15 Mr Pope's conversation, *Alice-For-Short*, p. 368, for an example.

Chapter 10

1 Photo of William Heinemann and Edmund Gosse – De Morgan Foundation.

2 Heinemann contracts. These are, as one would expect, very straightforward and simple. The publishers have the right to sell the books in the US, and else-

where, and give much higher royalties than authors get today. There is no mention in any of the contracts of advances, but it seems the author was not interested, as long as he could ask for cash when he needed it, and there was plenty there.

3 Cutting, Stirling, pp. 257, 280.

4 Asking publishers for money, Stirling, p. 314.

5 Stirling, p. 314.

6 Sidney Pawling was a partner in the firm from early days. For an account of his part in the firm see *William Heinemann*.

7 Copy among the Alan Green Papers. Birmingham City Museum and Art Gallery.

8 M.D.W., probably My Dear Wife.

9 Letter to William Heinemann, Stirling, p. 288.

10 Stirling, p. 286

11 Railways and the tube, etc., date the story around 1900.

12 *Somehow Good*, p. 23. A perfect description of a room in a west London villa in about 1900.

13 Ladbrooke Grove Road. Did he deliberately get this wrong, to obviate the risk of libel, as there is a markedly unflattering portrait of the mother of the family?

14 Not just because of the reference to the Norman Conquest, but even more because of the descriptions of the netsheds which exist in Hastings to this day. *Somehow Good*, p. 290.

15 *Somehow Good*, p. 338.

16 De Morgan must have been a very easy author to deal with, but it is evident that it upset him to be asked to prune.

17 Spencer Stanhope's death, Stirling, p. 315.

18 Letter to Janey Morris, Stirling, p. 315.

19 Letter to William Heinemann, Stirling, p. 315.

20 Various titles, Stirling, p. 316.

21 *It Can Never Happen Again*, p. 9.

22 Panhard car, *It Can Never Happen Again*, p. 29, sets the book at about 1900.

23 Charlotte Eldridge in *It Can Never Happen Again*, vol. 2, p. 4. One of the best, if very acid, portraits of a poison-tongued mischief-maker.

Chapter 11

1 The three last tenants were the De Morgans, the sculptor Stirling Lee, and Professor Oliver. Stirling, p. 318.

2 Stirling, pp. 318–19.

3 Stirling, p. 319.

4 One of the great pleasure-gardens of London – long since disappeared.

5 Beinecke Rare Book and Manuscript Dept., Yale University, 24 May 1910.

6 The De Morgans had to stay at the Sussex Hotel, 111 and 113 Queen's Gate, South Kensington, while the new house was being prepared.

7 *An Affair Of Dishonour* was published by Heinemann in 1910 at the usual price of six shillings.

8 Kipps Manor. A number of readers were curious to know where the house was in Suffolk, but the author was quite definite that it did not exist except in his imagination.

9 Two slum children from *It Can Never Happen Again* and *Joseph Vance*.

10 There is a remarkable similarity between the way Oliver Raydon talks and the pompous, stilted speech of Sir Willoughby Pattern in George Meredith's *The Egoist* published in 1879. But there is no evidence that De Morgan had read the book. He himself said that he read almost nothing in his years as a potter.

11 Stirling, p. 339.

12 The speech as it is printed in *The Author* is not a success – curiously muddled and inconsequential.

13 Stirling, p. 337.

14 It is very instructive to look at the typescript of the novel; the original is in the Huntington Library. The writing is amazingly clear and legible and gives the impression of having been written with ease and great fluency. There are very few alterations to the text, which differs very little from the printed book.

15 *A Likely Story*, p. 207.

Chapter 12

1 *When Ghost Meets Ghost* is 892 pp., and whatever the author might have thought about cutting his work, it would have benefited by a good deal of pruning.

2 Remarks on deaths, Stirling, p. 343.

3 Henry Holiday, *Reminiscences of My Life*. London, Heinemann, 1914. Stirling, p. 351.

4 Simeon Solomon. See chapter 1 n. 27. This talented contemporary at the Academy Schools ended his life as a down-and-out.

5 Letter to May Morris, 3 February 1914. Stirling, p. 352.

6 Augustus's preface to Sophia's book on spiritualism is a very honest and clear statement of his attitude, not only to spiritualism, but to the whole subject of the supernatural.

7 The only time one of De Morgan's books was published as a two-decker novel (*It Can Never Happen Again*), it met with great opposition from the libraries. But see De Morgan's letter to John Francis of 22 May 1915, saying that he preferred 2 vols for this one. Huntington Lib/Hm34250.

8 One of the early penal colonies; afterwards, Tasmania.

9 Australian penal colony.

10 *When Ghost Meets Ghost*, p. 590.

Chapter 13

1 Letter to Phelps. Yale University Library. Also quoted in Stirling, p. 360.

2 Stirling, p. 371.

3 Letter re explosion. Stirling, p. 371.

4 Julia Cartwright, 'William De Morgan, A Reminiscence', *Cornhill* 1917.

5 How his plots developed. Not at all an uncommon way of novel writing.

6 The unfinished sentence. See p. 555 of the novel.

7 See Gaunt, p. 148. Dates certainly tally as Baring was in London round about that time, at the end of 1916 and beginning of 1917. See Bickers, *The First Great Air War*, London, Hodder and Stoughton, 1988, and Baring's letters to Lady Juliet Duff, *Dear Animated Bust: Letters to Lady Juliet Duff. France 1915–1918*. Salisbury, Michael Russell, 1981 and A.M.W. Stirling, *The Merry Wives of Battersea and Gossip of Three Centuries*. London, Robert Hale, 1956.

8 London Univ. Lib. Pal. Section.

9 *Maurice Baring, A Citizen of Europe* by Emma Letley. London, Constable, 1991.

10 Sir George Frampton. A leading member of the late Victorian 'New Sculpture' movement.

11 Automatic writing. *The Results of an Experiment* published pseudonymously. London, Simpkin, Marshall, Hamilton, Kent & Co., 1909. See Chapter 7.

12 The letter from Lady Burne-Jones. Stirling, p. 374, also refers to trench fever.

13 Sir William Blake Richmond, Stirling, p. 373.

14 Edmund Gosse. English author and critic, old friend of the De Morgans. Also published by William Heinemann. Stirling, p. 381.

Chapter 14

1 Information supplied by the William Heinemann archives.

2 Published May 1922.

3 Copy of notes owned by the De Morgan Foundation.

Bibliography

PUBLISHED WORKS BY WILLIAM DE MORGAN

THE NOVELS

Joseph Vance: An Ill-Written Autobiography. London, Heinemann, 1906. Reprinted by Nelson, 1919, O.U.P. World's Classics, 1954. New York, Holt, 1906.
Alice-For-Short. London, Heinemann, 1907. Reprinted Nelson, 1919, New York, Holt, 1907.
Somehow Good. London, Heinemann, 1908. New York, Holt, 1908.
It Can Never Happen Again. London, Heinemann, 1909. Reprinted Nelson, 1919. New York, Holt, 1909.
An Affair of Dishonour. London, Heinemann, 1909. New York, Holt, 1910.
A Likely Story. London, Heinemann, 1911. New York, Holt, 1911.
When Ghost Meets Ghost. London, Heinemann, 1914. New York, Holt, 1914.
The Old Madhouse. London, Heinemann, 1917. New York, Holt, 1919.
The Old Man's Youth. London, Heinemann, 1921. New York, Holt, 1921, under the title: *The Old Man's Youth and the Young Man's Old Age*.

OTHER WORKS

'Lustre Ware'. A paper given to the Society of Arts 31 May 1892 and reprinted in the Society of Arts journal, 24 June, 1892.

Report on the Feasibility of a Manufacture of Glazed Pottery in Egypt. The Ministry of Public Instruction, Cairo, 1894.

After dinner speech to the Society of Authors. Reproduced in *The Author*, November, 1910.

Illustrated Catalogue of Painted Tiles and Pottery to be had of William De Morgan at Orange House Pottery 36, Great Cheyne Row, Chelsea, 1880.

Sketch Book. Unpublished. Given to Dr Reginald Thompson 8.7.89. Birmingham City Museum and Art Gallery.

Introduction to the Waverley ed. of *Our Mutual Friend*, by Charles Dickens, 1913.

The Results of an Experiment. Collaboration between William and Evelyn De Morgan, published anon. London, Simpkin, Marshall, Hamilton, Kent & Co, 1909.

ARTICLES AND BOOKS CONSULTED AND CITED

Adams, Stephen, *The Arts and Crafts Movement.* London, Quintet Publishing, 1987.

Adcock, St. J., 'William De Morgan'. *The Bookman.* August, 1910.

Arts and Crafts Exhibition Society Catalogues, 1888–1906.

Austwick, J. and B., *The Decorated Tile. An Illustrated History of English Tile-Making and Design.* London, Pitman House, 1980.

Baring, Hon. Maurice, *Dear Animated Bust: Letters to Lady Juliet Duff. France, 1915–1918.* Salisbury, Michael Russell, 1981.

Barrington, W.D.M., (Mrs Russell Barrington), 'The Potter As I Knew Him' (Includes piece by Halsey Ricardo). Alan Green Bequest papers, Birmingham City Museum and Art Gallery.

Bellott, Hale, *University College, London 1816–1926.* London, University of London Press, 1926.

Bickers, R.T., *The First Great Air War.* London, Hodder and Stoughton, 1988.

Blunt, R., 'Those Were The Days. Some Annals of an Undistinguished Life'. Unpublished. 1943. Chelsea Public Library.

Blunt, R., *The Wonderful Village. A Further Record of Some Famous Folk and Places by Chelsea Reach.* London, Mills & Boon, 1918.

Builder, The. 1871, p. 311, reference to stained glass at Layer Marney, Essex; p. 811, Reference to stained glass at Rocester, nr. Uttoxeter, Staffordshire.

Burne-Jones, G., *Memorials of Edward Burne-Jones.* 2 vols., London, Macmillan, 1904.

Caiger-Smith, Alan, *Lustre Pottery. Technique, Tradition and Innovation in Islam and the Western World.* London, The Herbert Press, 1991.

Cartwright, Julia (Mrs Adey), 'William De Morgan, A Reminiscence'. *Cornhill*, April, 1917.

Catalogue of the Exhibition of the Decorated Arts of Great Britain and Ireland at the Louvre, 1914.

Catleugh, Jon, *William De Morgan Tiles*, with essays by Elizabeth Aslin and Alan Caiger-Smith. Shepton Beauchamp, Somerset, Richard Dennis, 1983.

Clayton-Stamm, M.D.E., 'William De Morgan and his Pottery.' *Apollo*, January, 1967.

Conan Doyle, Sir Arthur, *History of Spiritualism*. 2 vols. London, Cassell, 1926.

Cooper, F.T., 'The Story of Two Long Rich Lives'. *New York Herald* (16 July 1922).

Coyser, A.W., *British Art Pottery 1870–1970*. London, David and Charles, 1976.

Crane, Walter, *An Artist's Reminiscences*. London, Methuen, 1907.

De Morgan, Augustus, *A Budget of Paradoxes*. London, Longman, Green, 1872.

De Morgan, Mary, *On A Pincushion*, ill. by William De Morgan. London, Jackson and Halliday, 1876.

The Necklace of Prince Fiorimonde, ill. by Walter Crane. London, Macmillan, 1886.

The Windfairies, ill. by Olive Cockerell. London, Seeley, 1900

A Choice of Chance (under the pen-name William Dodson) London, T. Fisher Unwin, 1887.

'The New Trade Unionism and Socialism in England'. *The Homemaker*, monthly magazine, January, 1881.

De Morgan, Sophia Elizabeth, *Memoir of Augustus De Morgan by his Wife Sophia Elizabeth De Morgan*. London, Longman, Green, 1882.

Threescore Years and Ten. Reminiscences of the late Sophia Elizabeth De Morgan. To which are added letters to and from her husband, the late Augustus De Morgan, and others. Edited by her daughter Mary A. De Morgan. London, Richard Bentley & Son, 1895.

From Matter to Spirit: The Results of Ten Years Experience in Spirit Manifestations. Intended as a Guide to Enquirers. By C.D. with a Preface by A.B. (Augustus De Morgan). London, Longman, Green, Roberts, & Green, 1863 p. 101.

DNB article on William De Morgan

Fitzgerald, Penelope, *Edward Burne-Jones. A Biography*. London, Michael Joseph, 1975.

Gaunt, William, and Clayton-Stamm, M.D.E., *William De Morgan*. London, Studio Vista, 1971.

Gaunt, William, *The Pre-Raphaelite Tragedy*. London, Jonathan Cape, 1942.

Godden, G.A., *An Illustrated Encyclopaedia of British Pottery and Porcelain*. London, Herbert Jenkins, 1966.

Gordon, Catherine, ed., *Evelyn De Morgan Oil Paintings*. With contributions by Andrew Michael, Judy Oberhausen, and Patricia Yates. London, De Morgan Foundation, 1996.

Greenwood, Martin, *The Designs of William De Morgan, A Catalogue*. Shepton Beauchamp, Somerset, Richard Dennis and William E. Wiltshire III, 1989.

Haley, Sir William, 'William De Morgan as Novelist'. *The Times Literary Supplement* 9 July 1954.

Hale, W.T., *William De Morgan And The Greater Early Victorians. Indiana University Studies*, vol. 8, no. 50. The University, Bloomington, Indiana.

Henderson, Philip, *William Morris. His Life, Work and Friends*. London, Thames and Hudson, 1967.
The Letters of William Morris To His Family and Friends, ed. London, Thames and Hudson, 1950.

Hilton, Timothy, *The Pre-Raphaelites*. London, Thames and Hudson, 1970.

Hodgkin, T., 'University College London Fifty Years Ago.' *The Northerner*, Newcastle-upon-Tyne, 1901.

Holiday, Henry, *Reminiscences of My Life*. London, Heinemann, 1914.

MacCarthy, Fiona, *William Morris: A Life For Our Time*. London, Faber & Faber, 1994.

Mackail, J.W., *The Life of William Morris*. 2 vols. London, Longman, Green, & Co., 1899.

Milne, J., 'The Romance of the De Morgans'. *The Graphic*, 24 July 1922.

Morris, May, 'Reminiscences of William De Morgan'. *Burlington Magazine*, August and September, 1917.

Pinkham, Roger, *Catalogue of Pottery by William De Morgan in the Victoria and Albert Museum*. London, 1973.

Ponting, N., 'William De Morgan: Assessment of his designs'. *Apollo*, 1955.

Porter, Venetia, 'Decorative Tiles at Leighton House'. Decorative Arts Society Journal, no. 16, 1992.

Reynolds, Simon, *William Blake Richmond, An Artist's Life 1842–1921*. Norwich, Michael Russell, 1995.

Ricardo, Halsey, 'The Potter As I knew Him.' Unpublished. Alan Green Bequest papers, Birmingham City Museum and Art Gallery.

Ricardo, Sir Harry S. *Memories and Machines. The Pattern of My Life*, London, Constable, 1960, p. 30 et seq. for material on his father.

Scott, T., *The Nation*. 13 September 1922.

Seymour, F. Warren, *William De Morgan. A Post Victorian Recital*, 1920.

Sparrow, Walter Shaw, 'William De Morgan and His Pottery'. *The Studio*, vol. 17, no. 78 15 September 1989.
'The Art of Mrs. William De Morgan'. *The International Studio*, 10, 1900, pp. 221–32.

St John, John, *William Heinemann: A Century of Publishing 1890–1990*. London, Heinemann, 1990.

Stirling, A.M.W., *William De Morgan and his Wife*. London, Thornton, Butterworth, 1922.
Life's Little Day: Some Tales And Reminiscences. London, Thornton, Butterworth, 1924.

The Richmond Papers. London, Heinemann, 1926.

The Merry Wives of Battersea and Gossip of Three Decades. London, Robert Hale, 1956.

Stoker, Bram, interview with William De Morgan, 'Habits of Work'. *Worlds Work*, vol. 16.

Sutherland, John, *The Longman Companion to Victorian Fiction*. London, Longman, 1988.

Swinnerton, Frank, *Swinnerton, An Autobiography*. London, Hutchinson, 1937.

Thirkell, Angela, article on The Vale in the Annual Report of the Chelsea Society, 1958.

University of London, Annual Reports, 1827–34.

Wilhide, Elizabeth, *William Morris, Decor and Design*. London, Pavilion Books, 1991.

Williams, Orlo, 'The Novels Of William De Morgan'. *The London Mercury*, October 1922.

Woodyatt, John, 'William and Evelyn De Morgan', with note by Sir Edmund Gosse. *Country Life*, 6 April 1948.

Index